THE TWO MICHELANGELOS

THE TWO MICHELANGELOS

Bette Talvacchia

LUND HUMPHRIES

First published in 2021 by Lund Humphries

Lund Humphries
Office 3, Book House
261A City Road
London EC1V 1JX
UK

www.lundhumphries.com

ISBN: 978-1-84822-449-0

A Cataloguing-in-Publication record for this book is available from the British Library

Copy edited by Pamela Bertram
Designed by Crow Books
Set in Centuar MT and Trajan Pro
Printed in China

The publisher gratefully acknowledges the support of the National Endowment for the Humanities.

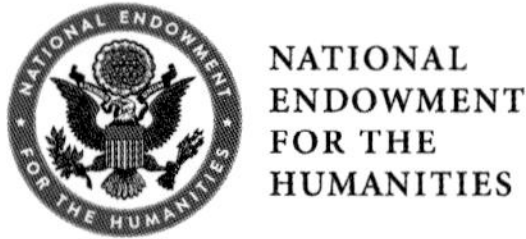

Any views, findings, conclusions, or recommendations expressed in this publication do not necessarily reflect those of the National Endowment for the Humanities.

of the book. Here, I especially want to acknowledge the path-breaking contributions of Paul Barolsky, whose scholarship and support were important to the realization of this book. He is a beacon for all writers of art history who strive for historical accuracy, articulation of key ideas and vivacity in their work. This is true especially for scholars who dare to imagine themselves trailing the footsteps of Giorgio Vasari, the Renaissance master of unparalleled eloquence, relevance and intrigue in recording the history of art.

I hope the reader will experience some of the pleasure it gave me to write this book, which I offer to enquiring minds of every description. I would like to thank Dr. Michael Kwakkelstein, Director of the Dutch University Institute for Art History in Florence, for his enthusiasm and the many conversations shared during the course of the project, which always renewed my energy. I would also like to acknowledge the constant support of my sister, Dr. Janet Talvacchia of Swarthmore College, which is essential in so many ways.

The volume began as a project supported by the National Endowment for the Humanities in 2015, when I received a Public Scholars Fellowship. This is one of the most cherished awards I have been given, with its commitment to furthering and promulgating the excitement of current research in the Humanities to a broad range of involved readers. I can only hope the result lives up to its noble inception.

Most of my writing took place during the horrific pandemic of 2020. While serenity was hard to come by, intense immersion into the past and a search for its meaning helped to sustain me.

I was joined in this endeavor by the Lund Humphries team, ably and graciously headed by my editor, Rochelle Roberts and supported from the start by Erika Gaffney, Commissioning Editor, who always went a step beyond. I extend sincere thanks to Walter Melion, who very kindly first introduced me to Lund Humphries. A generous contribution from the Italian Academy Foundation through its Chairman, Comm. Stefano Acunto, significantly aided production, for which I am most grateful. My research could not have been completed without the invaluable holdings of the New York Public Library and the constant help of its dedicated staff. Thanks to Chantal Lee, Librarian in The Miriam and Ira D. Wallach Division of Art, Prints, and Photographs and the many librarians hard at work throughout the library during its closure to the public, my endless queries and requests met with prompt, professional replies and a virtual mountain of scanned documents. They unfailingly supplied me with all the material needed to complete my research; their assistance also provided me with congenial collaboration and up-beat interaction during a challenging period of required isolation.

In recognition, I dedicate this book to the NYPL and all of its wonderful keepers and disseminators of knowledge.

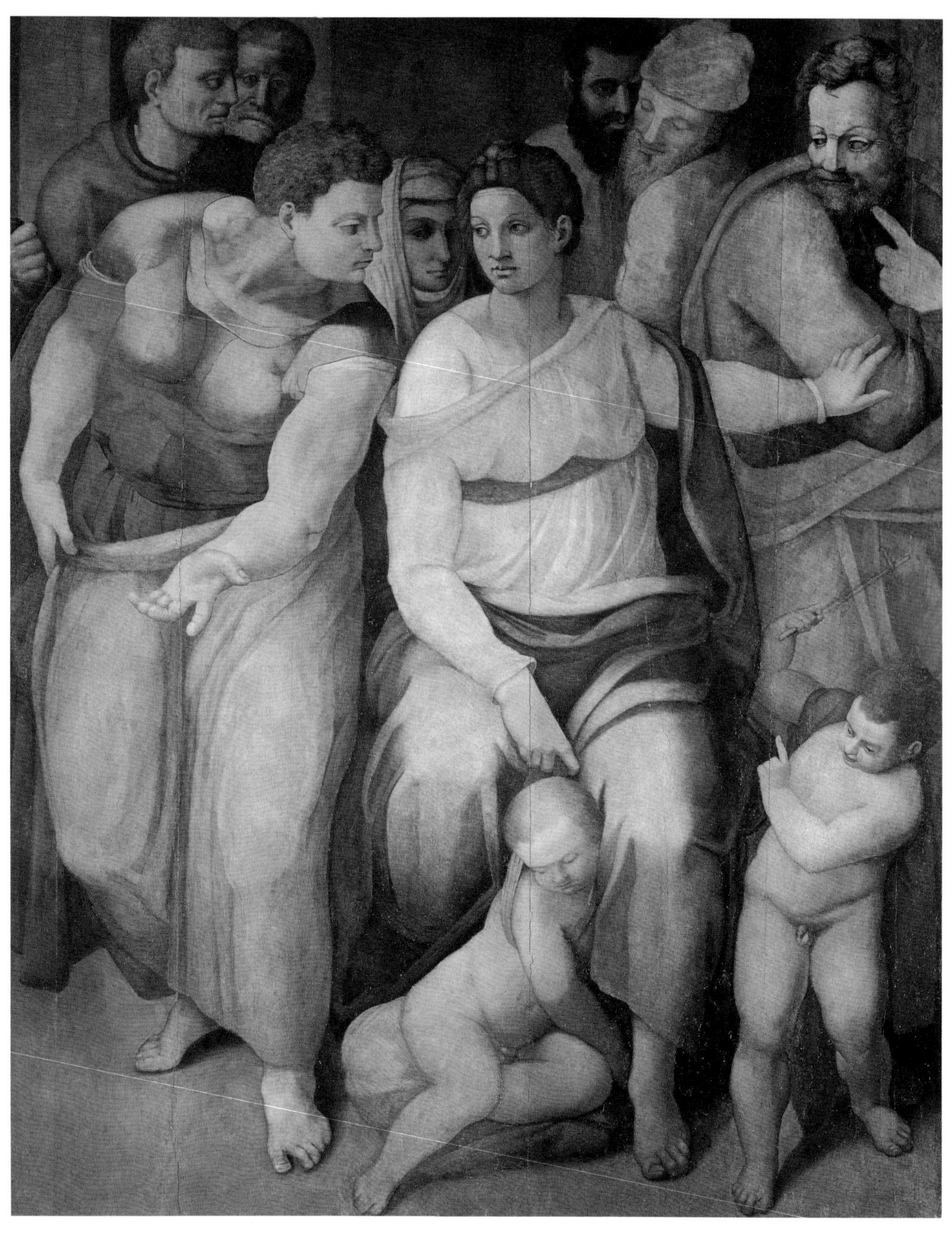

1 Ascanio Condivi, *Epiphany* (designed by Michelangelo), *c.*1554, wood panel, 240 × 187 cm (94½ × 73 ⅝ in), Casa Buonarroti, Florence

I

Introducing the Two Michelangelos

WHAT'S IN A NAME?

Shakespeare gives voice to the emblematic question through the musings of Juliet. She concludes that names do not define inherent qualities since 'That which we call a rose / By any other name would smell as sweet'. However, as Juliet is all too aware, on the surface a person's name is of crucial significance and has a compelling, almost magical power in forming our perceptions about others. The names of artists participate fully in the rich texturing of responses, characterizations and preconceptions called upon when we first meet their work. This is particularly true of art in the Renaissance, an era when artists began increasingly to emerge as celebrated personalities and to sign their works in clever ways. They could employ Latin phrases to show their solidarity with exalted classical precedent, insert visual puns to disclose their identity, or lodge disguised self-portraits within a narrative scene. The viewer's delight in uncovering these clues and affirming the maker's name provides a sense of immediacy to encounters with the past and alerts us to the awesome weight with which the name of the artist is freighted.[1]

Throughout the history of art perhaps no name has carried as much recognition as 'Michelangelo'(Plate 1). In our own day, the name evokes the artist as a superhuman creator; the production of art as making demands upon both skill and passion; and the artistic personality as rebellious and anti-social. Through historical coincidence that takes on an almost mythical character, Michelangelo was the given name not only of the Florentine sculptor who has come to epitomize the Renaissance, but also of the painter who grew up in Caravaggio, a provincial town in Lombardy, about 25 miles east of Milan.

Michelangelo Merisi da Caravaggio (Plate 2), commonly called by reference to his familial hometown when he moved to Rome, produced revolutionary paintings whose impact was arguably as great at the beginning of the 1600s as the older Michelangelo's art had been a century earlier. Each had outsized ambitions unquenched by his realization of success, fame and authoritative artistic styles. The two artists reached the highest levels of patronage despite tempestuous personalities and self-defeating patterns of behavior. In addition to their name, another surprising concurrence is that the two had many characteristics in common: they were abundantly talented, driven in their work, profoundly influenced by contemporary religious beliefs and apparently disdainful of the very authority that provided them with the privileges of success. With regard to their art, there is one notable shared quality: in each case, their works gravitated quickly toward an exploration of religious themes expressed through the human figure. Each in his own way became an expert and influential master of spiritual expression through carnal imagery.

Their similarities help us to think about who became famous in the 16th and 17th centuries, how the business of art was conducted and which works of art were most acclaimed, valued and fervently pursued for purchase. At the same time, an examination of the differences in the styles and careers of the two Michelangelos, following targeted themes, illuminates the changes in art during the transition from the Renaissance to the Baroque era, now often conceptualized as the start of the Early Modern period. Significantly, the two artists were both crucial protagonists in the creation of public religious art during two fraught episodes of church history, the birth of Protestantism and the response of the Catholic Church to it. The internal contrasts within the work of the two artists and the dramatic changes in the external world they inhabited, illuminate many of the transformations in Italian society during the 135 years that passed from the birth of Michelangelo Buonarroti to the death of Michelangelo Merisi.

During his own lifetime the Florentine Michelangelo's delivery into the world on 6 March 1475 was well documented and acclaimed as the arrival of the savior of art. Giorgio Vasari (1511–74), an important artist as well as a skillful writer, is his most exhaustive biographer (Plate 3); a Tuscan compatriot whose career, like his subject's, unfolded in Florence and Rome. Vasari's scheme in his monumental compilation of artists' lives, *Le vite de' più eccellenti architetti, pittori, et scultori italiani,* places Michelangelo at the pinnacle of current artistic developments. His significance is underscored in the first publication of the volume in 1550, where he is the only living artist honored with a biography. If this focus was diluted in the second edition of 1568, whose length was greatly extended by the inclusion of a large number of contemporary artists, the author compensated by amplifying the space dedicated to Michelangelo, whose chapter exceeds one hundred pages. The length and illustriousness of the subject turned the *Vita* [Life] dedicated to Michelangelo into a tome among the shorter notices in the volume. The inference that could be drawn from the disproportion was immediately acted upon and the biography simultaneously was published as an extract entitled *La vita del gran Michelangelo,* announcing the artist's greatness through a grandiose literary tribute.[2]

Vasari pointedly makes the most of the artist's name, which honors Michael, the mightiest of the archangels. The angel Michael's most significant role, vanquishing the rebel angels from the kingdom of heaven, opened a symbolic parallel for the earthly Michelangelo, who banished inferior practice from the realm of Italian art, which Vasari considered as universal. The leap from conqueror to savior came easily:

> . . . the most benign Ruler of Heaven in His clemency turned His eyes to the earth, and, having perceived the infinite vanity of all those labours, the ardent studies without any fruit, and the presumptuous self-sufficiency of men, which is even further removed from truth than is darkness from light, and desiring to deliver us from such great errors, became minded to send down to earth a spirit with universal ability in every art and every profession, who might be able, working by himself alone, to show what manner of thing is the perfection of the art of design. . . . He was pleased, in addition, to endow him with the true moral philosophy and with the ornament of sweet poesy, to the end that the world might choose him and admire him as its highest exemplar in the life, works, saintliness of character, and every action of human creatures, and that he might be acclaimed by us as being rather divine than human.[3]

Vasari's incomparable encomium was widely accepted throughout the Renaissance period; he was not the first to exploit the potential for symbolism in the artist's appropriately transcendent name. The poet Ludovico Ariosto (1474–1533) had already written a eulogistic pun in his epic *Orlando Furioso*, singling out the superhuman Michelangelo in a group of extraordinary artists as 'Michael, angel divine, more than a mere mortal' (Canto 33). Vasari took his cue from Ariosto and at mid-century would not have encountered much disagreement with this point of view. Praise of Michelangelo as divine expressed a consensus regarding the staggering level of the artist's talent and inventiveness and, going beyond his creations, indicates that the artist was also uncommonly worthy in his human comportment. Michelangelo Buonarroti was a heaven-sent model for all subsequent artists to emulate, both in their professional and personal lives. The artist's modest manner of living and his evident deep spirituality enabled a more or less factual basis to be magnified into hyperbole.

It was then, as it is now, a brave undertaking to write the biography of a living subject. Despite Vasari's eloquent homage to Michelangelo as the savior of art and its divine practitioner on earth, the artist quibbled with some passages in the *Life* and was deeply resentful of others. So concerned was Michelangelo to control his image that he enlisted an adherent to his cult, Ascanio Condivi (1525–74), to write what we would call an 'authorized biography' to respond to the misrepresentations he perceived in Vasari's account.[4] Published in 1553, *The Life of Michelangelo Compiled by Ascanio Condivi* took part in a duel of publications, with Vasari eventually having the final word in his second edition. Condivi's dexterity with both pen and brush was vastly inferior to Vasari's. However, his modest 'compilation' carries enormous weight since it was Michelangelo himself who directed the content, which most likely was then edited by a professional man of letters, Annibale Caro (1507–66).[5] The master's dictation of the text provided a verbal scaffolding for the pages of the book, just as he contributed drawings that afforded a strong design beneath the weak execution of Condivi's paintings, as in the *Epiphany*, a rare example of his work (Fig. 1).[6]

Michelangelo Merisi da Caravaggio also attracted the attention of biographers; his short and controversial existence, however, neither suggested nor received monumental treatment. None of the relatively brief accounts of his less than 40 years on earth allude to the potential symbolism of his name, most likely because his conduct was more criminal than heavenly. Several accounts were written in the 17th century and two of Caravaggio's biographers knew him personally. Giulio Mancini (1558–1630), a physician who had treated the artist, was also an art collector and writer. In the early 1600s Mancini began collecting information that he gradually developed into a very personal treatise on painting, which remained in manuscript until its publication in the 20th century. Mancini's account is succinct and selective, but precious for authoritative insights into Caravaggio's early years in Rome. He expresses full admiration for Caravaggio's art and is sympathetic to the artist. But Mancini was plainly bewildered by the extremes of Caravaggio's conduct, opining that 'his great knowledge of art was accompanied by an extravagance of behavior'.[7]

Giovanni Baglione (1571–1644), another contemporary living in Rome, included a biography of Caravaggio in his *Lives of Painters, Sculptors, and Architects*, which was published in 1642. Baglione was an embattled fellow-painter who saw Caravaggio as a malicious rival. While his account is shaded by his enmity, it has the value of being a first-hand record of someone who shared the Roman years of Caravaggio's career and whose own art was profoundly influenced by Caravaggio's style. The fact that Baglione compiled and published 'lives' of his fellow artists in Rome is one of the many continuations of the genre established by Vasari a century earlier, underscoring the impact of Vasari's literary testament to the profession of the fine arts.

While acknowledging the originality of Caravaggio's art and its influence on a large group of followers, the early written opinions vary as to its worth in establishing a new and controversial style of painting. There was nothing like the widespread consensus that Michelangelo Buonarroti received during his life. And no one considered Caravaggio to be the savior of art; so far from being compared to divinity, the violence and erratic behavior of the Lombard Michelangelo was decried by all who wrote about him. Vicente Carducho (1585–1638), a Florentine-born painter working in Spain, called Caravaggio both an 'Anti-Christ' and 'Anti-Michelangelo' in a scathing assessment published in 1633, which equates the end of the world with the extinction of good painting.[8] Lacking a systematic account of his full life, many gaps in our knowledge exist; what we do know is often skewed by the fact that the majority of documented occurrences in the artist's life come down to us in police reports. There is no possibility for a hagiography of an angelic Michael based on the Lombard Michelangelo's life. His earliest biographers made no attempt to be objective; Caravaggio's contemporaries were strictly partisan in their responses to his art, which were to some degree marked by their judgments of his rash actions. Unfortunately, that tradition has been followed continuously up to our own time.

There was long uncertainty about the precise date and even the place, of Caravaggio's birth. Documentary evidence has finally yielded the details: he was born in Milan on 29 September 1571.[9] The location of his birth confirms his family's ties to Milan in addition to the provincial town that later came to identify the artist and points to Caravaggio's early cultural formation in the Lombard capital. The date also unequivocally declares what would otherwise have been a vexing question as to the reason for his name. Caravaggio was born on Michaelmas, a major feast day in the Catholic Church, dedicated to celebrating Saint Michael the Archangel. It was common practice to name a child in honor of the saint whose feast coincided with the day of birth, especially when good fortune chose a significant heavenly protagonist who could take special interest in protecting the newborn. This must have seemed auspicious to the Merisi family; in retrospect we can perhaps say that the child eventually shared Michael's readiness for battle, if not the angelic nature of his patron saint.

On the other hand, we have no indication how the Buonarroti family selected the name of Michelangelo. Formerly it had not been traditional within the family, nor does there seem to have been a particular devotion to the saint, at least in any documented form. Vasari, however, blatantly contrived a mystical explanation for the decision of Michelangelo's father, Lodovico, which helped to create a cohesive symbolic structure for the artist's existence, complete with messianic overtones:

> . . . a son was born on the 6th of March, a Sunday, about the eighth hour of the night, to which son he gave the name Michelagnolo, because, inspired by some influence from above, and giving it no more thought, he wished to suggest that he was something celestial and divine beyond the use of mortals, as was afterwards seen from the figures of his horoscope, he having had Mercury and Venus in the second house of Jupiter, with happy augury, which showed that from the art of his brain and of his hand there would be seen to issue forth works marvelous and stupendous.[10]

Compare Vasari's stirring hyperbole to Baglione's prosaic (and inaccurate) opening line: 'Michelangelo was born in Caravaggio in Lombardy and was the son of a fairly well-to-do master-builder named Amerigi.'[11]

The biographies of the two Michelangelos could not be more different, both in fact and in literary narration. The Florentine artist reached dizzying heights of renown, yet lived a regulated, respectable life in a rather abstemious manner and he wanted it recorded in that way. Condivi takes the trouble to insist Michelangelo was 'healthy above all, both by nature and as a result of physical exercise and his continence with regard to sexual intercourse and food'.[12] Caravaggio's life was as infamous as his art was famous; he brawled, was repeatedly jailed, scuffled over women, was accused of sodomy and was violently impetuous to the point of committing murder. Yet these disturbing facts coexisted with other equally documentable parts of his background and character. Caravaggio began in what today might be characterized as a comfortable middle-class environment; his family owned property and practiced trades. The future artist was literate, indicating some amount of formal education; in an inventory of 1605, his stash of a dozen books was recorded, quite a respectable number for the time.[13] His station and economic circumstances, however, became precarious when his father and paternal grandfather both died of the plague on the same day in 1577 and he left his home without significant financial support.

The practice of religion is not usually stressed as characteristic of Caravaggio, but it was a force in his life that warrants further exploration. He is known to have attended religious services, documented as a participant with other artists in the observation of the 'Forty hours devotion' [*Quarant'ore*] in Rome.[14] This refers to a devotional practice of continuous prayer before the Eucharist, with the faithful participating in relays; it was a tradition fervently promulgated by Filippo Neri (1515–95) and Carlo Borromeo (1538–84). Caravaggio's art is demonstrably engaged with, and deeply committed to, a particular trend of religious practice in the Catholic Counter-Reformation Church that was galvanized especially in Rome and Milan by these two churchmen who were canonized shortly after death. The artist should not be ascribed with the interests of a theologian, but understood as an informed member of the Catholic congregation touched by the ideas and religious culture propagated by Neri and Borromeo. His art is manifestly that of a partisan who used his talent to give form to a fundamental vision of Catholic reform, *pauperismo*, describing a Church committed to a simplicity ennobled by poverty and dedicated to aiding its less privileged members. Caravaggio's Catholicism was formed in the zealous environment of Saint Carlo Borromeo's Milan, where the '*Chiesa pauperista*' was propagated, professing poverty as an ideal in Christian communities. Borromeo consciously emulated Saint Francis of Assisi in his negation of opulence within the Church and the Franciscan model also had repercussions in Caravaggio's religious expression.[15]

With family members who were property owners, tradesmen and clerics, Caravaggio was not from the wretchedly poor stratum of society where desperation begets criminality. Mancini describes the artist's family as well off, which is an exaggeration of their more modest circumstances; yet in the author's words, they were 'honorable citizens'. Caravaggio's intractable habit of merging into the lowest levels of street life continued even after he began his climb into high society and residencies in lordly mansions. His behavior was that of a young man from a respectable family who enjoyed 'slumming' in nightly forays; his eminent protectors indulged and enabled such behavior.

If Caravaggio satiated himself by contravening social standards, Michelangelo vaunted the Buonarroti family's claims to nobility as part of his heritage. He saw to it that Condivi introduced his subject as 'descended from the counts of Canossa, a family from the region of Reggio which was noble and illustrious as much for its own merits and antiquity as for its connections with imperial blood'.[16] Michelangelo internalized the Buonarroti claim to nobility, disdaining the formation of a workshop, believing the distinction added to the status of his profession. It distanced his production from the marketplace and perhaps helped to assuage his family's initial concern that the practice of art, particularly the physical demands of sculpting, was tainted by the component of manual labor, ill-suited to the mantle of noble heritage.

Caravaggio had no qualms about selling in the marketplace, which is exactly how his work began to circulate in Rome. He did not head a traditional workshop, in part because he quickly found entry into lordly households, but also because his habits were too loose and far from managerial. It is ironic that while neither of the two Michelangelos taught apprentices within traditional workshop organizations (each for his own reasons), the styles they developed became canonical for generations of artists throughout Italy and beyond.

Given the number of replicas and close copies of Caravaggio's works, we can deduce his collaboration with a close circle of artists to satisfy the requests for his most famous paintings. The novelty of this arrangement attests both to Caravaggio's professional acuity and the immediate demand for examples of his original style. While he vaunted the merit of his manner of painting, Caravaggio made no claim to ennobling genealogy, whether imagined or factual; rather, once in Rome, he repudiated the brother who tried to contact him. Professional status, however, mattered greatly to Caravaggio. One increasingly important measure of an artist's success in the Early Modern period was the reception of a title or honorific and Caravaggio was both ambitious and a man of his times. When forced to flee Rome, he eventually landed on his feet in Malta, where the path was cleared for him to enter into the Order of the Knights of Saint John. Caravaggio attained this notable honor in 1608, yet within a year he managed to turn the prize into an utter catastrophe, setting into motion a series of events that comprised the final, tormented few years of his life.

Ordinarily, a man with a criminal record would not be accepted into the order, but Caravaggio benefited from the intervention of powerful protectors. His arrival in Malta was facilitated by the direct descendants of Marcantonio II Colonna (1535–84), the celebrated hero who commanded the papal fleet in a decisive victory against the Turks at Lepanto and who was later invested as Viceroy of Sicily. Marcantonio's daughter, Costanza Colonna (*c.*1556–1626), was the wife of Francesco I Sforza, the Marquis of Caravaggio. After the early death of the Marquis in 1583, Costanza was given the right to rule the Sforza fiefdom, along with guardianship of her small children. Letters attest to Costanza's impressive character and abilities. She was held in high esteem by Carlo Borromeo, with whom she shared a close friendship; valued enough that he made the trip to Caravaggio to visit Costanza after her husband's death. Further meetings and correspondence indicate Borromeo's role in mentoring her development.[17]

The Merisi family had valued positions within the Sforza-Colonna household, which became more intimate in the course of Costanza's life. Earlier accounts speculated that Caravaggio's father, Fermo, was employed by the Marquis. In reality, the relationship came about through the family of the artist's mother, Lucia Aratori; her father, Giovan Giacomo, was a land surveyor with significant responsibilities in the administration of Francesco Sforza's holdings. The Marquis Francesco held the Aratori-Merisi family in high esteem, attested by his appearing as a witness to the marriage of Caravaggio's parents. The Marchioness Costanza employed Caravaggio's aunt and later his sister, who both were devoted, life-long members of her domestic staff, as nurses (nannies) to her children. We may presume this intimate family relationship was a compelling reason for the Marchioness's personal involvement from the start of the artist's career, well beyond his status simply as one of her subjects. She proved to be a constant shield against the consequences of his calamities.[18] Caravaggio's support system turns out to have developed in large part along lines of matriarchal influence. It grew from the initial professional engagement of his maternal grandfather and developed through his aunt's and sister's dedicated service to the Marchioness and her children. It was Costanza who interceded with men of power to protect Caravaggio in his moments of most dire need.

The role played by Costanza Colonna, the Marchioness of Caravaggio, in support of the artist has been underestimated in the past and can now be substantially revised. Caravaggio's relocations and flights from adversities follow a discernible thread through the network of the Marchioness and her alliances, especially familial. Costanza was in Rome during 1592, the year Caravaggio is most likely to have arrived. Although we cannot pinpoint the precise date, documents tell us that he sold the last parcel of land from his patrimony on 11 May 1592, an action indicative of a definitive move, while the last notice of him in Caravaggio dates to July of that year. The Marchioness's temporary residence in Rome was an advantageous moment for Caravaggio to plan his arrival. The artist could benefit from his advocate's ability to smooth his transition to a city where she held a place of distinction, a member of one of Rome's most distinguished families. Indeed, it seems she was responsible for placing the young artist in the household of Monsignor Pucci (infamous for feeding Caravaggio parsimoniously on a diet of salad greens) as his first domicile in the Urbs.[19]

Caravaggio repeatedly called upon Costanza Colonna's support to extricate him from many sorts of scrapes and several arrests in Rome, which appear to have accelerated along with his reputation as an artist. The Marchioness was again in Rome by the end of 1600, staying for the next six years in her family's grand palazzo near the church of the Santissimi Apostoli. In the summer of 1605, Caravaggio temporarily removed himself to Liguria, escaping prosecution for assaulting a notary, Mariano Pasqualone, his rival for the affections of a woman called Lena. Costanza's help is evident in this move, since Caravaggio was immediately welcomed in Genoa by the princely Doria family, which had recently become part of the Colonna familial network through marriage to Costanza's niece. The readiness of the Marchioness to intervene on behalf of Caravaggio in his flight from Rome for aggravated assault is a premonition of her hand in facilitating his urgent departure three years later after committing a murder.

After Caravaggio's irrevocable crime of homicide in 1606, he found refuge in the territory owned by the Colonna family just outside of Rome and papal jurisdiction. When the artist continued his flight south, Costanza, who had been in residence at the Palazzo Colonna in Rome between May and October 1606, subsequently went to a family residence in Naples and was in a position to help Caravaggio from that city. The route of his escape was punctuated by, and likely based upon, the locations of Colonna sanctuaries, arguably masterminded by Costanza. Caravaggio's movements track from immediate succor in Palazzo Colonna, followed by a quick escape to Paliano (originally a fiefdom of Costanza's father, inherited by descendants through her brother), then moving south to Naples, another city where the Colonna had an extremely influential presence (where Costanza's stay from June 1607 to early 1609 can be documented); and then finally to the island of Malta.[20]

Having spent eight months in Naples, in June 1607 Caravaggio left for Malta, transported on one of the Order's ships, with passage easily arranged by the Marchioness through her son, Fabrizio Sforza Colonna, a captain of the Maltese galleys. Costanza was on good terms with the French nobleman Alof de Wignacourt (1547–1622), Grand Master of the Order of the Knights of Saint John, having had occasion to correspond with him on behalf of Fabrizio during 1605–06. It was Wignacourt who obtained permission from Pope Paul v to contravene the rules of the Order and to make an exception for a man with a criminal record to be received into their ranks. Caravaggio was thus admitted and soon produced an outstanding, full-length portrait of the Grand Master attended by his young page, now in the Louvre Museum. Caravaggio's renown and skills as an artist undoubtedly made his membership in the Order very attractive to its cultured, aristocratic leader, recently invested as a Prince of the Holy Roman Empire. Throughout his exile Caravaggio carried out paintings and commissions along the way, from Lazio to Malta, cushioned by introductions and protection within the network of Costanza Colonna and her family.

Without a doubt, Costanza Colonna's ministrations were crucial to Caravaggio's survival; she had the contacts necessary to arrange for his escape from Rome and to ensure safe havens along the road. It cannot be

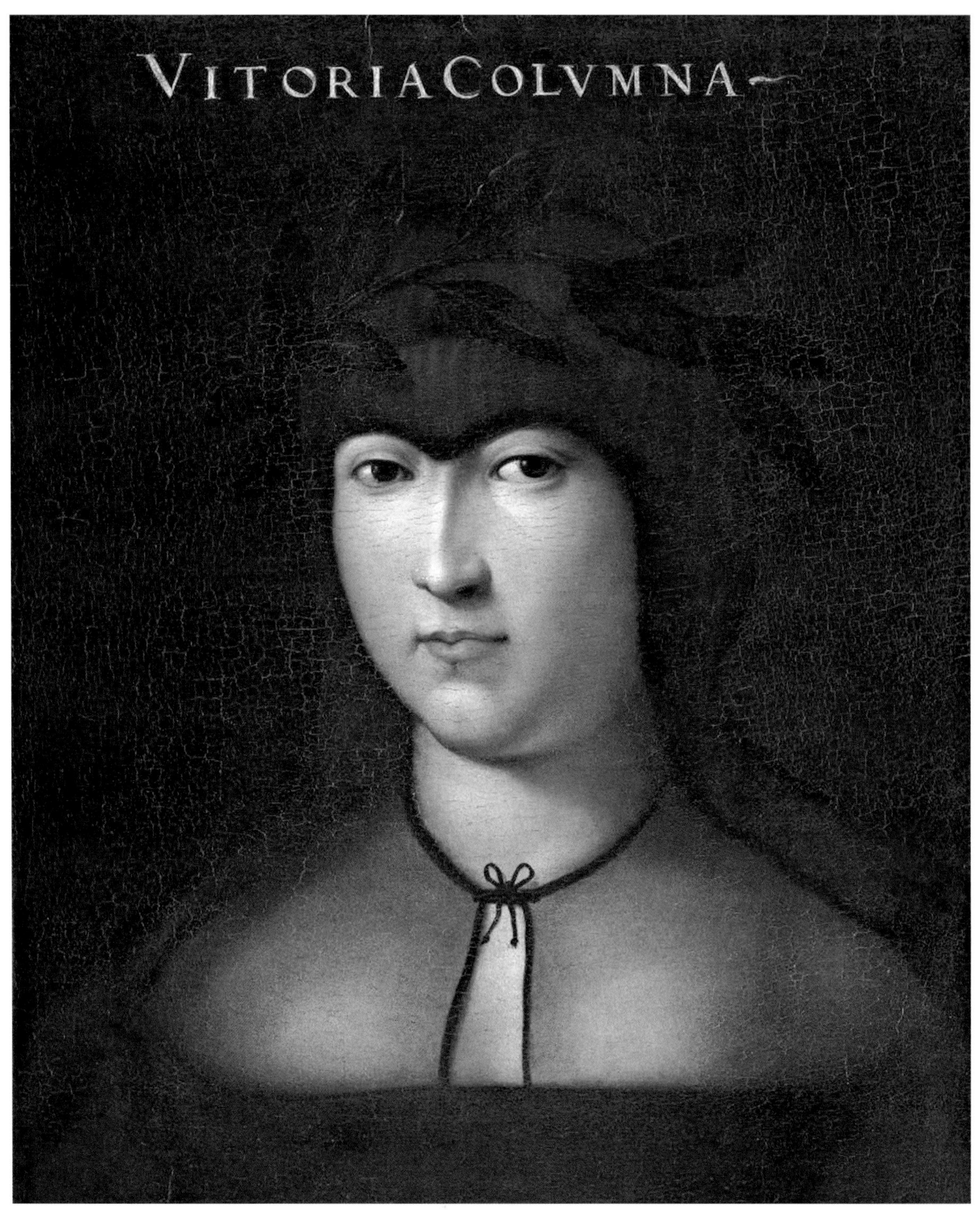

2 Cristofano dell'Altissimo, *Portrait of Vittoria Colonna*, before 1568, oil on wood, 71.5 × 56 cm (28 ⅛ × 22 ¹⁄₁₆ in), Uffizi Galleries, Florence

a coincidence that his footsteps followed her and her family's residences and spheres of influence at the start of his career, during his time in Rome and throughout the remainder of his troubled life as a fugitive from justice. Caravaggio's guardian, Costanza or 'Constance', was as propitiously named as he. It is also worth noting that the Colonna were relations of the Borromeo family (Anna Borromeo was Costanza's sister-in-law), reinforcing Caravaggio's network in both secular and religious concentrations of power. Our favored image of Caravaggio as a street thug with no connections to the privileges of the elite could not be further from the historical truth.

Despite the dramatic differences in the lives of the two Michelangelos, there were also points of contact capable of prompting Caravaggio's engagement with the memory of his namesake. After all, the poet Vittoria Colonna (1490–1547), an intimate friend of Michelangelo Buonarroti, with whom he exchanged sonnets, made gifts of drawings and shared convictions about the reform of Catholicism, was a high-profile member of the same branch of the Colonna family that steadfastly safeguarded Caravaggio (Fig. 2). Vittoria was the aunt of Costanza's father, thus a close blood relation of Caravaggio's life-long protector. Costanza was signally placed to cherish the memory of her great-aunt, an influential woman who was a celebrated writer lauded by Ariosto in the *Orlando Furioso*, as was Michelangelo. During Vittoria's lifetime, 13 editions of her poetry were published.[21] She was an esteemed member of a group active in Catholic reform in Rome and had international contact with leaders of the movement. Michelangelo self-avowedly looked to her for spiritual guidance and shared impassioned conversations about unconventional approaches to the doctrines of Catholicism. Condivi affirms the closeness of Vittoria to Michelangelo in impassioned terms: 'he greatly loved the Marchioness of Pescara [Vittoria's title by marriage], with whose sublime spirit he was in love. She, from their first meeting, loved him passionately'. Michelangelo reaffirmed this by remarking he always kept a portrait of Vittoria in his house, as Calcagni annotated.[22] The Marchioness of Caravaggio must have been thrilled to follow her illustrious great-aunt in extending patronage and friendship to the Michelangelo of her own era.

Another intriguing point of contact between the ostensibly unrelated circles of the two Michelangelos exists in the person of Cardinal Francesco Maria Del Monte (1549–1626), who was the key to Caravaggio's initial Roman success (Fig. 3). Del Monte was wealthy, worldly, superbly well-connected and a man of culture who invited the artist to reside in his household in 1595. Del Monte was Venetian in origin, born into a cultured family that gave him access to the most celebrated circles of the city's dazzling art. It is recorded that Francesco's father was friends with Titian (1488/90–1576), who was a *padrino* [godfather] at his son's baptism; an auspicious start for a future art patron and collector. Caravaggio's early style, a product of four years in the workshop of Simone Peterzano (1535–99), who proudly signed a major work as a 'pupil of Titian', was positioned to resonate with the connoisseur/cardinal. Del Monte would have understood the stylistic basis of Caravaggio's first paintings and their worth, even when he found them displayed among undistinguished works sold in bulk. The cardinal was likely to have come across the paintings in the piazza of San Luigi de' Francesi just beyond his door, where we know a man by the name of Costantino Spata had a shop whose inventory included works by the youthful Caravaggio.[23]

The mansion from which Del Monte stepped was the Palazzo Madama, the traditional seat of the Medici family in Rome. Del Monte was more than an ally of the Florentine dynasty, hand-picked by the former Cardinal de' Medici as his replacement when Ferdinando gave up his clerical career in 1587 to become the Grand Duke of Tuscany. Del Monte represented Medici concerns in Rome, became Ferdinando's confidant and was in constant communication with the Grand Ducal Court in Florence. He made presents of Caravaggio's paintings to Ferdinando (which remain in the Uffizi collection), ensuring that the young artist

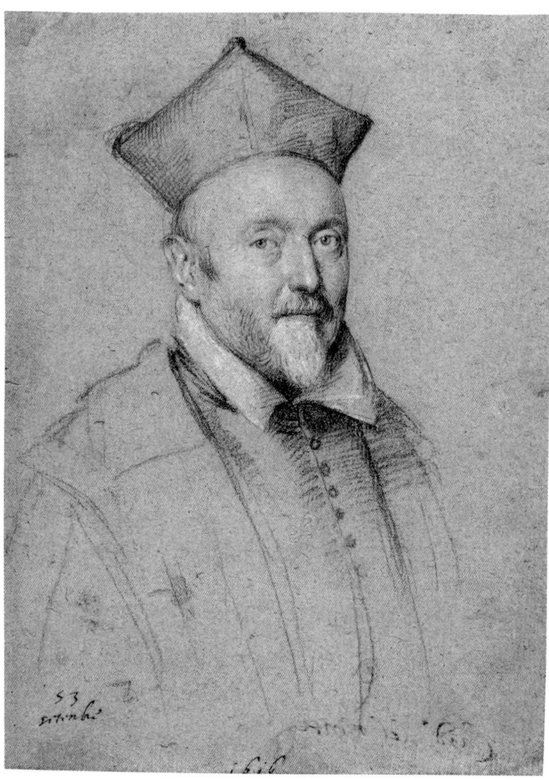

3 Ottavio Leoni, *Cardinal Francesco Maria Del Monte*, 1616, black chalk heightened with white on blue paper, 22.9 × 16.5 cm (9 × 6½ in), Collection of the John and Mable Ringling Museum of Art, the State Art Museum of Florida, Florida State University, Sarasota

would be mindful of having to excel in the orbit of his predecessor, given how inseparably the name of Michelangelo was connected to the Medici family.

The association of Medici patronage with Michelangelo Buonarroti had become legendary even during the artist's lifetime, but the aggrandizement of what in truth was a less than consistent reality developed from an auspicious start. After a short apprenticeship in the workshop of the accomplished painter Domenico Ghirlandaio (1448/9–1494), Michelangelo was singled out for special tutoring by the sculptor Bertoldo di Giovanni (*c*.1430/40–1491), who curated the Medici collection of antiquities. In that setting the precocious skill of the barely adolescent Michelangelo came to the attention of Lorenzo the Magnificent (1449–92), who invited him into his household. The privileged residency came to a sudden end when Lorenzo died a year later. However, the brief experience was hugely formative for the young artist, who dined with Lorenzo's sons and absorbed the captivating ideas of Angelo Poliziano (1454–94), tutor to the Medici children and resounding voice of neoplatonic philosophy. Michelangelo absorbed much from this refined intellectual environment and was galvanized by its precepts; it sustained him throughout his life and work.

Michelangelo retained love and nostalgia only for his first patron, Lorenzo de' Medici, and continued to work for the family only as circumstance, pressure and opportunity required. Cardinal Giulio de' Medici (1478–1534), later Pope Clement VII, illegitimate son of Lorenzo's brother Giuliano, was the only member of the subsequent generation with whom Michelangelo developed a positive rapport over time, at one point going so far as to identify himself as 'the cardinal's man', a declaration of alliance, if not of affection. Giulio was a perceptive patron, fully involved in the projects he commissioned to memorialize the Medici family. He earned Michelangelo's respect, but commanded his obedience, tightly controlling the work his premier artist was allowed to carry out for others and at times forbidding it. Giulio's priorities were made absolutely clear, enforced by the power of his rank. While pope, Giulio issued a brief prohibiting the artist, under pain of excommunication, from working on any project apart from those he himself sanctioned. Michelangelo was fully aware of Giulio's vigilance regarding his activities and therefore feared for his life after supporting the renegade Florentine Republic, established in revolt against Medici rule in 1527. When, with the backing of imperial muscle, the dynasty retook the city in 1530, Giulio immediately pardoned the artist and put him to work once more. The pope had everything to gain from his leniency, seamlessly employing the artist for the glory of his family and papal reign. In compensation, Michelangelo was handled with kid gloves and given consequential commissions worthy of his capacities; a fulfilling exchange for the artist, if not one that encouraged the bonds of devotion.

Condivi does not mention any of the Medici in his iteration of friends in whose company Michelangelo delighted; instead we are specifically told: 'He loves and honors without exception all members of the house of Farnese, because of the living memory he has of Pope Paul, whom he remembers with the greatest reverence.'[24] In singling out one of Rome's most powerful families for such unqualified personal tribute, Michelangelo repudiated by inference any current connection to the house of the Medici, even as the heirs of Lorenzo Magnifico continued to burnish the luster of their heritage, taking conspicuous advantage of their patrimony.

Despite the fact that Michelangelo left Florence definitively in the autumn of 1534, major architectural projects left unfinished for the Medici popes were continued by proxy or left as esteemed works in progress, awaiting the return of the illustrious native son, who in the end never reappeared. Just short of 30 years after his definitive departure, Michelangelo was elected *in absentia* as one of the two presiding officers of the newly established *Accademia del Disegno* [Academy of Fine Arts], second in prestige only to Duke Cosimo I de' Medici, its official patron. Although Michelangelo purposefully kept his distance from members of the lateral branches of the original dynasty, invested as dukes by the emperor, the new regime traded on his eminence as a representation of Florence and Tuscany. After the master's death, the lore of Medicean support assumed increasing grandeur, even as its factual basis faded, enhancing the cultural status of the Medici dukes and grand dukes as a prop of their political dominion. The memory of Michelangelo was central to the public face of the later Medici dukes.

The environment into which Caravaggio alighted upon invitation to his first residency was directly inherited from Grand Duke Ferdinando de' Medici (1549–1609) by his appointed successor, Cardinal Francesco Del Monte. The cultivated and wealthy household was perhaps not quite as formative for Caravaggio as Lorenzo the Magnificent's home had been for Michelangelo, but certainly it had enormous impact and similarly set the artist on the path to success through a close-knit network of patronage. When he became a part of Cardinal Del Monte's household, which was after all an extension of Grand Duke Ferdinando's domain, Caravaggio entered a tangential sphere of Medici interests and cultural influence, which made a comparison with the historical Michelangelo inevitable. It is without question that the 24-year-old Caravaggio took the rivalry to heart as he strove for recognition in the Roman world of art and for a time enlisted the work of his predecessor as a measure of his own. The specter of Michelangelo Buonarroti manifestly reigned in the Papal City, foremost for painters on the ceiling and altar wall of the Sistine Chapel, but also in fabled sculptures on public view and in monumental architectural projects, all literally overshadowed by the colossal dome of Saint Peter's Basilica. Although in the late 16th century it was common for ambitious artists to emulate Michelangelo Buonarroti and imitate his work, Michelangelo Merisi had reason to give this practice a personal twist.

Caravaggio's earliest powerful and stalwart protectors/patrons, Costanza Colonna and Francesco Del Monte, had lasting ties by either blood or alliance to individuals who were central to the life of Michelangelo Buonarroti at different points during his career. Surrounded by those who had every reason to mark the portentous import of his forename, Michelangelo Merisi began his ascent to fame within circles that garnished luster by association with the history of Michelangelo Buonarroti. The circumstances can only have been an impetus for Caravaggio to launch his unique style in a spirit of rivalry, determined to extinguish the brilliant manner of painting established and perfected by his namesake and replace it with his own brand of fireworks.

Michelangelo, while proclaiming sculpture to be his true medium, nonetheless perfected a manner of painting that was a culmination of the Tuscan style as developed in the 1400s. It was based on anatomical study of the human figure, the creation of illusionary consistent spatial depth on a flat surface, analysis of ancient art and the observation of nature. These skills were mastered through constant, almost obsessive, drawing, which translated all that was seen and conceived into a linear form and later translated into painting. Caravaggio's method was more immediate. Working almost exclusively in oil paint, he prepared his design directly on the canvas and created his figures from models posed in front of him. Although some drawing may have been involved, it was not Caravaggio's primary technical tool. The illusion of space is provided in his compositions mainly by the placement of the figures and their interaction in the foreground of the pictorial space. The figures tend to emerge from a dark background and are dramatically lit. The contrast of light and dark in Caravaggio's compositions is pronounced and creates relief, while in Michelangelo's paintings the lighting is even, with subtle gradations of tone to produce shadows and create volume.

The one value shared by the two Michelangelos was their dedication to the observable world as a point of departure for their art, yet their individual understandings of how to represent nature were strongly divergent. Both artists followed nature as a guide, but while Michelangelo strove to surpass his model, Caravaggio was grounded in the norm. The Tuscan approach was to select with discernment the best of nature, recombine its elements and improve the finished product to reach an idealized state of perfection. The Lombard style insisted on inclusion of the flaws and infelicities found in life, combined especially when a startling effect was desired. Beauty was also given its due, but with less idealization, producing an earthier, less cerebral allure. This was shocking to the eyes of Caravaggio's contemporaries in Rome, accustomed to the quest for an otherworldly perfection as a hallmark of 'high art'.

The Renaissance viewers' attitude can be encapsulated by their admiration for figures that appear 'alive' rather than 'real'. Reading widely through Vasari's biographies confirms his consistency in using the term as a compliment of the highest order; he repeatedly admires painted or sculpted bodies that are so close to living organisms that they lack only breath to become fully animated. This concept is recorded in a moving expression of esteem and awe by Giovanni di Carlo Strozzi, in a verse praising Michelangelo's sculpture of *La Notte* [Night] for the Medici Chapel in San Lorenzo:[25]

> La Notte che tu vedi in sì dolci atti
> Dormir, fu da un Angelo scolpita
> In questo sasso, et perchè dorme ha vita;
> Destala, se nol credi, e parleratti.

> *La Notte*, whom you see sleeping so gracefully, was sculpted by an Angel in this stone; and as her sleeping shows, she has life. Rouse her, if you do not believe it, and she will speak to you.

In an exquisite exchange of verse, Michelangelo gives his sculpture a despondent voice in response to her proposed awakening, with a politically charged reference to the degradation of the present time:

> Caro m' è il sonno, et più l'esser di sasso,
> Mentre che 'l danno et la vergogna dura,
> Non veder, non sentir m' è gran ventura;
> Però non mi destar, deh, parla basso![26]

> Sleep is dear to me, and being of stone is dearer; while injury and shame endure, not seeing, not hearing, to me is great good fortune. Therefore, do not awaken me: Ah, speak softly!

Baglione, in contrast, wrote a terse criticism of Caravaggio's approach, despite admitting the powerful transcription of the visible world shown in his paintings. Saying that although the artist had 'great ability' in painting from nature, he then proceeds with a barb: 'He lacked judgment in choosing the good and omitting the bad in the things which he represented.'[27] Begrudging his rival's talent, Baglione maligns Caravaggio's *giudizio*, his judgment in making a selection from nature, which was one of the skills Buonarroti had praised as crucial to a good artist. Caravaggio's revolutionary innovation was to make a show of rejecting selection, instead embracing all of nature in whichever way it was presented in his models. This was, of course, another stylistic strategy, always open to the artist's manipulation, which Caravaggio turned into the defining aspect of his art. His followers took up the method and pushed it to its limit, just as the followers of Michelangelo in the previous century exaggerated the anatomical refinement of the master's figural style.

Michelangelo's distilled Tuscan style is usefully defined as 'idealized naturalism', which attests to his working method of intense study, selection and enhancement of what is found in nature. While we have come to call Caravaggio's approach 'realism', this is a helpful term only if his 17th-century version is separated in our minds from the 19th-century movement, labeled 'Realism' with a proclamation and established under that banner. Realism is always a style, not a direct transcription of the visible world. For example, the brilliant lighting that can skip, dance, or hobble across the surfaces of Caravaggio's paintings, creating vivid patterns and drama, punctuating his construction of space and guiding us through his compact narratives, is always a painterly fabrication. It may be based on the effect of a strong light entering a room from above, but it is altered and manipulated in order to achieve Caravaggio's pictorial goals.

In the eyes of his fellow painters and connoisseurs of the 1600s, the unsettling effect of Caravaggio's novel style was largely due to his insistence on privileging pure painting technique over preparation of his subjects through drawing. This is generally couched as the artist's revolutionary use of color, which sounds puzzling to us, accustomed as we are to shocking color schemes in later art. But if we think of these descriptions as the beginnings of the much more familiar controversy in subsequent centuries opposing *disegno* to *colore*, or line *vs.* color, we come closer to appreciating the significance of his contemporaries' remarks. Giulio Mancini makes this consideration the opening line of his biography: 'Our age owes much to Michelangelo da Caravaggio for the manner of coloring which he introduced and which is now quite generally followed.'[28] The implacably negative Baglione turns the technique into a caustic criticism when, after defaming Caravaggio's character, proceeds to savage his adversary's accomplishment: 'Some people consider him to have been the very ruination of painting, because many young artists, following his example, simply copy heads from life without studying the fundamentals of drawing and the profundity of art and are satisfied with color values alone.'[29]

The phrase 'color values alone' is shorthand for the artist building figures *alla prima* on the canvas, which means composing them directly on the support with his loaded paintbrush, rather than using a painstakingly prepared drawing as an intermediary step to the realization of the figure. *Alla prima* technique was valued for its directness and was thought to enhance the immediacy of the viewer's perception of the painting. The the step-by-step method of drawing from the model, translating observations into linear form, then giving volume to the lines through shading and light effects and finally transferring the results to canvas, was prized for the level of perfection that was attainable. In Caravaggio's style, emotive drama triumphed over abstracted precision; it was in tune with a developing aesthetic preference of the era and influenced its expansion.

The status of the Tuscan manner of painting, based on the supremacy of drawing and the careful illusionism of graduated shading that created volume, cannot be overestimated. It was a congenial method for organizing extensive fresco programs and monumental paintings and was thus in demand for projects of the highest standing. Tuscan artists traveled throughout Italy, spreading the technique and their fame with commissions of consequence. And, most important, they established the style in Rome, which was consolidated by the careers of Michelangelo and Raphael. The latter was not Tuscan by birth, but was consecrated as an honorary Florentine by virtue of his art in Vasari's scheme of the Renaissance. This was the state of painting when Caravaggio arrived in Rome from Lombardy, by way of Venice through his training. The contrast of Michelangelo Buonarroti and Michelangelo Merisi was fuel for an early partisan skirmish between the forces of line and those of color, later systematically taken up with vehemence and the fervor of devotees in the curriculum of the newly developing academies of art.

Federico Zuccari (*c.*1540–1609), the first president of the Roman Academy of Saint Luke, weighed in at the earliest emergence of Caravaggio's controversial style in a major public site. 'What's all the fuss?' he is quoted as asking dismissively, 'All I see here is the reflection of Giorgione.' An authoritative upholder of the Tuscan style, Zuccari's put-down was to scorn Caravaggio's striking effects as the result of building form through color, 'mere' *alla prima* painting, basically saying he had seen it all before and was not impressed. Knowledgeably, but with a cutting edge, the eminent artist categorized Caravaggio's painting as part of the Venetian tradition of *colore*, by naming one of its most brilliant practitioners from the early 16th century, Giorgione da Castelfranco.

In addition to the underlying differences between their traditional styles in art, there are many distinctions that separate the strong regional cultures of Tuscany and Lombardy and some enduring antagonisms. Vasari incidentally characterized Lombards as dullards in matters of art when he made a small group of them antagonists in a tale about Michelangelo and the reception of his *Pietà*, now in Saint Peter's Basilica[30] (Plate 4). The crux of the story is that overhearing the Lombards attribute his work to one of their countrymen, Michelangelo returned surreptitiously to the site of the installation and carved his name prominently on Mary's garment. It remained the only work he ever signed.

If the point of the story is to underline the importance of the *Pietà* in Michelangelo's early Roman career, one of the entertainments of the narration is to show up the group from Lombardy as provincials lacking sufficient understanding of the masterpiece. The Lombards' candidate for kudos was 'our Gobbo from Milan'. The *gobbo* [hunchback], refers to Cristoforo Solari (1489–1520), a sculptor with a local reputation, though modest talent. Vasari's mockery is palpable, as if a humdrum practitioner could ever bring into the world a sculpture of such awe-inspiring majesty and technical wizardry. It may also be Vasari's subtle gibe at an earlier, brief *vita* of Michelangelo. The short account ends by naming Solari among three sculptors who followed in the master's footsteps 'at a great distance', but are worthy of esteem: 'Gobbo Lombardo has also obtained recognition and honour. He has filled the Cathedral of Milan with statues of various saints.'[31] Although these few words do not constitute great praise, Solari was the lone Lombard singled out for mention in a group otherwise consisting solely of Tuscans: Michelangelo as the star, followed by Andrea Sansovino and Baccio Bandinelli. Vasari may have resented the inclusion of the northerner who helped to embellish the Milanese Cathedral. After all, the author was on record as believing the ancient Lombards to have 'shaved the back of their heads, with long locks in front, and they dyed themselves as far as the chin'; and castigated the buildings of their descendants for being constructed in 'the most ugly and haphazard manner'.[32]

Michelangelo himself had contrived a witticism at the region's expense in his humorous sonnet describing the physical travail of frescoing the Sistine ceiling. The artist complained that his uncomfortable habitual position, with head thrown back, neck stretched to its limit and chest colliding with chin, has resulted in the growth of an unsightly swelling. The lump is similar, he avers, to the affliction suffered by the *contadini* in

Lombardy as a result of drinking the local water: 'I've grown a goiter from this labor, as do peasants from the water they drink in Lombardy, or whatever other similar place.'[33] While painting physical perfection in the Tuscan manner on the ceiling, Michelangelo saw his own body, straining and drawn, become increasingly brutish and presumably less Florentine, in appearance. He poked wicked fun at his situation in verse, although sharing the ridicule by maligning Lombardy and its residents in the unflattering comparison.

There are many instances in Florentine Renaissance literature where Lombards are set up as the butt of jokes and consultation of etymological dictionaries attests to the use, even today, of the adjective *lombardo* employed to signify an uncouth or simpleminded person, especially in opposition to *fiorentino* as a paradigm of sophistication.[34] Without doubt, the trajectory of the Tuscan dialect to its preeminence in literature allowed for its terms of chauvinism to prevail in the definition. However, the foundation for Florentine disdain goes back a very long way, to the derivation of the Tuscans from the ancient Etruscans, with their elegant and highly accomplished civilization. These indigenous roots were opposed to the origins of Lombardy, initially populated by a tribe of invaders from the North, the *Longobardi*, an appellation that singles out their uncouth, long-bearded appearance.[35] Early Modern Tuscans called upon history from the 7th century to fuel their regional prejudice, but with a good dose of jocularity.

Michelangelo Merisi may or may not have been aware of these literary jests at the expense of his compatriots, but he would have been all too cognizant of the regional competitiveness and biases that generated them. Indeed, the appellation 'Caravaggio' was neither playful nor affectionate. Rather, it was factual and distancing, conspicuously marking him as an outsider in Rome and identifying him by his family's roots in the Lombard town. In terms of art, Merisi was at the opposite end of the spectrum, far away from the Florentine Michelangelo; this larger cultural antipathy might have been a further spur to the Lombard Michelangelo's determined and eventual overthrowing of the heroic artistic mode of his Tuscan namesake.

Their places of birth and the masters with whom they studied determined the pathways the two Michelangelos traveled toward their decisive mature styles. Michelangelo Buonarroti's apprenticeship began in the Florentine workshop of Domenico Ghirlandaio, notable for his proficient synthesis of the most exciting tendencies of late Quattrocento [15th century] painting, for his expertise in bringing impressive fresco cycles to realization and for his astute professional demeanor, all of which won him commissions from the most illustrious patrons, most of whom operated within the sphere of Medici influence. A tenet of Ghirlandaio's system was, in solid Tuscan manner, an exhaustive grounding in drawing, proceeding from copying the master's own drawings, to the rendering of three-dimensional objects, finally to study from life. Michelangelo's initial works attest to his training, with panels incorporating some of Ghirlandaio's traits and a drawing style formed by his master's pen and ink technique.[36] Although later mythologizing of Michelangelo's genius prefers him to have had no need of teaching, in reality he went through the gradual steps of education in ways similar to his contemporaries, if more accelerated. A rare document pertaining to his time with Ghirlandaio captures the adolescent Michelangelo fulfilling a novice's errand, although one showing a certain level of trust, to the Ospedale degli Innocenti, where he knocked on the door to collect a payment on behalf of his master for a completed painting.[37]

The future 'divine artist' rapidly progressed and did not remain at length as a trainee in Ghirlandaio's organization. He was soon promoted into the company of an elite group of aspiring artists who studied ancient art from the Medici collection in the garden near San Marco owned by the family and tutored by one of their retainers, the sculptor Bertoldo di Giovanni (*c.*1440–91). This experience truly began the ascent of the young artist toward becoming the divine Michelangelo, instructed to measure his progress against the achievement of antiquity, living among the members and supporters of the ruling family of Florence and conversing with the same teacher who had educated the children of Lorenzo the Magnificent. Michelangelo was only too happy to recount this extraordinary episode from his past for the benefit of Condivi's biography, at the same time that he denied any connection to Ghirlandaio's workshop, an element in his formation that was too close to the norm to make the story sparkle.

Nor did Caravaggio ever give recognition to the master with whom he studied, Simone Peterzano, despite having carried out a regular four-year apprenticeship for which we have solid information.[38] Peterzano had a successful career in Milan, producing important fresco cycles and obtaining commissions from the city's most illustrious patrons, although he is now most often mentioned purely in connection to his famous pupil. Peterzano's family was from Bergamo, a provincial center under Venetian rule during the 16th and 17th centuries. The family moved to Venice during Simone's childhood, setting the venue for his artistic training. Peterzano eventually was apprenticed to Titian and afterward followed opportunities as an independent master, reaching Milan by 1572, where he achieved success.

Caravaggio's training under Peterzano resulted in the style we see in the young artist's first known Roman works, recognizably Lombard in its lighting and subject matter, but with an underlying Venetian technique favoring the building of volume through color values. The transmission of Titian's tradition was clearly paramount in Peterzano's creed, even if the technique was modified in practice by the adaptation of local preferences once the artist became active in Milan. This is made clear in a self-portrait that has come down to us with the proud signature SIMON PETERZANUS VENETUS TITIANI ALUMNUS FECIT MDLXXXVIIII, repeating the affirmation of his painterly heritage found on other major works (Fig. 4). This proclamation of having formerly passed through Titian's workshop, insisted upon in 1589 on such a personal image, tells us something of the environment in which Caravaggio, who had left Peterzano's workshop just a year after that date, learned his art. The influence was, as mentioned, apparent to the artists in Rome who first commented on Caravaggio's provocative style.

The antithetical traditions of painting absorbed, developed and personalized by the two Michelangelos were congenial to their talents and enabled their art to soar to extraordinary levels of expression. United only in their refusal to acknowledge the fundamental importance of their training, their divergent styles are indicative of not only their different regions of birth, but also of the dramatic changes along the entire peninsula of Italy between what we refer to as the Renaissance and Baroque periods in art. Many of the most sensational adjustments came from revolutions within religious culture. Their bearing on art was enormous, affecting institutional power, systems of patronage, devotional practices and perhaps most crucially, attempting to legislate the very manner of conceiving and representing sacred subjects. Both Michelangelos became authoritative exemplars of religious painting and explored their sacred subjects as practicing members of the Catholic community; both were responsive to trends of thought and articulations of belief that were edgy and progressive in their own moment. However, times had changed to such an extent that if we posit the Tuscan Michelangelo as the archetype, his Lombard namesake becomes the anti-Michelangelo in his Counter-Reformation Catholicism, his manner of life and the stylistic goals of his art.

Caravaggio's approach to making art was tenaciously experiential where Michelangelo's was resolutely theoretical. The former staged his characters, representing their existence in the actual world, while the latter placed his figures in an idealized realm. And if Michelangelo's spatial illusionism could fool the eye of willing viewers into entering a world of perfection, Caravaggio sought not to entice his viewers, but to move them, encouraging emotional responses to his narrations. If Michelangelo surpassed nature in his conceptions, producing an art of sublimation, Caravaggio was complicit with nature's shortcomings, making an art of imperfections. Each, however, proceeded with finely honed artifice to achieve his vision.

There is every reason to believe that, assessing the artistic environment upon his arrival in Rome, Michelangelo Merisi quickly became aware his chief rival was the legacy of Michelangelo Buonarroti. The Renaissance artist who had during his lifetime been hailed as 'divine', whose exceptionally long career left a physical mark on the city of Rome, continued to have an impact on the psyche of all ambitious artists who hungered for success in the Eternal City. They either emulated, amended, or repudiated him, but all had to come to terms with the inescapability of Michelangelo's art and the manner in which it had dominated most of the 16th century.

We can imagine Michelangelo Merisi belligerently embracing the references evoked by his given name at the same time that he strove to diminish their domination. An obvious strategy for professional success would be to position himself as the new Michelangelo, who would outdo both the style and the significance of his predecessor. To my knowledge, the importance of this parallel has not been fully explored in the vast literature on the two artists. Caravaggio's immediate contemporaries would take for granted the vast gulf between the Tuscan and Lombard Michelangelos in terms of style, status and comportment, which would not bear comparison. The longer historical view changes things as one era builds upon its forerunner and we are in a position to see the relation of one to the other. However, to keep references to the two artists clear and to endow Caravaggio with a recognizable identity when the rediscovery of his work began in the 1950s, writers utilized 'Caravaggio' almost exclusively to refer to Michelangelo Merisi; the name 'Michelangelo' already had a unique, dedicated use in the history of art, not to be repeated. By now, Caravaggio's given name has been generally disregarded and the potential for instructive connections to his namesake have been largely overlooked. It is as if, to invoke Shakespeare's Juliet once more, her plea 'O, be some other name!' has been taken to heart in our treatment of Caravaggio.

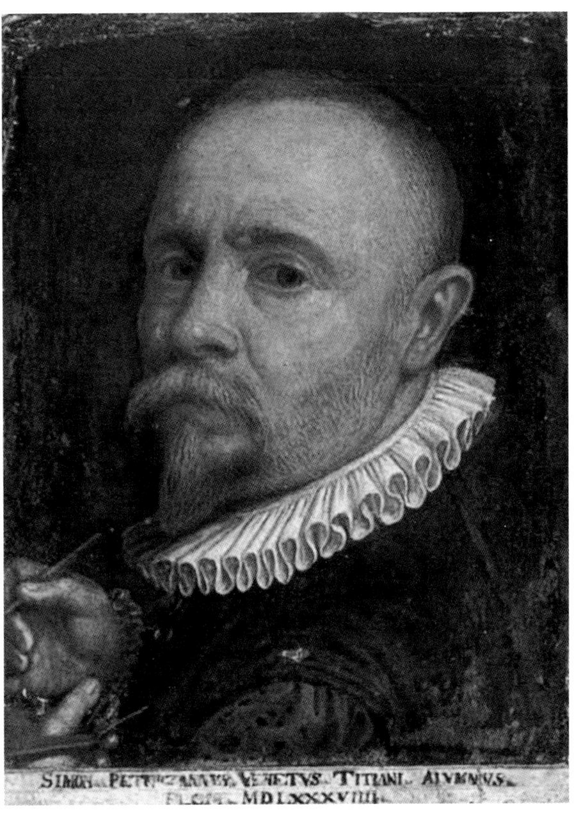

4 Simone Peterzano, *Self-Portrait*, 1589, oil on panel, 23 × 17 cm ($9\ {}^{1}/_{16} \times 6\ {}^{11}/_{16}$ in), Private Collection, Rome

Michelangelo Merisi began by openly smirking at the artistic patrimony of his namesake. Yet, as he brought his own striking style to maturity, sobered by all manner of struggle in life and in art, the example of Michelangelo Buonarroti continued to emit a signal that sparked a creative, if argumentative, response. What follows is an exploration of those encounters and their explosive impact on the art of the Early Modern era, whose enthralling history ignited a resurgence of interest in the mid-20th century and is still gathering steam as the 21st century moves ahead.

2

Mythological Characters as Agents of Provocation

Michelangelo's apprenticeship in Domenico Ghirlandaio's late 15th-century Florentine workshop exposed him to an accomplished working method featuring reminiscences of antique art as virtuoso passages within a framework of modern design. His subsequent experience in the Medici Garden at San Marco privileged ancient models as the source of good design and the vehicle for perfecting the human figure. The study of classical texts, expertly engaged by those who surrounded Michelangelo during his adolescent years of close attachment to the Medici family, encouraged his familiarity with ancient mythology, understood as complementary, rather than in opposition to, the Christian canon. Michelangelo Buonarroti's specialized training and the first steps of his career both were marked by his study of ancient art. One of the remarkable objects in the Casa Buonarroti, the Florentine museum housed within the former residence of the family, is a marble relief known as *The Battle of the Centaurs*. It dates from *c.*1492, when Michelangelo was still an adolescent; yet it remains a startlingly lucid announcement of his future art.

The sculpture is a student piece, although one that displays extraordinary technical confidence and declares the potential of the carver. At this early stage of development, Michelangelo was guided by the two masters introduced in the last chapter, whose output was dedicated to recapturing the classical past, turning its cultural achievements into a rejuvenated idiom that spoke to their own contemporary world. Bertoldo di Giovanni, proficient in relief sculpture as well as curator of Medicean antiquities and Angelo Poliziano, scholar of neoplatonic texts, contributed their expertise to the exercises of the young artist. As a result, Michelangelo's education as a sculptor took the fusion of antique form with classical content as an unquestioned premise for creative activity, manifest in the *Centaur* relief. It was his artistic birthright, bequeathed by a talented group in the circle of Lorenzo de' Medici, who were giving shape to exhilarating new ideas in art and literature which would energize the coming century. Michelangelo stepped forward on the momentum of this cultural whirlwind.

The artistic formation of Michelangelo is remarkable for its privileged access to the most stimulating tendencies in Quattrocento culture and his work became instrumental in passing on this heritage to succeeding generations. Michelangelo's art was so identified with models of antiquity that when the classical paradigm was later contested, his personal approach became a point of controversy. The early works of Caravaggio shout this contention. At the start of their careers, each artist had significant moments of measuring himself against the classical canons. Michelangelo saw the ancients as his true masters and rivals and he strove to surpass their achievements; Caravaggio was intent on establishing an alternative that poached from classicizing precedent but ignored its strictures. The alliance that Michelangelo had formed with the ancient tenets was renounced by Caravaggio, yet his refusal did not exclude reference to antiquity when it suited his objectives. Even Gian Pietro Bellori (1613–1696), an influential 17th-century biographer who criticized the artist for his anti-classicism, cited a classical example to elucidate what he perceived as the deficiencies of Caravaggio's style:

> Demetrius, the ancient sculptor, is said to have been so eager to render the likeness of things that he cared more for imitating them than for their beauty. We have seen that the same is true of Michelangelo Merisi: he recognized no other master than the model and did not select the best forms of nature but emulated art – astonishingly enough – without art.[1]

Bellori, whose life of Caravaggio was written polemically by a partisan of an opposing school of thought, one that embraced the classical model in alliance with study from life, skewed an ancient prototype to invent a cautionary tale. Pliny's *Natural History* provides a more positive view, using the story to explain the strategy of a painter who disregarded customary training and attained glory by exalting nature as his exclusive guide:

> Lysippus of Sicyon is said by Duris not to have been the pupil of anybody, but to have been originally a copper-smith and to have first got the idea of venturing on sculpture from the reply given by the painter Eupompus when asked which of his predecessors he took for his model; he pointed to a crowd of people and said that it was Nature herself, not an artist, whom one ought to imitate.[2]

Pliny's story seems tailor-made to have hugely pleased Caravaggio. It not only applauds the practice of copying nature to produce art, but also makes the painter the hero. In Pliny's account, one of the most famous sculptors in the ancient world extolls a painter who is distinguished by his denial of debt to any human master; without doubt, a sympathetic exemplar for Caravaggio. Further, Pliny recognizes Eupompus as nothing less than the initiator of a new manner of painting: 'Eupompus's own influence was so powerful that he made a fresh division of painting'.[3] Bellori recognized the applicability of Pliny's account to Caravaggio's case, paraphrasing it twice. However, the appropriation was modified each time to disparage the Lombard's work. Further on in the cited passage, which opens the biography dedicated to Caravaggio with a classical template in order to denounce the artist's anti-classicism, we read:

> He not only ignored the most excellent marbles of the ancients and the famous paintings of Raphael, but he despised them, and nature alone became the object of his brush. Thus when the most famous statues of Phidias and Glycon were pointed out to him as models for his painting, he gave no other reply than to extend his hand toward a crowd of men, indicating that nature had provided him sufficiently with teachers.[4]

Bellori's variants of Pliny's ancient testimony, rearranged to denounce Caravaggio's lack of respect for the classical legacy of art, show a clever manipulation of texts. The stratagem is matched, or perhaps outdone, by Caravaggio's own tactical citation of antiquity precisely in order to disrupt the continued domination of that paradigm. Caravaggio's mutinous fervor against classicism was matched in intensity in an earlier era by Michelangelo's ardent efforts to conquer the antique on its own terms. Both attitudes find remarkable expression in the representations of Bacchus each artist produced in the early years of their careers in Rome.

Bacchus, the Roman version of the Greek mythological deity Dionysus, is a god of vegetation, particularly the grape harvest and wine and is associated with fertility. The state of inebriation is part of his domain, but also that of ritual frenzy or *mania* [ecstasy]; he also presides over impersonation and the theatrical arts. During the Quattrocento the iconography of Bacchus was elaborated in neoplatonic texts, where his indulgence in wine was taken to be a path to the liberation of the spirit. The transformed state of being was capable of lighting a divine spark, inducing a creative frenzy. The classical tradition allowed this altered consciousness to apply to the transcendence required for creative acts such as composing poetry, where the human realm most closely approaches the celestial. The stirring state of ecstasy that allowed contact with the supernatural in the ancient world was Christianized by the Florentine Neoplatonists to symbolize the progress of the soul toward the divine. Pico della Mirandola (1463–94), whose *Oration on the Dignity of Man*, written in 1486, was foundational for Renaissance thought, explains: 'We shall be possessed by these Socratic frenzies, which will so place us outside of our minds that they will place our mind and ourselves in God.'[5]

The Christianized Renaissance meaning was also broadened to attribute the inspired creative impulse to the visual arts, linking them closely to the afflatus of poetry. The production of art is understood to arise from the same heightened sensations that link visual artists to poets, to whom Plato first attributed the mystical process of creation linked to divinity. Artists in the Renaissance were beginning to enjoy a rise in status through the theory of their participation in the otherworldly and transcendent exercise of their imaginative facilities.

The imbibing of Bacchus was thus a symbol of inspiration, both divine and artistic, with spiritual connotations that were noble, as well as earthly implications that were open to less glorious results. Associations forged in neoplatonic thought were part of the heritage Michelangelo brought with him to Rome and would have resonated with great immediacy for the young artist who had heard their exposition at first hand. Pico della Mirandola was also a protégé of Lorenzo the Magnificent, had been under his protection in Florence from 1488 and was a close friend of Poliziano. The lessons in ancient culture Michelangelo received from Lorenzo's circle of humanist scholars were inevitably called upon for his first major commission in Rome.

Upon arrival in the Eternal City, Michelangelo immediately sought out Cardinal Raffaele Riario (1460–1521), with a letter of presentation from Lorenzo di Pierfrancesco de' Medici (1463–1503). This Lorenzo was a cousin of the Magnificent and lived for some years under his guardianship; an estrangement later occurred over a dispute regarding the younger relative's patrimony. Lorenzo di Pierfrancesco helped Michelangelo to start his career in Rome, providing introductions to the powerful cardinal as well as to an extensive Florentine network in the papal city. Raffaele Riario belonged to the Della Rovere family; he was a prestigious grand-nephew of Pope Sixtus IV (1414–84) and a relation of Michelangelo's future, beloved patron, Pope Julius II (1443–1513). When the young artist met the cardinal, Riario was involved in the lengthy process of constructing his palatial Roman residence, later confiscated by the Medici and eventually housing papal administrative offices, known by its function as the *Cancelleria* [Chancellery]. The Medici and Riario/Della Rovere families sustained bitter enmity across generations. However, as often occurred in Renaissance history, artists were forced to tread narrow paths between their patrons' feuds and followed the most advantageous commissions. Riario was favorably impressed by the young artist upon their first meeting and freely invited him to view his outstanding collection of ancient sculpture during their ensuing conversation. Treating the newcomer with surprising respect, the cardinal then requested Michelangelo to give his opinion of the antiquities he had inspected. Upon Riario's swift offer of a commission, the young sculptor modestly demurred (according to his own account), averring he would not be able to outdo the ancients, but all the same was willing to prove himself to the discerning collector. This lively scenario comes to us in Michelangelo's own words from his earliest surviving correspondence, addressed to Lorenzo di Pierfrancesco:

> This is only to let you know that we arrived safely last Saturday and at once went to call upon the Cardinal di San Giorgio [Riario] to whom I presented your letter. He seemed pleased to see me and immediately desired me to go and look at certain figures; this took me all day, so I could not deliver your other letters that day. Then on Sunday, having gone to his new house, the Cardinal sent for me. I waited upon him, and he asked me what I thought of the things I had seen. In reply to this I told him what I thought; and I certainly think he has many beautiful things. Then the Cardinal asked me whether I had courage enough to attempt some work of art of my own. I replied that I could not do anything as fine, but that he should see what I could do. We have bought a piece of marble for a life-sized figure and on Monday I shall begin work.[6]

The result of this encounter was a free-standing, life-size figure of Bacchus (Plate 6). Although the sculpture survives to this day and enjoys the most authentic documentation possible from its mention in Michelangelo's letter, we have only partial information to explain what happened once the sculpture was completed. There are indications of intrigue, which remain perplexing. It seems Riario never welcomed the *Bacchus* into his collection, even though a document attests to a final installment of the full payment of 550 *fiorini d'oro* [gold florins] having been made on 3 July 1497; it was an enormous amount to pay for a work by an unknown sculptor, 22 years of age.[7]

There is compelling evidence that the original idea was to place the figure in the company of classical statues in a theater designed with strict adherence to ancient prototype.[8] This extravagant feature, projected to be contained within the courtyard as a focal point of Riario's vast residence, was to be the site for performances of Greek and Roman plays. For reasons that are not clear, the *Bacchus* was instead eventually installed in the garden of Jacopo Galli, one of Michelangelo's newly acquired Roman protectors, who opened his home to the artist in an atmosphere of close friendship. Galli was the cardinal's banker and intermediary, who had journeyed to Florence to meet Michelangelo on Riario's behalf.[9] Many reasons have been hypothesized for the displacement of the sculpture, fueled by Michelangelo's later, deeply disparaging remarks to Condivi about his experiences with Riario. The artist delivered a version of the story about the *Bacchus* to his biographer that prickles with displeasure and scorn five decades after the fact. The brief account amounts to a full-scale *damnatio memoriae,* an erasure of all testimony to the good deeds of the cardinal, condemning him to a state of insignificance in Michelangelo's personal saga. The put-down is so effective that only recent research has begun to piece together the real situation: 'And the fact that the cardinal of S. Giorgio had little understanding or enjoyment of sculpture is made abundantly clear to us because in the whole time that Michelangelo stayed with him, which was about a year, he never worked on any commission whatever from the cardinal.'[10]

The elderly Michelangelo cancelled the credibility of his first Roman patron by reviling him as a philistine and retroactively deaccessioning the *Bacchus* from the cardinal's patronage. The eager, thinly veiled bragging evident in the letter Michelangelo sent home to Florence in 1496 describing the warm reception given by the cardinal was forgotten by the person who wrote it. The survival of the missive's testimony, however, confirms that things happened differently.

The cardinal's initial enthusiasm makes his ultimate rejection of the *Bacchus* more than puzzling, especially in view of the considerable amount he paid for it. Various explanations have been proposed, including the suggestion that Michelangelo's sculpture was too modern in conception to complement Riario's reconstruction of an authentic classical theater along Vitruvian principles. As we will see, the *Bacchus* was certainly revolutionary enough to give credence to this possibility. Or, a more practical consideration may have annulled the original intention: Riario was unable to bring to completion his ambitious *all'antica* theater.

At the end of 1499, Cardinal Riario found it prudent to leave for France after falling foul of Pope Alexander VI's politics and the territorial ambitions he cultivated for his son, Cesare Borgia. While Riario was able to maintain ownership of his urban palace, construction slowed to a halt. The cardinal returned to Rome only after a lapse of four years, his future and fortune once again assured by the ascendance of Pope Julius II to the papacy in 1503. Riario's dream, however, of resuscitating the theater of antiquity in his private residence was never realized; perhaps its time had passed and funding had dwindled. Perhaps it was not a good idea to outdo the papal court in ostentation while his relative sat on the papal throne; Julius II was seeing to his own monumental building programs. Without the theater for which it had been envisioned, the *Bacchus* may have become an irrelevant detail to the cardinal in the midst of his larger concerns; or worse, an unwanted reminder of a cherished project never to be completed. Jacopo Galli's property was in all probability the site of carving the *Bacchus*, which then awaited its final destination in the future theater. Not being able to have it installed in what was still a construction site before his departure, Riario could have easily been magnanimous enough to leave the sculpture permanently with Galli in recognition of his services, or it may have become a *de facto* gift. After the decade of Julius II's reign, Riario's fortunes went from decline to disaster. In 1517, he conspired in an unsuccessful plot to assassinate the Medici Pope Leo X; he was stripped of rank and wealth and ended his life in embittered exile in Naples. His glorious residence was taken over by Leo's cousin, the future Pope Clement VII.

Any number of subsequent events in the tangle of Michelangelo's Roman experiences may have poisoned the memory of Cardinal Riario for him; the only certainty is that the artist re-wrote history to make Jacopo Galli responsible for the commission of the *Bacchus*. Pronounced with such unreserved conviction, Michelangelo's wishful thinking became the version of record. Following the insults heaped upon Cardinal Riario, Condivi describes Jacopo Galli as 'a Roman gentleman of fine intellect' and 'a connoisseur' who knew how to recognize the fledgling artist's talents by making excellent use of them. Time has proven Galli and his descendants worthy of the prize; the *Bacchus* stayed in the family's possession for three-quarters of a century.

A curious thing happened to the *Bacchus*, however, while it resided with the Galli family. At some point the sculpture was mutilated by the removal of its right hand and sexual member. The penis was detached, not broken or damaged, nor was it ever restored; the signs of it having been 'chiseled away' are still evident.[11] The escapade of the hand is even more baffling. We do not know precisely when the hand came off, nor if the damage occurred through mishap or calculation. A famous drawing executed in the early 1530s by the Dutch artist Maarten van Heemskerck (1498–1574) records the sculpture presiding over the garden of the Galli home in its damaged state, fitting in perfectly with the ancient ruins in whose company it is positioned (Fig. 5). This lively and eloquent document tells us a great deal about the presentation of the statue.

Heemskerck gives it pride of place in the composition, so close to the edge of the pictorial space that the base of the sculpture is cut off. It appears to

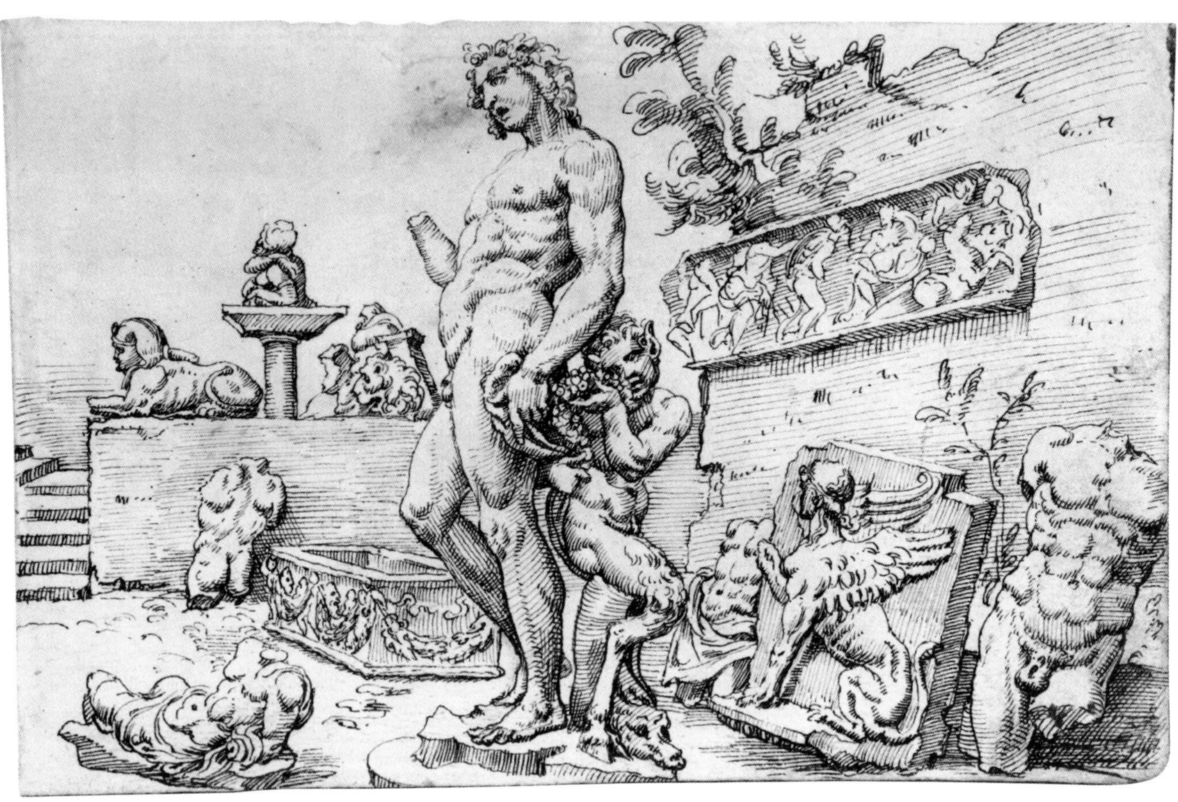

5 Maarten van Heemskerck, *Garden of the Casa Galli*, 1532–5, drawing, 13 × 20.5 cm (5 ⅛ × 8 ¹⁄₁₆ in), Staatliche Museen, Berlin

be monumental in comparison to the reliefs and bits of fragmented sculptures arranged in artful chaos within a walled garden. The affinity of the *Bacchus* to the rest of the collection is strikingly made: the statue's right arm is shown at such an angle as to appear a mere stump and its broken outline is silhouetted in open space just to the left of the composition's center. Heemskerck masterfully shows us that Michelangelo's *Bacchus* could not only stand proudly in competition with all manner of ancient art, but could also fool the unwary observer into mistaking it for a classical piece impaired by the hazard of time. There is every reason to believe that Michelangelo was directly involved in the sophisticated trickery. As we will see later, Michelangelo took his first shot at entry into what we would call 'the Roman art scene' by a similar feat of virtuoso deception and it involved all the same players who participated in the genesis of the *Bacchus*.

Despite his ostensible humility in response to Cardinal Riario's collection during their first conversation, Michelangelo had supreme confidence in his ability to prevail against all rivals from antiquity and this attitude pervades his early work. If we accept the connection of the cardinal's original commission to his great project of constructing a classical theater, it comfortably follows that Michelangelo was asked to contribute a free-standing figure of the principal deity of the dramatic arts, a *Bacchus* which could hold its own when placed in an assembly of ancient figures. When the challenge of that siting failed to materialize, Galli and his artist imagined an analogous, less grandiose yet more creative and teasing, installation.

The pseudo-antique, brilliantly modern sculpture was instated as the reigning divinity of Galli's collection of classical fragments. All the *Bacchus* needed to be fully in character for its duplicitous role was a bit of discretionary damage. We do not know exactly when the hand was severed from the wrist of the figure, nor when it was repaired. Condivi's description, however, with its emphasis on the position of the hand holding a generously proportioned, two-handled vessel, is evidence of restoration having taken place before mid-century. The biographer reveals nothing about the puzzle of the missing hand. Rather, he emphasizes the gratification of Bacchus as he contemplates his wine, goblet poised for imbibing: 'He holds a cup in his right hand, as if about to drink, and gazes at it as if taking pleasure in that liquor which he invented; for this reason Michelangelo encircled the head with a garland of vine leaves.'[12]

It is remarkable that more than half a century after the completion of the *Bacchus*, its creator desired that the motif of the raised cup, implying eventual agreeable inebriation, be singled out as worthy of note. Was this observation a subtle way of setting the record straight, declaring that the sculpture had been reintegrated, obscuring the youthful deception? The rest of the description enforces a reading of the iconography that also modifies the original concept, introducing a moralizing intention cautioning against debauchery. This retunes the sculpture to harmonize with the times, much more in keeping with the early signs of Catholic Reformation than with the neoplatonism and proud rivalry with antiquity that were hallmarks of Michelangelo's references around 1500.

It is, therefore, crucial to remain anchored in the aesthetics of the 1490s when thinking about Michelangelo's approach to the ideation and carving of *Bacchus*. His strategy for outshining the ancient models is so apparent that we can stipulate precisely his contributions to the conventional classical iconography. Maximizing his knowledge of Bacchic themes derived from the Medici neoplatonist circle, Michelangelo began by assembling an image from the literary sources, as Condivi approvingly states in his description of the statue, 'whose form and appearance correspond in every particular to the intention of the writers of antiquity', citing particularly 'the mirthful face and sidelong, lascivious eyes of those too much possessed of the love of wine'[13] (Fig. 6).

Even though at the age of 78 the artist hewed closer to the current ideological temper, silenced any mention of divine frenzy and changed the emphasis to moralizing against unrestrained indulgence, Michelangelo was still proud of how his *Bacchus* stood up against its predecessors. Or, more precisely, how the figure barely manages to remain standing as he reels from the effects of wine. As his astounding contribution to the iconography, Michelangelo manipulated the defining trait of ancient figural sculpture, the *contrapposto* stance, so that Bacchus seems to be swaying before the viewer's eyes. *Contrapposto*, as perfected in classical art, contrived one leg as straight and weight-bearing, freeing the other to lift off the ground, bend, twist, or otherwise shoot the hip upward, allowing the torso to be given life-like movement. While eradicating stiffness from the body, the *contrapposto* stance is also a balancing act, calculated to give stability to the figure.

Michelangelo's unique feat was to make his marble Bacchus appear unsteady. While the typical *contrapposto* of the legs is retained, Bacchus's torso is positioned to move slightly backwards and its left side is tilted appreciably downwards; his head slants a bit to the right and a little forward. The most audacious of all Michelangelo's technical bravura consists in his decision to carve the figure on the diagonal from within the original rectangular block, working from front left to back right, producing an internal dynamic that would yield fully satisfying arrangements from every viewing angle. All of these nuanced adjustments are activated by the viewer's movement around the statue, transferring

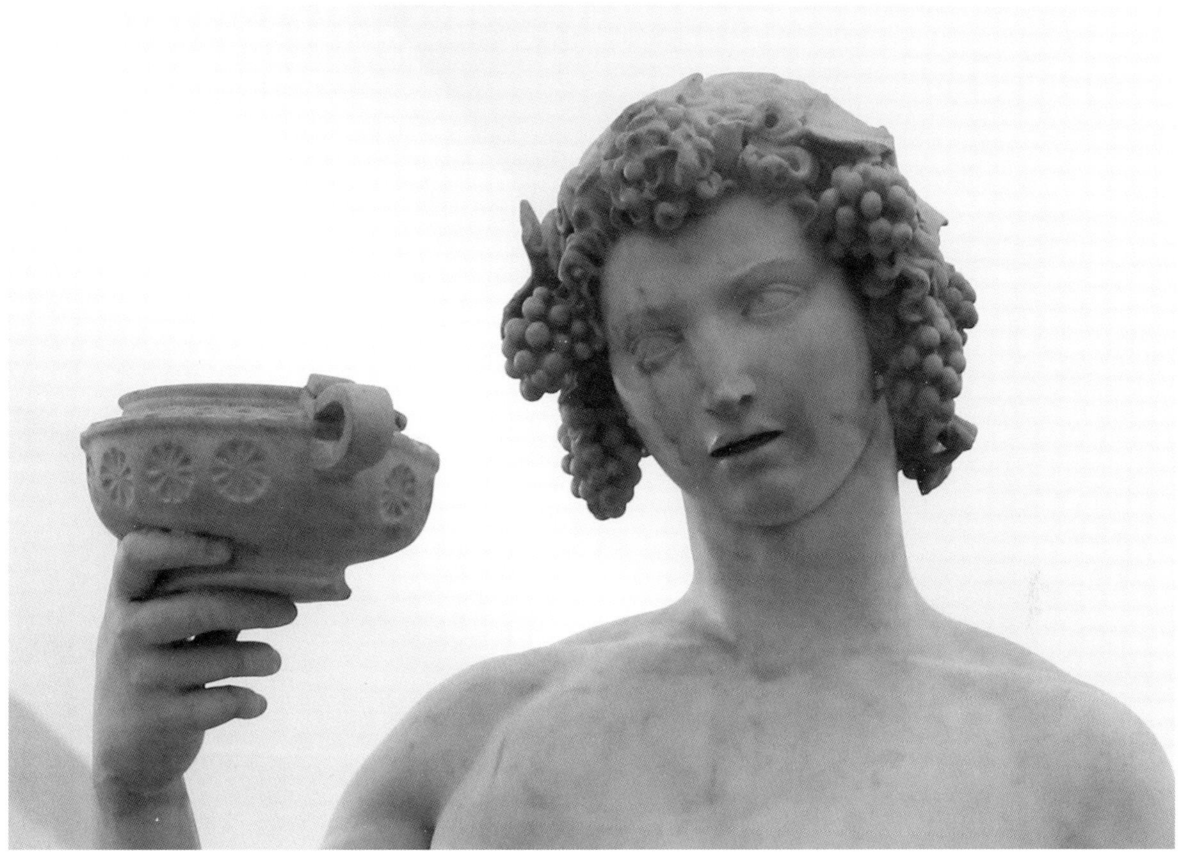

6 Michelangelo, *Bacchus*, 1496–7 (detail), marble, 203 cm (79 15/16 in), Bargello Museum, Florence

an illusion of a lurching motion to the swaying posture. With brilliant control, Michelangelo has imparted an impression of mobility, supplied by the actual motion of the viewer.[14] This sets the *Bacchus* apart from the ancient canon; it was a virtuoso touch that defined the sculpture as truly modern, even while it was indebted to classical paradigms in both form and content. The *Bacchus* was composed not only to be seen from every angle, but conceived to change along with the position of the viewer.

The effect of the magisterial work was startling to its original audience for its combination of classicizing form with contemporary technique. The awesomeness of its impact was indissolubly tied to the revolutionary way in which the *Bacchus* both followed and departed from its models. We are lucky to have a first-hand account of how an expert, visiting in 1540, participated in the game of ancient/not ancient that had been organized in Galli's garden:

> Now, in Rome a marble god Bacchus with a young satyr carrying a basket of grapes on his back was shown to me as an antique and marvelous work. It appeared to me to be the work of an able artist, and yet not an antique one, even if in the color of the marble and in all its perfections it was; and

> when some Romans asked what I thought, I said that it was very fine and done by an able artist, but I declared that it was not antique, and this because its arms and hands were raised halfway, which was outside the limits and rigor of antiquity, for they were neither very low nor raised very high, and likewise that the movement and placement of the legs of the Bacchus were weak and lacking the stability and firm implantation of the antique, even though the perfections and the invention and the proportions and the satyr with the basket looked antique. Then they were amazed by my words and told me in response that it was a work that Michelangelo had done days earlier in order to deceive the Romans and the pope with that antique object, and Michelangelo learned that his work had not deceived me.[15]

Francisco de Hollanda was the Portuguese artist who, brimming with pride, tells us in such a beguiling manner of how his *giudizio*, or faculty of good judgment, prevailed in the challenge he was set. His triumph in passing the test by recognizing the true nature of the *Bacchus* is capped by Francisco's delight that Michelangelo himself was informed of the deed. The story records, beyond Francisco's glee, the Renaissance practice of testing the informed viewer's critical acumen in discerning the constituent qualities of a work of art. The observer is handed an opportunity to shine eloquently in the company of other connoisseurs and learned friends, or fall into disgrace with an unimpressive assessment. This type of courtly, or high-society diversion with high stakes, was conducted with different categories of examination. In addition to the argument of ancient versus modern drawn in Hollanda's glowing report, a contest between the mediums of painting and sculpture was famously set as the quintessential subject for disputation, codified as the *paragone*. It will be considered again and amplified with a very particular twist, to suggest contests centered on the works of the two Michelangelos.

At this point, however, it is illuminating to recall Cardinal Riario's disregard for the *Bacchus* and the venom with which Condivi condemns his (literal) lack of vision. Michelangelo's skill in carving marble was perhaps so blinding that Raffaele Riario really was not able to fully appreciate its revolutionary merits. Riario's *giudizio* did not live up to Michelangelo's expectation; the cardinal utterly failed the test in which Hollanda later excelled. The Galli family evidently understood and valued the achievement embodied in their *Bacchus* and boasted uninterrupted possession of the masterpiece for many decades. They gave it up only in 1572, to a recipient who would have been very difficult to deny. The *Bacchus* was purchased by Francesco I de' Medici and destined for the Grand Ducal collections in Florence. It was joined around 30 years later by another astonishingly innovative version of the Bacchic figure, which had been presented to Francesco's brother and successor, Ferdinando. On this occasion it was a painting rather than a sculpture and it was created by Caravaggio (Plate 5).

Cardinal Del Monte was responsible for the commission, in all probability intended from its inception as a gift for his friend and mentor, Grand Duke Ferdinando, the ruler of Florence at that time.[16] The request, therefore, directly involved an eventual comparison to Michelangelo's interpretation of the theme, as well as a late entry to the most popular contest in 16th-century intellectual sport, the *paragone*, or confrontational comparison, between the merits of painting versus sculpture. To add to the challenge, the contest was to take place on what could be considered Michelangelo's home ground, the production of an outstanding modern work that engaged classical subject matter and responded knowingly to classical form. Caravaggio proved himself equal to the task on both counts.

Just like Michelangelo, Caravaggio would have had to begin by considering ancient traditions in his conjuring of Bacchus, an allusion inherent in the subject. Despite Caravaggio's later persona as an enemy of ancient art and his reputed ignorance of it, he was well aware of the power of the antique. He called upon it as a source in a number of early works, yet he manipulated his citations in a manner antithetical to that of his precursor. Where Michelangelo strove for an energizing dialogue with the ancients that had embellished their original language, Caravaggio engaged a resolute argument that disguised his comprehension of their vocabulary. His sense of competition, however, was just as keen and it extended the rivalry to encompass not only the ancients, but his 'old master' namesake. There is every reason to think that the terms of his commission asked Caravaggio to incorporate specific references from antique models into the requested painting, again shadowing what his predecessor had encountered almost exactly a century earlier in undertaking the sculpted *Bacchus*.

One group of sculptures from the classical past may have particularly interested Caravaggio and his patron as they imagined potential concepts for the novel Bacchus, one to be executed according to Caravaggio's preferred techniques. What could be a more appropriate challenge to Caravaggio's declared adherence to an effect of realism than an encounter with a highly idealized model? The perfect foil could be found in the portrait type of Antinous, the young lover of Emperor Hadrian (76–138 CE), whose recognizable features were consistently harmonious, well-proportioned and regular. The choice of an Antinous type as a starting point for a representation of Bacchus was eruditely apt. A tradition had arisen in antiquity that merged the comely features of Antinous with images of the venerated deity of wine, especially as the emperor sought to assuage his grief with effigies immortalizing the deceased beloved. The ancient world canonized the parallel and produced numerous variations of the Antinous/Bacchus configuration, which were known and imitated in the Renaissance.

The findings of several scholars have uncovered a compelling context for Caravaggio's commission, citing the many pertinent classical examples of the Antinous and Bacchic types that were collected and copied at the time, arguing their applicability to Caravaggio's painting. A recent, expertly researched discussion concludes that Caravaggio's *Bacchus* was directly influenced by a lavishly praised ancient bust of Antinous in the possession of Giovanni Francesco Peranda in Rome.[17] When objects from the distinguished collection became available for purchase, wide-ranging covetousness ensued, attested by excited correspondence among informed collectors throughout Italy. Passionate attention focused on an elegant bust of Antinous. The *Antinous* ultimately became part of the Gonzaga collection in Mantua, Duke Vincenzo having prevailed over other notable, and notably acquisitive, connoisseurs. Several were from the circle of Caravaggio's closest patrons; Cardinal Del Monte was among them, as was his mentor, Ferdinando de' Medici. It is arguable that Del Monte devised a commission for Caravaggio that re-invented the unobtainable Antinous as a very available Bacchus. It is tempting to think that Del Monte found a remarkable way to declare his friendship to Ferdinando, providing him with an unprecedented, modern presentation of Bacchus to compensate for the Grand Duke's failure to procure a much sought-after antique work of high status. The elements that make up Caravaggio's *Bacchus* appear calculated to delight Del Monte's eminent protector and indeed all learned viewers, with a painting that was keenly mischievous in its handling of classical iconography, remarkably innovative in style and exuding a naughty sensuousness appropriate to the god of wine. Put concisely, Caravaggio's *Bacchus* was worthy of entering a collection that boasted Michelangelo's revolutionary treatment of the subject, matching it in originality and bravura.

The persuasive contextual argument for Caravaggio having looked to classical prototypes as the basis for his depiction of Bacchus is strongly supported by the visual evidence. The abundant curly hair in artful disarray, long, straight nose, generous lips and broad cheeks of the Antinous portrait type present a fine fit for the traditionally sensuous and androgynous lineaments of the god of wine. All of these features can be discerned as underlying Caravaggio's figure, although they are exaggerated to the point of producing an entirely different effect. The hair is composed of massive curls that go beyond copious to give the appearance of a wig; clusters of grapes, although plentiful and depicted with enough detail to differentiate two varieties, are almost lost in the dense coiffure. The traditional wreath of vine leaves has been nearly transmuted into a helmet by its enormity. And the increased fleshiness of all the facial features transforms the regularity of Antinous/Bacchus's beauty into a distinctly plump sensuousness, which is not, however, echoed in the decidedly sinewy torso, shoulder and arm. The teasing amalgamation of ancient prototype and live model causes the discrepancy, with purposely uncamouflaged seams. Caravaggio created other visual clues alerting us to details incorporated from an unmistakably living subject, including the dirty fingernails of the hand holding the wine, which contrast so vividly with the elegance of the curving fingers. The ruddy complexion of this Bacchus comes not only from the flush of his cheeks in response to the wine, but from the high coloring of a young man living under the Roman sun. The naturalistic effect is reinforced by the noticeably tanned hands, pale at the wrists where the long sleeves of his street clothes obscured the sun's rays.

Caravaggio entered whole-heartedly into the stratagem of delineating a classical deity with particulars culled from the everyday world. The 'toga' of Bacchus is formed by a contemporary white *camicia*, or voluminous shirt that men wore beneath their outer garment. Its appearance is cleverly altered by slinging the material over just one arm and draping the rest across the figure's torso. It is jumbled below with a slightly grayer bed sheet, haphazardly bunched up behind the figure. The elaborate folds of the sheet scarcely obscure the bed from which the linens were presumably taken. The coarse striped canvas mattress peaks out, for the amusement of the attentive viewer, to confirm the arrangement's unexalted origins.

Caravaggio continues his virtuoso performance of turning mundane contemporary objects into the attributes of an Olympian deity with the still life elements in the foreground of the painting. The carafe and chalice are glassware of modern luxury, yet their transparency and graceful simplicity endow them with a timeless quality well suited to their assignment as the god's attributes. The display of fruit on the ledge that establishes the pictorial space between the figure and viewer at first glance seems opulent, as befits the god of harvests. A closer inspection, however, reveals a more disquieting message; the fruits closest to our gaze are unappetizingly overripe, marred by dark blotches and bursting skins. Leaves have turned brown and brittle and cast inky black shadows beneath the bowl and across a crumpled napkin. This very convincing, masterfully painted still life tells a moral tale in itself, piled with the produce of nature, half of it gleaming and tempting, the other half rotting and sinister. Caravaggio's regional skills as a painter of still life, for which he was particularly known at the early stages of his career in Rome, have been featured in a starring role, almost outdoing the impact of the subject's protagonist. It is the visual declaration of a remark attributed to the artist, an inflammatory exclamation that painting an excellent still life is just as difficult as fashioning a human figure.

The role played by the still life elements that identify Bacchus in Caravaggio's composition is in fact a major one. In addition to the moralizing implications of the decaying fruit, the presentation of the wine suggests a further narrative thread. The uneven level of the wine in the carafe and the bubbles on its surface show that the vessel has just been set down on the table; the movement of the wine is repeated in the pronounced rippling effect of the liquid within the chalice (Fig. 7). Bacchus is portrayed in the act of offering a luscious, inebriating libation to the viewer as he stretches his arm outward. The gesture is conveyed in a delicate rather than a thrusting manner, whether to show a slight hesitancy or to prevent spillage from

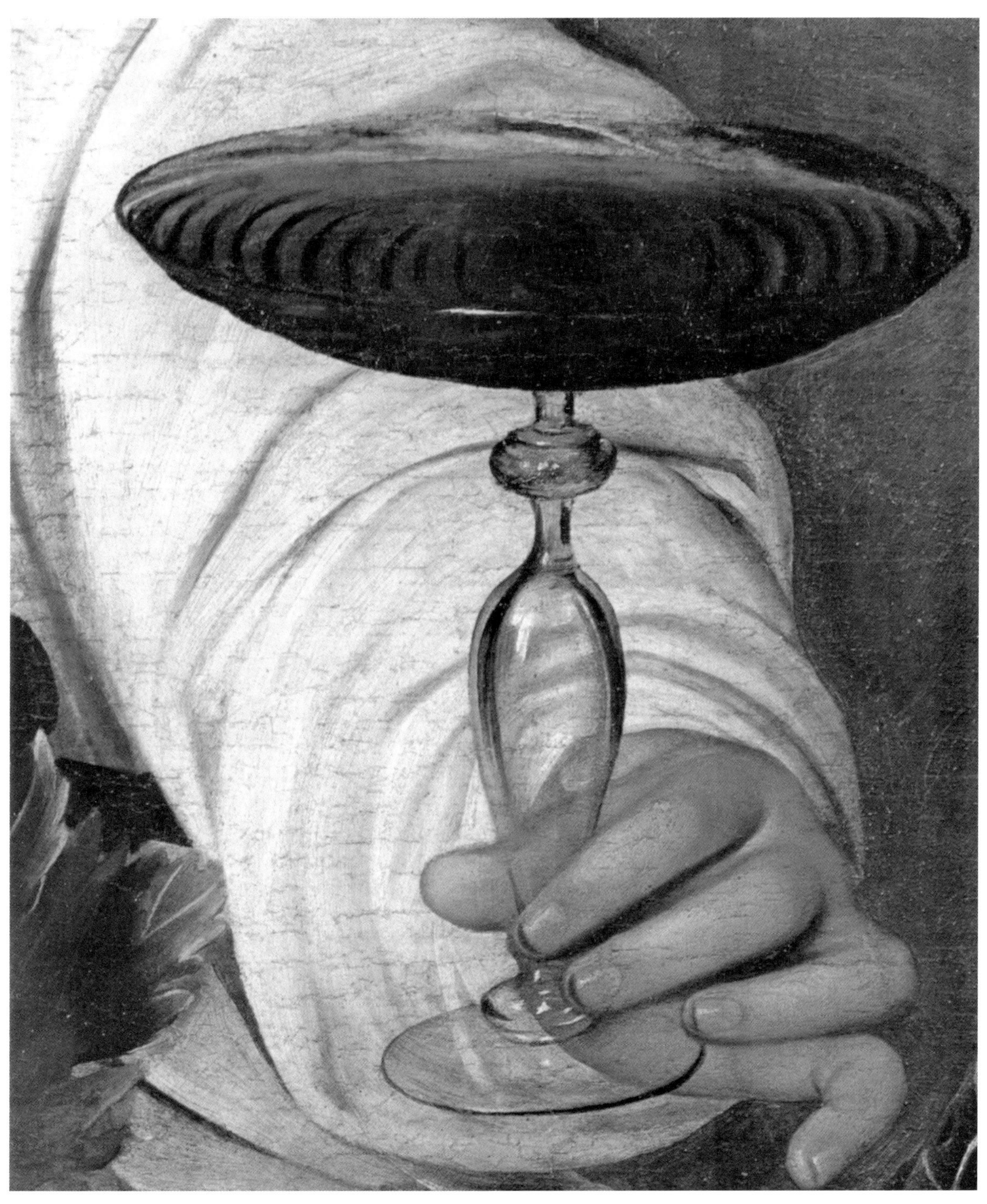

7 Caravaggio, *Bacchus*, *c.*1597 (detail), oil on canvas, 98 × 85 cm (38 9/16 × 33 7/16 in), Uffizi Galleries, Florence, Inv. 1890, no. 5312

the glass that is full to the brim. The passage is painted so brilliantly that it may take some time to recognize the secondary offer placed to the left of the chalice, just about at the center of the composition. The right hand of Bacchus, a deity connected to the fertility of the grape harvest, is ready to pull open the large black bow that holds his makeshift garment in place, offering another path to carnal intoxication. His heavy-lidded gaze, calculated to focus directly on the viewer, buttressed by the knowing arch of his brows, adds the finishing touch to the seductive characterization of the figure.

The teasing eroticism of this Bacchus has often been mistakenly read as an expression of Caravaggio's homosexuality, or at least as an image necessarily constructed in this vein. In reality, this particular painting tells us nothing about the artist's sexuality, but follows easily recognizable elements in the imagery traditionally employed in the evocation of the deity. Caravaggio played with the convention of depicting Bacchus as androgynous or effeminate, a type of youthful male beauty inherited directly from classical prototypes. The characterization passed from the ancients through Renaissance variations, on to Caravaggio's own time. Michelangelo drew on the same set of traditions. Vasari commented approvingly that the sculptor had seamlessly blended in his *Bacchus* 'the smoothness of a male youth and the fleshiness and roundness of a woman', customary focuses of desire in that era. Nor is there any reason to deny an erotic charge to female viewers in response to the fantasy of the image; after all, the *Bacchae*, the revelers who were a central part of the god's entourage, were female. Bacchus can be appreciated as a seducer across all categories of gender.

Bacchic seduction in the service of ecstasy, whether carnal or spiritual, is enabled through intoxication. Escape from sensory limitations is part of the jurisdiction of Bacchus and both Michelangelos allude to this release in their works. The sculpture and the painting alike focus attention on the offering of wine; Michelangelo's staggering Olympian displays it as the source of creative ecstasy, while Caravaggio's saucy deity directly proffers it for the viewer's consumption. The three-dimensional forms of Michelangelo's sculpted group are activated by the viewer's movement around them as the swaying of the drunken god is perceived; the participation of the viewer is required for the full realization of the sculpture. In the painting, the foreshortened arm of Bacchus extends out toward the viewer, dissolving the boundary between the pictorial space and the inhabited world; the viewer's involvement in receiving the wine is, similarly, fundamental to the conception of the painting. The exaltation of wine in the cup of Bacchus, at the core of traditional iconography yet handled so innovatively by each artist, makes a spectacular connection between the two works. Caravaggio's response to Michelangelo's motif is dramatically declared in the tendering of the wine. The virtuosity of the sculpture's nuanced, gently inebriated sway is answered in the painting by the swagger of the contemporary young man who plays the role of the god, openly seducing his viewers. Fresh variations on Bacchic motifs become a battleground *par excellence* for the two Michelangelos; luckily, we can with all authority claim the viewer to be the winner.

The ultimate destination of Caravaggio's *Bacchus* was to be part of the Medici collections, its presence traceable to 1609.[18] The early date is a further indication that Cardinal Del Monte actively provided Grand Duke Ferdinando with an eloquent attestation of friendship in arranging the pairing thus providing a razor-sharp *paragone* to demonstrate the mastery of his newly acquired artist to delight Ferdinando and his court. The superb gift might well have been initiated as a compensation for the Grand Duke's frustrated desire to own the antique bust of Antinous. If, however, this specific cause and effect remains speculative, it is evident that upon arrival Caravaggio's *Bacchus* functioned in a particular way to enrich the Medici family collections. It bequeathed a contemporary spin on a cherished ritual of comparison, pitting Ferdinando's brand-new painting against the 'old master' sculpture acquired by his brother Francesco, the preceding Grand Duke. The thrilling *paragone* set up between the two Medici collectors, as well as the two Michelangelos, would be a vehicle for sophisticated courtly conversations that covered and extended the fertile terrain of fierce artistic competition at its highest level.

The role played by Francesco Del Monte in spurring Caravaggio to a level worthy of rivaling Michelangelo in a new stylistic idiom was crucial. Residence in the cardinal's household gave the artist not only economic stability and the attention of potential patrons, but also access to important collections of art, the shared ideas of the cardinal's erudite group of friends and the benefit of conversation with learned connoisseurs. Caravaggio was quick to grasp and capitalize on advantages within his reach once he entered Del Monte's orbit. This is demonstrated through comparison of an antecedent example of the Bacchus theme carried out just before the artist came under the cardinal's influence. The treatment is clever and imaginative, but nowhere near as nuanced and complex as attained in the Medici *Bacchus*.

The painting known as the *Bacchino malato* [Sick little Bacchus] (Plate 8) was carried out around 1594, just before Caravaggio entered Del Monte's household. The composition shows the artist already in command of the stylistic components that will mark his mature work: dark background, strong light from the left, figure dramatically close to the pictorial plane. Salient elements that reappear in the Medici *Bacchus* are also present, such as the bare shoulder and half-revealed torso with a *camicia* cunningly wrapped around it, once again held in place by a suggestive bow which, in this case, thrusts toward the viewer. The impeccably painted still life features are present, with peaches and grapes placed on a low table in the foreground that establishes the pictorial space. The conventional attributes of Bacchus, which identify the subject and afford more possibilities for bravura still life passages, are on view in the ivy wreath, large in scale with an almost animated effect and in the cluster of grapes the young god holds up toward his lips. Although the fruit on the narrow table is pristine, some of the ivy leaves and a few grapes closest to the boy's mouth have turned an unappetizing shade of yellow-brown. The traditional inclusion of objects open to moralization is quietly introduced here; eventual deterioration lurks in the midst of the robust beauty of nature. Caravaggio's later painting for Del Monte goes far beyond this simple allusion to foreground the contrast of decay and luxury as a major iconographic motif.

While the many individual similarities between Caravaggio's two paintings of Bacchus can be neatly enumerated, they do not add up to the conceptually unified layers of meaning that fill Cardinal Del Monte's commission, nor does the earlier composition achieve the same monumental effect. Caravaggio's trademark strategy of blending the ancient with the modern is inescapably and instantly revealed in the *Bacchino malato*; the supposed deity is not only represented by an unidealized, living model, but has the recognizable features of the artist. The joke of the self-portrait in the role of a god hits the mark and produces a hearty laugh. But its immediacy does not allow for the elegance of a gradual, long-lasting smile induced by the later *Bacchus*, with its refined prototypes and live model so artfully melded. The rather coarse humor of the *Bacchino malato* is further exaggerated by the sickly pallor that characterizes his face, with strong light and highlighting picking out the effect under the figure's right eye, nose and lower lip. The ploy is so compelling that writers have whole-heartedly agreed to accept the image as an unmediated representation of Caravaggio suffering from a specific malady at a given time. But the fashioning of the *Bacchino malato* cannot have been so forthright. Perhaps the artist did recall the disturbing results of looking into a mirror during a prolonged illness. Had he been that unwell, however, it is doubtful that his first reaction would be to set up his easel and prepare a painting.

In a plausible reconstruction of Caravaggio's working method, it is more likely that the artist first came up with an idea about how to approach his subject, then made use of direct visual experience to express it. When appropriate to his pictorial goal, he combined 'real' elements with borrowings from older art, to create novel interpretations of a given subject. This *modus operandi* is evident in several paintings from his first years in Rome, which present adolescent boys in half-length, placed front and center and almost filling the pictorial space, wearing a flowing *camicia* that falls to expose a shoulder, accompanied by expertly painted still life compositions. The series includes *Boy with a Basket of Fruit* and *Boy Bitten by a Lizard*, becomes more refined in *The Lute Player*, more complicated in *The Musicians*, and culminates in the Uffizi *Bacchus*. The type was used consistently by Caravaggio throughout the 1590s, even extending to the very solid angelic apparition in *Saint Francis of Assisi in Ecstasy*. The sleeve of the angel's torso-baring *camicia* radiates with celestial brightness, while its shadowed side flaunts an enormous, undulating bow that terminates in a fluttering tail, highlighted as a telling sign of the speedy arrival of the heavenly aide into the otherwise still, dark scene.

It has been suggested that the single figure compositions were formally influenced by draped classical busts, then turned into a contemporary genre by the mediation of live models and given added texturing by the still life additions.[19] In the *Bacchino malato*, Caravaggio/Bacchus dons the off-the-shoulder *camicia* and superimposes a recollection of his own wan visage on the classical description of the intoxicated god of wine, generating an unexpected version of the deity caught the day after Bacchic reveling. The result is a playful twist on classical *imitatio*. It was Caravaggio's way of both absorbing and rejecting antique traditions, a strategy capable of yielding richly nuanced images and great critical success.

The shrewdness and ultimate triumph of Caravaggio's initial approach to his Roman subject matter and audience parallel the dexterity with which Michelangelo first brought himself to the attention of influential Roman patrons. Not surprisingly, however, the comparable trajectories that can be drawn run in opposite directions. Caravaggio discovered a way to transform the classical past into a current idiom based on observation of the modern world; Michelangelo learned that he could disguise his own works to become counterfeits of antiquity. The sculptor's urge at the start of his career, strongly encouraged by his supporters, was to have his audience declare him equal to the ancients by initially fooling them into receiving his works as antiques. Michelangelo himself allocated Lorenzo de' Medici the honor of being the first to instruct him in the strategy of rivaling the ancients through subtle 'counterfeiting' of their art. His ingenuous compliance with the advice assured the initiate's induction into Lorenzo's privileged circle of patronage. Vasari dispatches the episode without too much elaboration in his first edition. He records that Michelangelo began his tutelage under Bertoldo by working figures in clay, which were well received by the Magnificent. Animated by Lorenzo's attention, Vasari continues, the young artist set to work on a piece of marble, copying an antique head from the collection. The result delighted Lorenzo to such an extent that he celebrated the talent of the exceptional adolescent with the reward of a monthly stipend, a fine mantle and further, a secure income for his father as a customs agent.

Vasari's summary rendition, ending with a list of payments that any artist might receive, was clearly not stately enough for Michelangelo's taste; the job provided for his father is tacked on almost as an afterthought, giving a rather crass impression. Sticking to basic facts, Vasari's spare scenario does not endow the occasion with the stunning significance it held in Michelangelo's memory. In reply, the artist devised a story that only he could tell with authority, supplying particulars of the sequence of events, culminating in Lorenzo the Magnificent elevating him to the status of adopted son. Condivi duly rectified Vasari's anemic version with the inclusion of a vigorously expanded, enlivened presentation that gives rise to the splendid story of the marble faun.[20] Its purpose is to anoint Lorenzo de' Medici as the true founder of Michelangelo's exalted career. The artist's story recounts at length the propitious, epoch-making encounter between the adolescent Michelangelo and the puissant, cultivated statesman, surrounded by the remains of the antique world. The irresistible anecdote deserves to be quoted at length:

> One day he [Michelangelo] was examining among these works the *Head of a Faun*, already old in appearance, with a long beard and laughing countenance, though the mouth, on account of its antiquity, could hardly be distinguished or recognized for what it was; and, as he liked it inordinately, he decided to copy it in marble. [. . .] He set about copying the *Faun* with such care and study that in a few days he perfected it, supplying from his imagination all that was lacking in the ancient work, that is, the open mouth as of a man laughing, so that the hollow of the mouth and all the teeth could be seen. In the midst of this, the Magnificent, coming to see what point his works had reached, found the boy engaged in polishing the head and, approaching quite near, he was much amazed, considering first the excellence of the work and then the boy's age; and, although he did praise the work, nonetheless he joked with him as with a child and said, 'Oh, you have made the Faun old and left him all his teeth. Don't you know that old men of that age are always missing a few?'[21]

The impressionable youth was swayed by this reasoning and obliged by knocking out one of the faun's teeth and carving a hollow in the gums. He then eagerly made a second presentation, which was received by Lorenzo with huge amusement. The dénouement of the incident, however, is not Lorenzo's laughter at the boy's earnest response to his jocular remark. Instead, the story ends on a note of triumph, with the auspicious invitation to join the Medici family. When Lorenzo 'weighed in his mind the perfection of the thing and the age of the boy, he, who was the father of all *virtù*, resolved to help and encourage such great genius and to take him into his household'.[22]

One can almost hear the trumpets sounding when, in a final remark, Lorenzo calls for Michelangelo to have his father brought to him. The scene of the colloquium between the Magnificent and Lodovico Buonarroti ensues, as the gifted son is transferred from his biological father to the 'father of all *virtù*'. Signor Buonarroti is allowed to take the stage and promptly makes use of the spotlight to profess the nobility of his ancestry and the sobriety of his family. Once the elder Buonarroti is dismissed, we immediately learn about the privileges Michelangelo is to receive as a new and cherished member of Lorenzo's clan, destined to sit above the salt at the illustrious table, even, on occasion, directly beside the ruler of Florence. Vasari's two-line reference was put to shame by the fireworks of Michelangelo's recollections; without shame the astute author assumed it and indeed enhanced the tale's symbolic richness in his revised second edition.

Michelangelo's story sets up Lorenzo as the first great co-conspirator in a life-long rivalry with the ancients and inflates their initial interaction far beyond its roots in the first steps of an artist's traditional training, the copying of an authoritative model. Instead, a later phase of development is indicated, that of convincingly imitating the style of a challenging prototype. The apprentice's exercise of copying [*contraffare*] found in Vasari's report, is replaced in Condivi's narration with *ritrarre*, which connotes a more complex process of reproducing or representing a model in the sense of a portrayal. We can presume that while dictating the tale of Lorenzo de' Medici and the faun to Condivi, Michelangelo mandated the *ritrarre* we find in the text, condemning the nuance that accompanies Vasari's *contraffare* by excluding it. The choice of the term is important; *contraffare* more or less matches our contemporary definition of counterfeit, to render a perfect copy of something valuable, with intent to deceive.

There is, however, a clear difference in the era's reception of the counterfeit; often during the Renaissance the origin of the potential deceit was not concealed for long. The 'intent to deceive' was part of the *concetto* and it was indissolubly affixed to a desire to reveal. It was necessary for the victim of the 'con' to become aware of the deception. The goal was to amaze with the skill of the apparent imitation, adhering closely to the virtuosity of the prototype, yet always adding something extra to mark the inescapable originality of the ostensible forgery. The result was then embraced as extraordinary, all the more commanding for its challenge to the viewer's power of discernment. Following these Renaissance criteria, to mistake a modern work for an ancient one was to pay the highest possible tribute; it acknowledged a level of proficiency generally believed to have been attained only in antiquity and thus beyond the reach of all contemporaries.

The crux of the story of the faun depends on Michelangelo's inventive improvisation, culling from his fantasy what the original sculpture lacked: a mouth opening in laughter, revealing the creature's teeth and tongue. Far from being a workshop exercise, Michelangelo's *Faun* improves upon its model and it is precisely the upgrading that attracts Lorenzo's attention. We can posit that Condivi's avoidance of *contraffare* was calculated to keep the history of Michelangelo's early development as far away as possible from that of conventional workshop practices. In the text, the story of '*Il Magnifico and the Faun*' follows closely upon Michelangelo's heated disavowal of having learned anything of value from his first master, Domenico Ghirlandaio. But if the usual workshop routine of perfunctory copying is banished from Michelangelo's biography, his practice of creative counterfeiting accompanies the advent of his career.

The scenario of Michelangelo in the garden of San Marco, manipulating one of his sculptures to endow it with an authentic appearance of age, was repeated some years later on the advice of the younger Lorenzo de' Medici, Lorenzo di Pierfrancesco, whom we have already encountered as the patron who facilitated Michelangelo's trip to Rome. In Condivi's account, the crafty Medici scion counseled Michelangelo with regard to a *Sleeping Cupid* he had sculpted:

> 'If you would fix it so that it looked as if it had been buried, I would send it to Rome and it would pass for an ancient work, and you would sell it much better'. Upon hearing this, Michelangelo, to whom none of the ways of genius were obscure, reworked it immediately so that it looked as if it had been made many years earlier.[23]

It is important to keep Michelangelo's reconstruction of the event for Condivi in mind, because it neatly twins Lorenzo di Pierfrancesco's counsel with the prior advice of Lorenzo the Magnificent. If *Il Magnifico* had set Michelangelo on his path to future glory, the younger Lorenzo sent him to Rome, where the artist's most grandiose works would be realized. The continuity of Medici support is a central point of the story; acting for a second time under the guidance of a benevolent Medici patron, Michelangelo again created a work of art that imitated the ancients so successfully it surpassed them, as well as outdoing modern masters. On the second occasion, however, financial gain was added to the equation, with dramatic consequences that put neither Pierfrancesco nor Michelangelo in the best light.

Several versions of the sequel have come down to us, but they all agree on a crucial fact: the sale of the *Sleeping Cupid* led directly to Michelangelo's arrival in Rome. It was purchased by none other than Cardinal Raffaele Riario, vetted by Lorenzo di Pierfrancesco de' Medici through contact with Jacopo Galli as the cardinal's representative. This interaction, as we have seen, was the background for Michelangelo's immediate meeting with Riario upon arrival and to the rapid commission for the *Bacchus*. However, one more personage must be introduced at this point to complete the story. A certain Baldassare del Milanese took part in the intrigue, responsible for selling the sculpture to the cardinal with a huge price tag attached, one worthy of an authentic antiquity. Baldassare was twice dishonorable. First, he had no intention of eventually revealing the true identity of the artist, which condemned the *Sleeping Cupid* to be considered a forgery rather than a marvel. Second, the dealer then compounded the insult to Michelangelo's talents by sharing only 30 of the 200 ducats obtained in the transaction. With his mastery and his bank account offended, the artist quickly left for Rome to rectify the situation.

When informed about the deception Cardinal Riario did not react as expected. According to the edicts of the true connoisseur, he should have been properly astounded at the level of virtuosity displayed by an artist barely in his twenties, perhaps even adding to his monetary reward and above all, bragging about owning a work so fine that even he had initially been duped. Instead, Riario behaved in a churlish manner, offloaded the sculpture and demanded his money back. Upon meeting the young artist, the cardinal must have reconsidered his position, at least to the extent of giving Michelangelo the chance to prove himself with the *Bacchus*. We have seen that commission also to have been fraught with complications and, ultimately, a final placement in another collection. Perhaps in the end, Riario's taste and expectations were not susceptible to Michelangelo's daring maneuvering within the classical tradition. Unfortunately, we can reconstruct only a few tantalizing details of what transpired; but we know that the cardinal's rebuff was enough to sustain the artist's indignation for more than half a century. Vasari takes Michelangelo's side with touching solidarity:

> This affair did not happen without some censure of Cardinal San Giorgio, in that he did not recognize the value of the work, which consisted in its perfection; for modern works, if they are excellent, are as good as the ancient. What greater vanity is there than that of those who concern themselves more with the name than the fact?[24]

Vasari's final rebuff bravely forges a path that leads toward Shakespeare's more pithy question, 'what's in a name?'. Sadly, Vasari abruptly drops the thought and goes on to bemoan the existence of men swayed more by appearances than reality.

Without the willing participation of the connoisseur/purchaser, Lorenzo di Pierfrancesco's *jeu d'esprit* fell flat. Michelangelo was chagrined by the incident and made unsuccessful efforts to get the *Sleeping Cupid* back into his possession. Instead, the sculpture was acquired by Cesare Borgia, who then passed it on to Isabella d'Este, the Marchioness of Mantua (1474–1539), one of the most ingenious collectors of the Renaissance. She knew how to make the most of her prize acquisition through a spectacular display. She enthralled and entertained her distinguished visitors by setting up a *paragone* between Michelangelo's *Sleeping Cupid* and an example of one of its ancient ancestors.[25] The sculpture became legendary and its mystique survives to this day. Although it has been lost, references are often made to it and from time to time various candidates are brought forward, either as Michelangelo's original or the prototype that inspired him.

There is every reason to believe that Caravaggio's appropriation of the subject, a *Sleeping Cupid* painted for a Florentine patron (Plate 7), became another instance of his edgy dialogue with the elder Michelangelo and an unsettling amplification of the theme of the drowsing Cupid. The work was commissioned late in Caravaggio's career, during his residence in Malta. The subject of the painting is handled in a deeply enigmatic manner, yet the circumstances of its commission emerge lucidly. An inscription on the reverse of the canvas records the work as that of 'Sr Michel Angelo Maresi da Caravaggio, Malta, 1608' and a letter identifies the man who purchased the painting as Francesco Dell'Antella, a high-ranking knight of the Order of Saint John, the secretary of the Grand Master.[26] Surviving correspondence not only documents the circumstances and the patron, but in one of those felicitous fusions of history, comes down to us from the descendants of Michelangelo Buonarroti. Fra Francesco Buonarroti, living in Malta as a knight of the order, shares information in a letter to Michelangelo the Younger, his brother and namesake of their illustrious great-uncle. Fraternal contacts permeate the discussion:

> For your information let me tell you that on two or three occasions I have been in conversation with Signor Antella, who tells me that he has sent there [to Florence] a picture by Michelangelo da Caravaggio, showing a Cupid sleeping, to the house of his brother, Signor Niccolò; the Commendatore is delighted with it, and is very happy for people to go and look at it, so he can hear others' opinions on it, and also that somebody has written sonnets after seeing it, which he has shown me, so I imagine that he would appreciate your going to see it.[27]

Dell'Antella's decision to send the work to the family home in Florence places it in the setting that would most strongly evoke its legendary precursor, at that date presumably still visible in the Gonzaga collection in Mantua, before the bulk of it was sold in 1627. If Michelangelo's original sculpture resided in Lombardy, the history of its maker and making indisputably reigned in Florence, reinforced by the visible presence of the Buonarroti family, whose increased social standing shone from the reflected glory of their 'divine' antecedent. Reading between the lines, Michelangelo the Younger is being asked to add his particular authority to an assessment of Caravaggio's painting, one that would carry enormous weight; his word amounted to a living connection to the *Sleeping Cupid* of his great-uncle. The comparison, once more involving painted and sculpted versions of the same subject, is another, and very explicit, demonstration of the *paragone* in action, again with the added spice of testing the strengths of the two Michelangelos along with the merits of their preferred genres. The indirect invitation that Francesco Buonarroti passes on to his brother in effect bids him to weigh in on this novel *paragone*, adding a note of distinction to the excitement the painting has stirred up.[28]

Michelangelo the Younger must have complied, as inferred from Francesco Dell'Antella's compliment, 'Now I hold my *Cupid* in much higher regard than before, since it has been praised by your Lordship.' What more could the owner desire than to have a contemporary Florentine Michelangelo, who was a man of letters, an intellectual and noted collector, gift him with a glowing evaluation of another Michelangelo's work? Especially since, just as we have seen before, Caravaggio acknowledged his model by actively sparring with him, rather than being coolly conversant with his achievement.

Caravaggio's image of the reclining Cupid follows the brief description of Michelangelo's sculpted version we have from Condivi, who tells us the boy is 'six or seven years old, lying in the position of a man asleep'.[29] The painting's effect, however, is so unsettling and the body of the child so unidealized, that viewers have searched for explanations rooted in a supposedly diseased child who served as model; or they suspect Caravaggio of having blatantly used a baby's corpse for his subject. Such reasons attest more to the power of the representation and to the potency of the artist's imagination, than to logic. Studies of Caravaggio's technique support what the visual evidence shows, that while depending heavily on models during the first decade of his career, after 1605 Caravaggio drew more upon types and recollections of earlier figures, especially as his life was itinerant and his working conditions unstable.[30] In the case of the *Cupid*, Caravaggio would not have had easy or constant access to view sleeping children, nor to seek out one suffering from a disease that would suit his iconographic purposes. Especially given the subject – a surprising departure from the religious scenes Caravaggio had been principally painting – consultation of antique sculptures, descriptions and recollections would have been more likely.

It is worth pondering if at this moment, geographically and emotionally so removed from his exuberant days in Rome, Caravaggio reconsidered his relationship to classical models as he conceived the commission for a sleeping Cupid. Whereas his earlier adaptations of ancient motifs were abundantly clever and irreverent, there is a bitter edge to his rendition of the graceless child. Michelangelo's famed sculpture of Cupid, which initiated the Renaissance artist's affirmation as an equal of the ancients and became his legendary ticket to Roman success, now meets its antithesis in Caravaggio's treatment of the subject. If Caravaggio revisited his parodic approach to the Florentine's classicism while painting his Maltese commission, the laughter now has a harsher character, in keeping with more troubled times.

Transforming his idea into an apparently unmediated transcription of reality was at the core of Caravaggio's process of realizing a painting. And, certainly, it is most probable that part of the original commission was engaging the paradigm of Michelangelo's legendary sculpture, showing a child of around six years old, as authoritatively described by Condivi. Indeed, Caravaggio's Cupid is not an infant, although the chubby belly, brought into relief by the strong light, may at first render this impression. The relatively long, slender legs, however, are indicative of a small boy beyond the toddler stage, as are the fully developed features of his face, with strongly developed nose and mouth, large ears, thick dark eyebrows and a head of curly dark hair. Nor is the child's pose infantile. He draws his knee over his thigh, befitting a young god of sensuousness, emphasized by the warm light that suffuses this section of the painting. One of Cupid's hands tenaciously holds his weapon; the fingers of the other hand are strangely curved, a detail that has fed the speculation of distortion due to a disease. The clenched gesture is, however, explained by a *pentimento*, an underlying form that has been covered over and eliminated in the final state of the painting.[31] In this instance, upon second thought, Caravaggio eliminated a poppy held by the child and its eradication accounts for the strange curvature of the small hand, whose fingers now encircle a void rather than the stem of a flower. Rethinking traditional iconography is much more in line with Caravaggio's practice and gives us a more plausible explanation of the visual effect than the improbable procedure of actually setting up canvas, paints and brush repeatedly in front of a sleeping child wracked by disease.

The initial inclusion of the poppy provides a buried key to the underlying meaning of the painting. The narcotic plant is associated with sleep and may metaphorically refer to death, aptly given verbal form in our expression of being 'dead to the world' while in deep slumber. The erasure of the flower withdraws the conventional reading that a traditional symbol authorizes and adds to the disquieting effect of verisimilitude. Rather than limit the image to a symbolic sleep, the painting disturbingly reminds us of 'real' death. It is a fully developed example, in a macabre note, of Caravaggio undermining an ancient motif and negating Michelangelo's Renaissance exemplum that stemmed from it.

Caravaggio cites enough references to establish a conceptual connection to his models, but they are overlaid by details that come from his observation of the visible. The mischievous son of Venus, often portrayed as a chubby, joyous toddler is here presented as an ungainly, even perhaps ugly little boy, somber and harshly lit in his oblivious sleep. Caravaggio accentuates the atmosphere of death with ambient darkness and the lack of idealization is enforced by the appearance of Cupid's wings, gray like a sparrow's and a little worse for wear as they peek out from under the weight of the child's body. The sober key, devoid of the bawdy joyousness we usually associate with the god of love, dominates the painting. There is only one exuberant

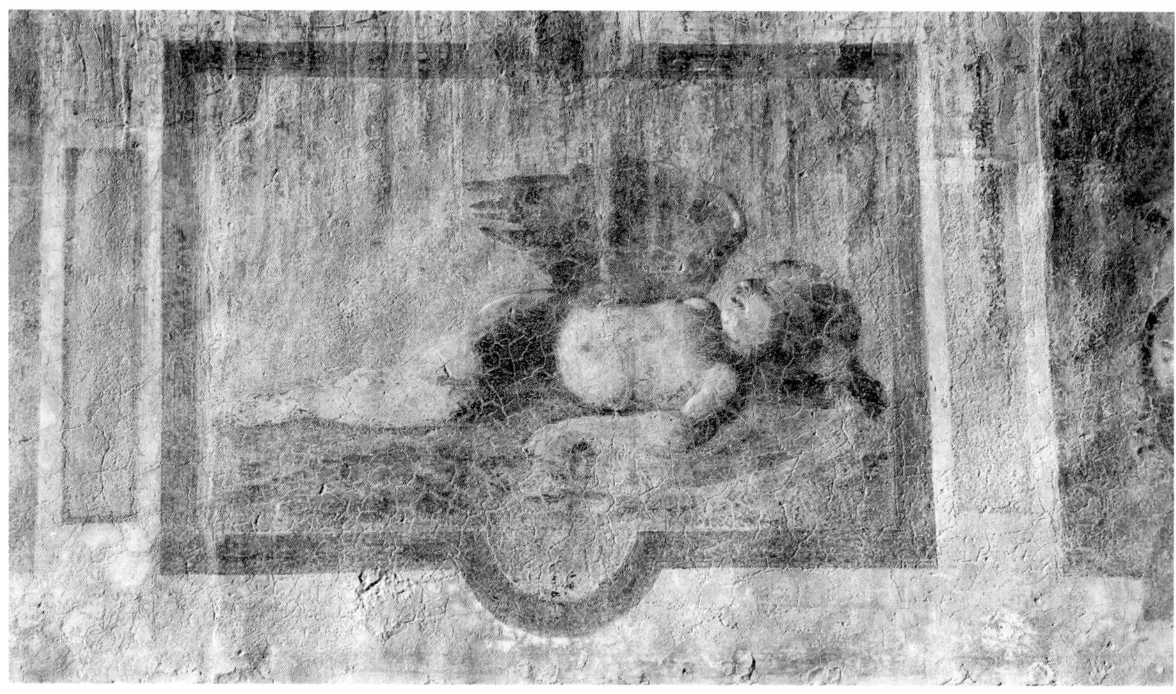

8 Giovanni da San Giovanni, originally 1619, after Caravaggio's *Sleeping Cupid*, fresco, lower register of the facade, Palazzo Dell'Antella, Piazza Santa Croce, Florence

detail, picked out in gold along the wooden bow that lies on the ground. So subtle as to have almost gone unnoticed, the design sketches a trail of tiny grotesque figures, most likely copied directly from a weapon; perhaps one belonging to the patron.[32] The specificity of the decorated bow is akin to the still life elements of Caravaggio's early works, whose careful inclusion refers to the artist's declared adherence to imitating the objects found in the visible world.

The decidedly unconventional representation, solemn as it is, delighted the Dell'Antella family. So far from disappointing, the exceptional appearance of their *Sleeping Cupid* worked remarkably well to convey a message worthy of a noble Knight of Malta bound by a vow of chastity, expressing a moral position in step with the time and place of its commission. The subject shows that the supremacy of Venus, enforced by Cupid and his arrows of seduction, is shattered; the mythological scene has been amended to announce instead a renunciation of carnal pleasures. This reading is further implied by the area of deep shadow that conceals the recumbent Cupid's groin, in stark contrast to the exhibitionism of the Cupid painted for Vincenzo Giustiniani (See Chapter 3). In Caravaggio's brilliantly calculated reversal of a classical motif, Cupid's impenetrable sleep, along with his literally obscured sexuality, imposes not only a temporary ceasefire of the volley of his arrows, but symbolizes the death of his goddess-mother's realm, where buoyancy and beauty no longer reside.

The triumphant overturning of classical predecessors and Michelangelo's paradigm must have provided satisfying provender for expansive discourses on the *paragone*, not only among the distinguished guests of the Dell'Antellas invited to view their art collection, but eventually by less exalted observers. In 1619, the family commissioned Giovanni da San Giovanni to include a reproduction of Caravaggio's painting in the series of frescoes carried out on the facade of their palazzo in Piazza Santa Croce (Fig. 8). Still discernible, it is an extraordinary testament to the pride of possession aroused by one of Caravaggio's paintings, enduring long after its initial purchase and the death of the artist. It was not until 1667 that the original painting left Palazzo Antella; at that date the collection was relinquished to the Medici and joined the other works by Caravaggio obtained by previous rulers.

The histories, facts and legends surrounding the treatments of Bacchus and the Cupids of the two Michelangelos reveal much about the attitudes of the artists toward antiquity and that of their patrons and contemporaries. Michelangelo's resounding admiration for ancient paradigms informs the virtuosity of his early Roman works, in which the young artist attempted to vie with his classical predecessors on their own terms. A competitiveness with antique art characterized all the early works known to us and it was singled out by Michelangelo's contemporaries as the benchmark of his achievement. The first biographical note about Michelangelo, termed a 'eulogy' by its author, identifies the artist as the vanquisher of antiquity in its opening lines: 'In painting and in marble sculpture the Tuscan Michelangelo Buonarroti has come very close to achieving the same worth and significance as that attained by the artists of antiquity, and this is generally agreed, owing to his equal fame.'[33]

This assessment, written *c.*1524/7 by Paolo Giovio (1483–1552), classifies Michelangelo, then almost fifty years old, as praiseworthy in direct proportion to his achieving the level of worth established by the ancients. Even in his maturity, the artist was understood and valued through the prism of his relation to antiquity. The anecdote of the sleeping Cupid was in fact introduced by Giovio:

> Michelangelo attained the highest fame in sculpture when he made a Cupid of marble, and, after having kept it buried in the earth for a time and then bringing it to light again, so that, owing to the spots and stains it had acquired and to the other small imperfections which had been intentionally inflicted upon it, the Cupid simulated a work of antiquity. He sold it then for a great price through a middleman to Cardinal Riario.[34]

Giovio's exposition is compact, attributing all the action to Michelangelo, with the additional help of an unnamed middleman to make the sale. The sequence of clauses, iterating cause and describing effect, each one rapidly following another, recites the story in a cut and dried manner, with the delivery of a factual news bulletin. Perhaps Giovio had access to reliable information; at any rate, his points are those elaborated upon and altered to Michelangelo's advantage in the account recorded by Condivi. The fact remains that the fame of Michelangelo Buonarroti was established and remained bound, to his triumphant modern variation of antique style. This evaluation accompanied him throughout his life, long after his art and his interests, reached beyond the narrow categorization.

Caravaggio's fame rested on starkly different terms of praise, ones that glossed over his informed tampering with the antique canon, in part because his references were defiant. Caravaggio was keenly aware of the old masters and antiquity and was surrounded by their art in the stately palazzi and cultural pursuits of his Roman patrons, but his paintings refer to antique and Renaissance exempla in an argumentative mode, not an appreciative contest of creative imitation. Caravaggio's creation of a modern style required the study of archetypes in order to tear them down; he engaged his models in dispute rather than dialogue. His paintings of Bacchus and Cupid compellingly demonstrate that for Caravaggio, surpassing the ancient canon was synonymous with revoking the flawless perfection that Michelangelo had so stunningly pilfered from the ancient models.

Significantly, both artists decisively moved away from mythological subject matter as their art developed and both became heroic interpreters of religious subjects, each responding to the very different spiritual climates of Catholic Rome during his lifetime. However, before exploring the profound religious expressions of the two artists, there is a revelatory chapter in Caravaggio's intense dialogue with Michelangelo that commands attention. It was an encounter that triggered the abundant audacity of the younger artist. It occurred in the wake of Caravaggio's first great Roman success, as if his newly gained prestige demanded an open confrontation with his namesake. Caravaggio targeted Michelangelo's sublime Sistine ceiling. He appropriated several of the extraordinary figures found there and used them as templates, first for a provocative erotic theme and then for a religious subject whose unsettling ambiguity is fostered by the irreverent reference to its prototype. Caravaggio encroached on Michelangelo's epochal spiritual territory in the Sistine Chapel with the clear intention of stealing the Florentine's thunder and retooling it for the needs of his novel modern style. Caravaggio's dialogue with his namesake turned into 'persiflage', to use a marvelously fitting term. The characterization was proposed in an early study that took seriously Caravaggio's most egregious attempts to vanquish his divine predecessor by mocking him with irreverent imitation.[35] The strategy, in all of its rich complexities and seditious results, is explored in the following chapter.

Colour Plates

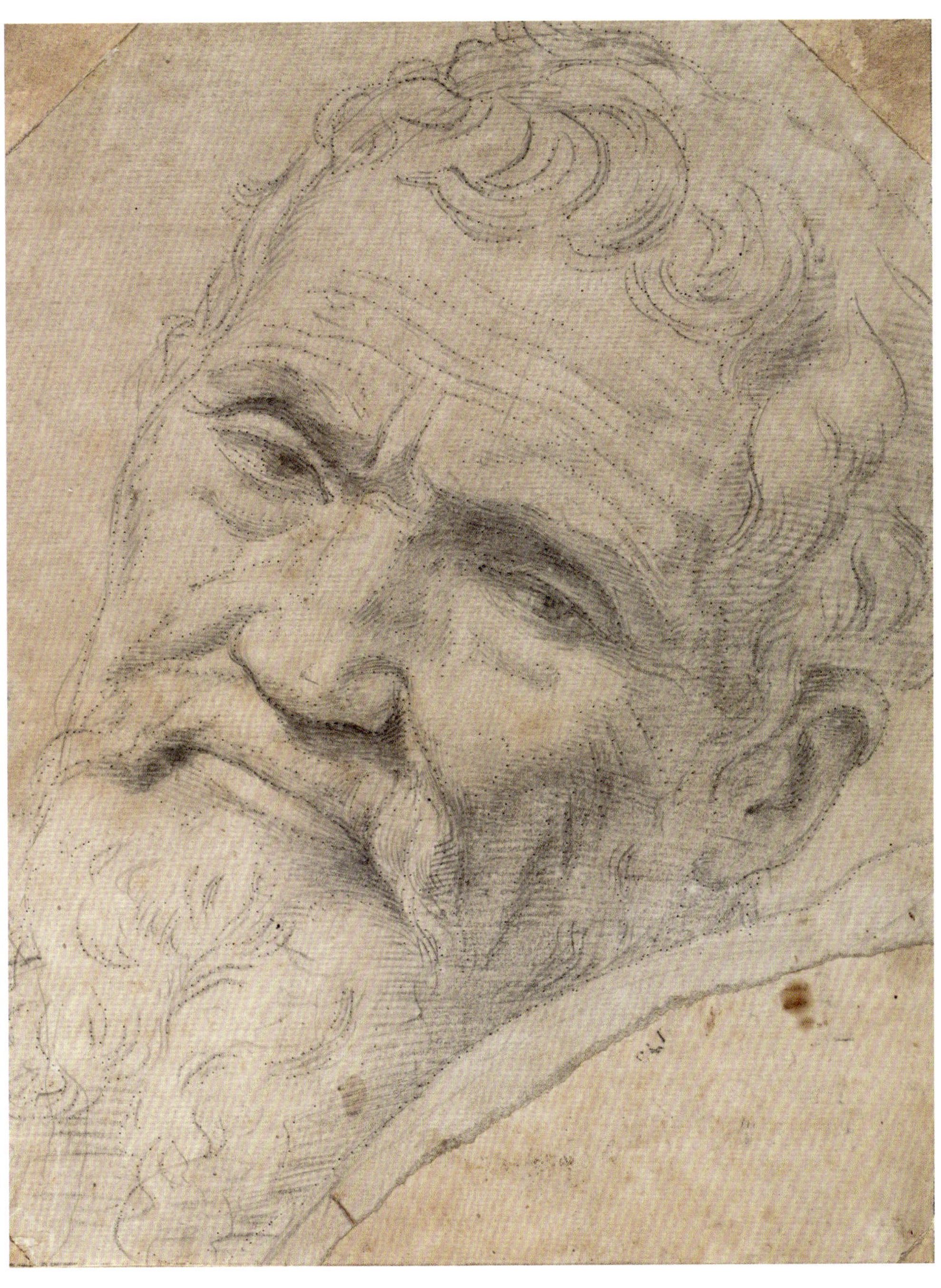

1 Daniele da Volterra, *Portrait of Michelangelo*, 1550–55, drawing, 29.5 x 21.8 cm (11 5/8 x 8 9/16 in), Teylers Museum, Haarlem

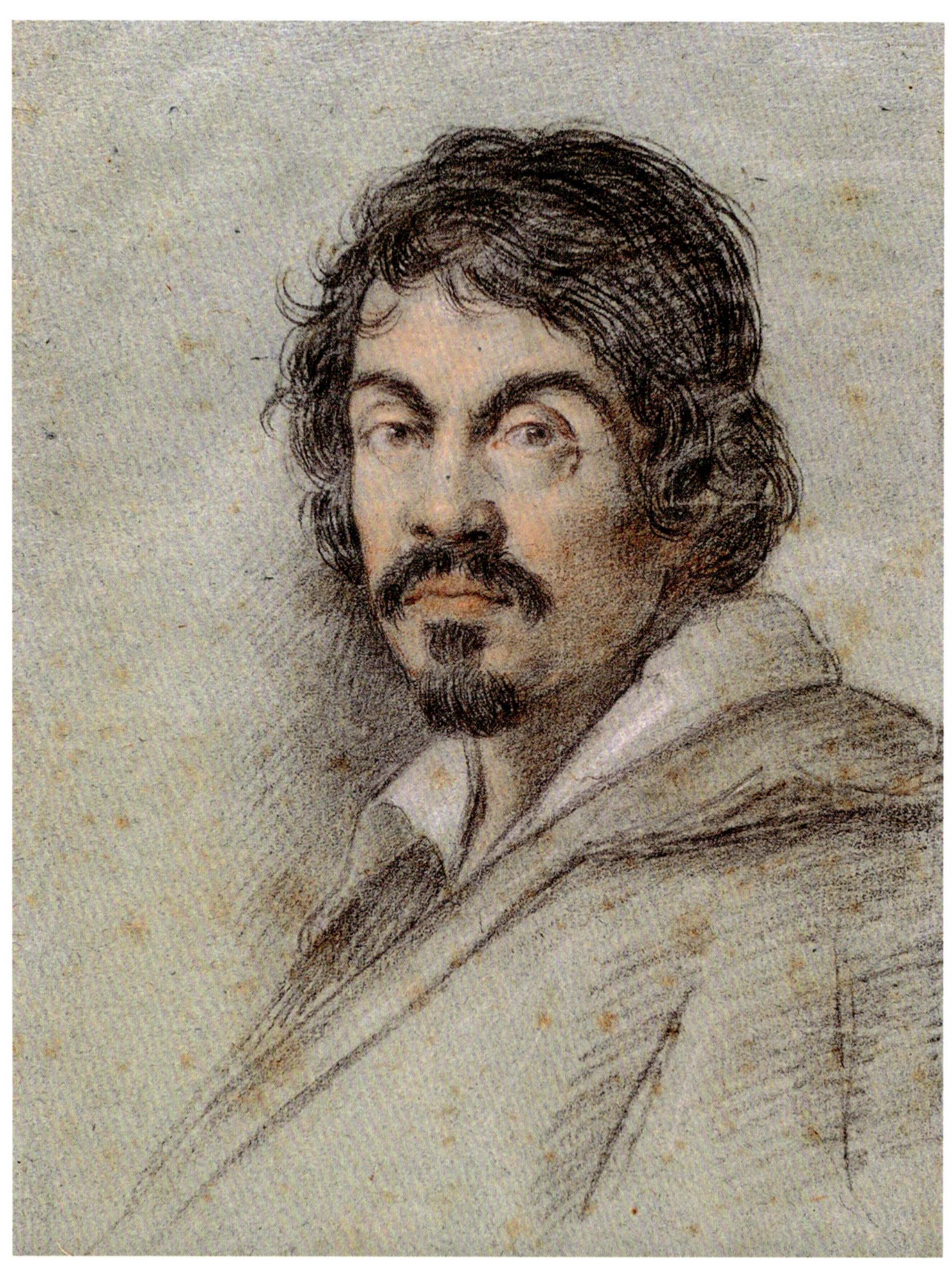

2 Ottavio Leoni, *Portrait of Michelangelo Merisi da Caravaggio*, 1621, chalk on paper, 23.4 × 16.3 cm (9 3/16 × 6 7/16 in), Biblioteca Marucelliana, Florence

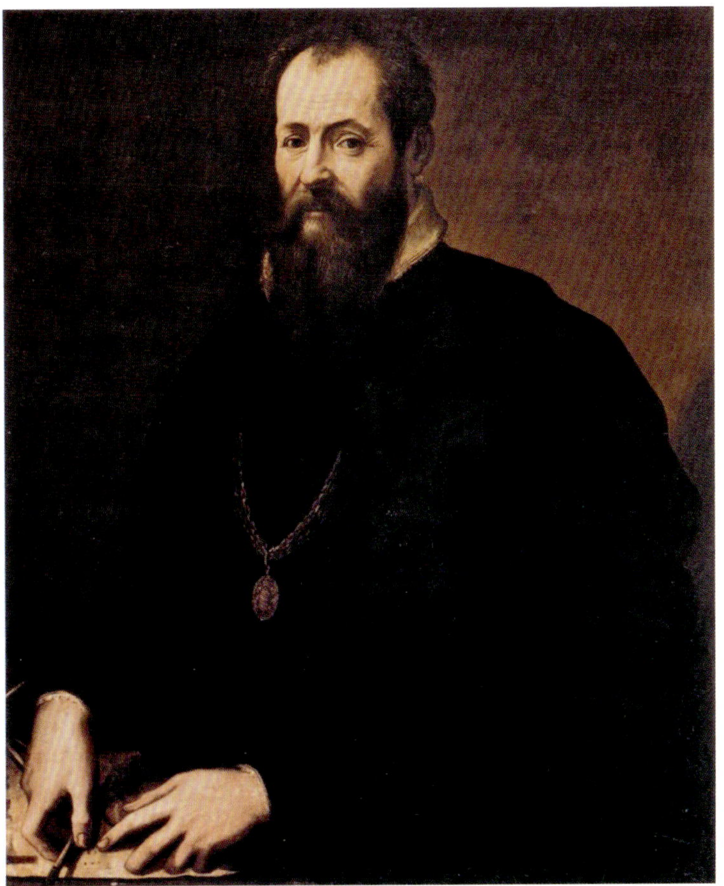

3 Giorgio Vasari, *Self-Portrait*, 1566–8, oil on canvas, 100.5 × 80 cm (39 9/16 × 31 1/2 in), Uffizi Galleries, Florence

4 Michelangelo, *Pietà*, 1498, marble, height 174 cm (68 1/2 in), Saint Peter's Basilica, Vatican, Rome

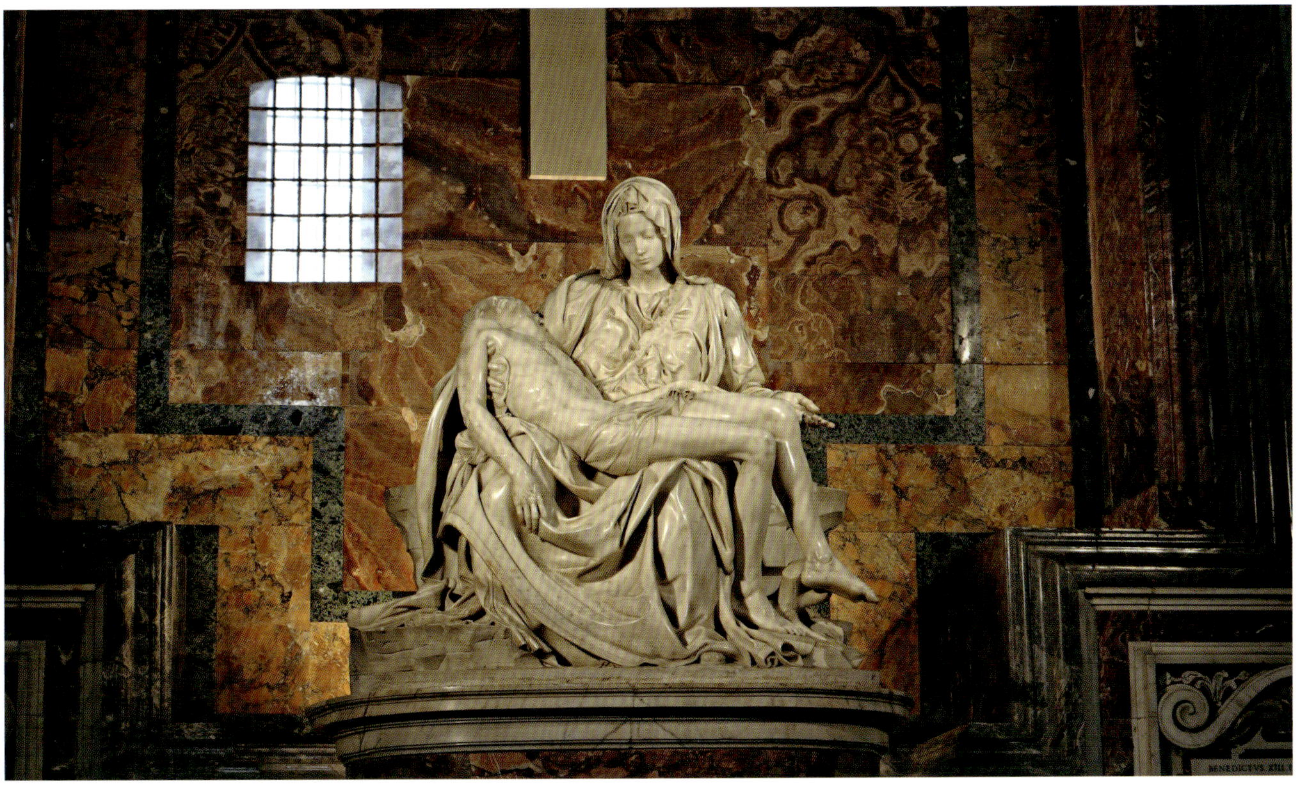

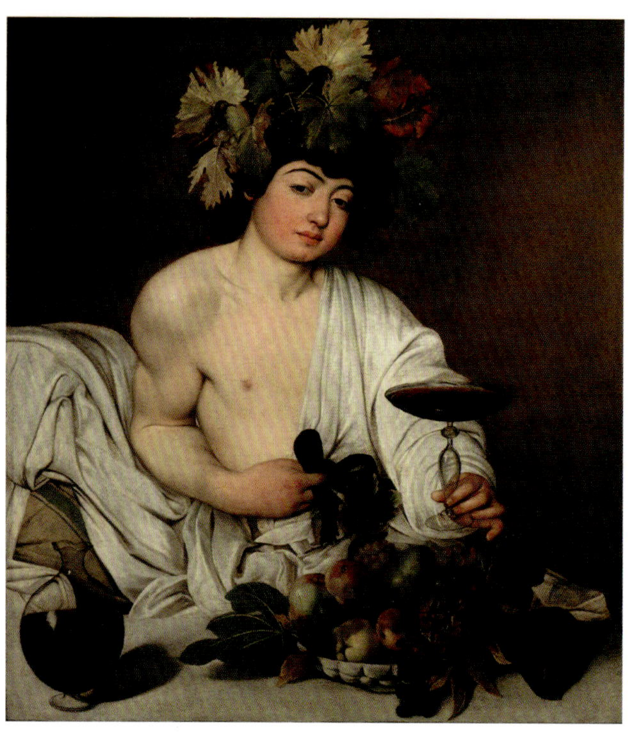

5 Caravaggio, *Bacchus*, *c.*1597, oil on canvas, 98 × 85 cm (38 9/16 × 33 7/16 in), Uffizi Galleries, Florence, Inv. 1890 no. 5312

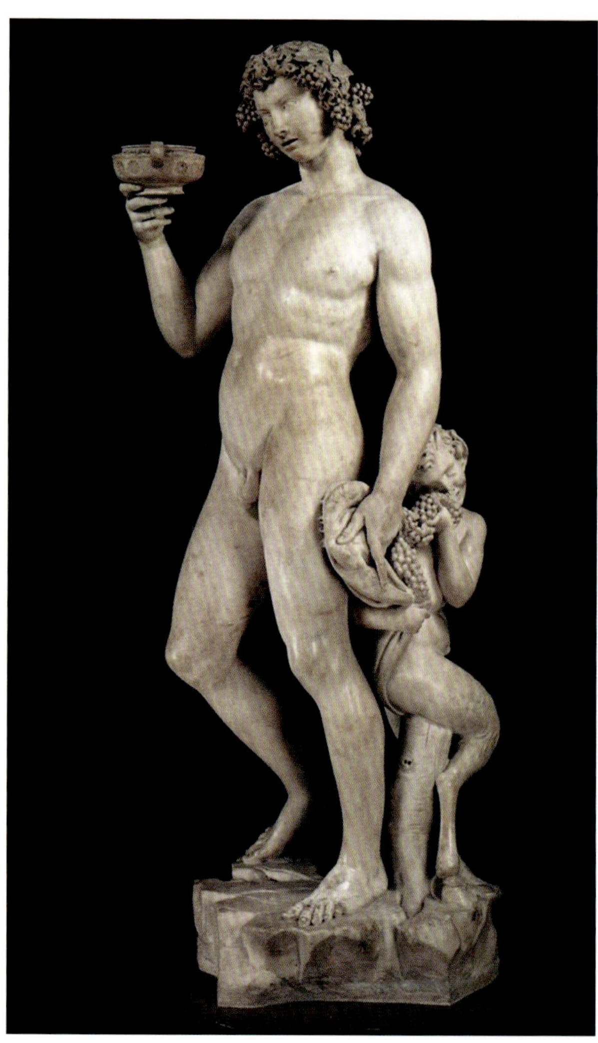

6 Michelangelo, *Bacchus*, 1496–7, marble, height 203 cm (75 15/16 in), Bargello Museum, Florence

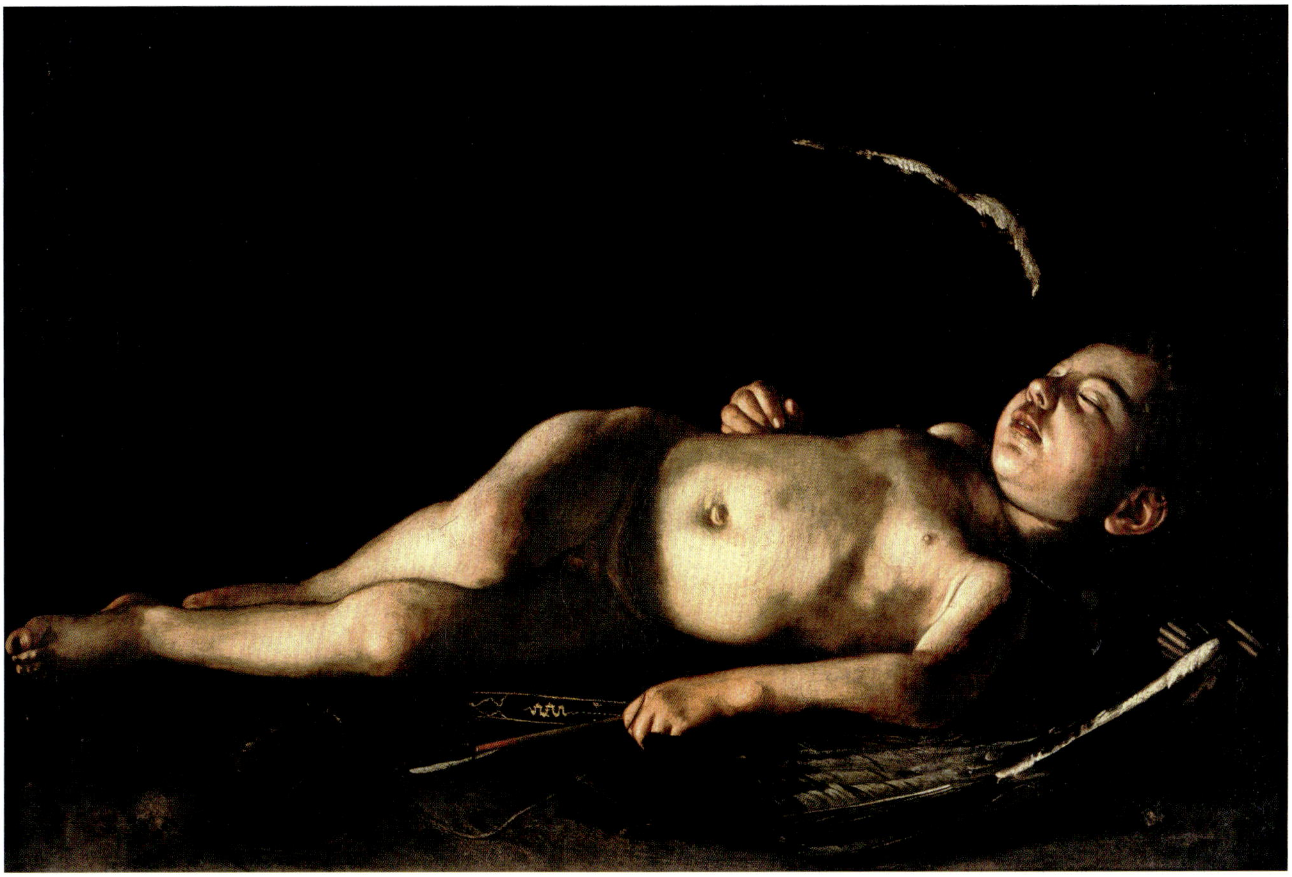

7 Caravaggio, *Sleeping Cupid*, 1608, oil on canvas, 72 × 105 cm (28 3/8 × 41 5/16 in), Pitti Palace, Florence

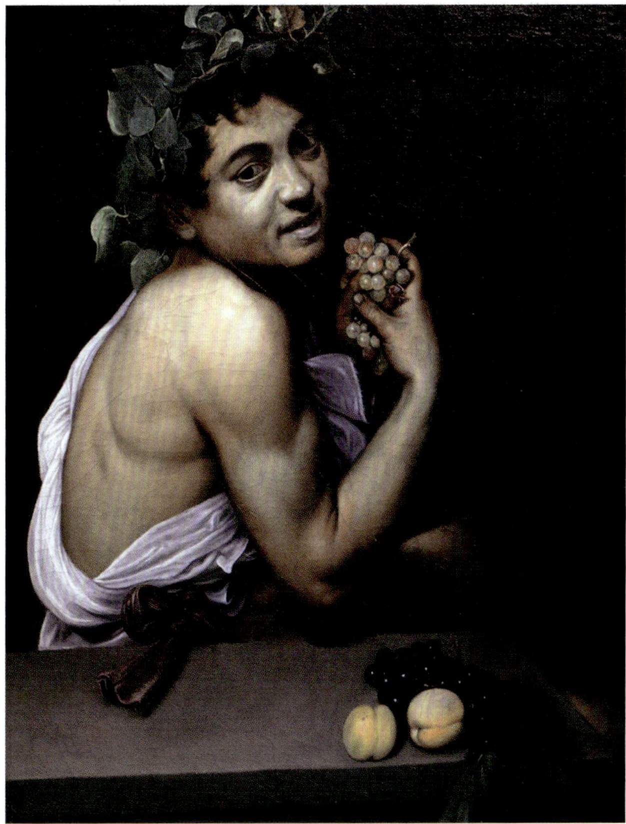

8 Caravaggio, *Bacchino malato*, 1593–4, oil on canvas, 67 × 53 cm (26 3/8 × 20 7/8 in), Borghese Gallery, Rome

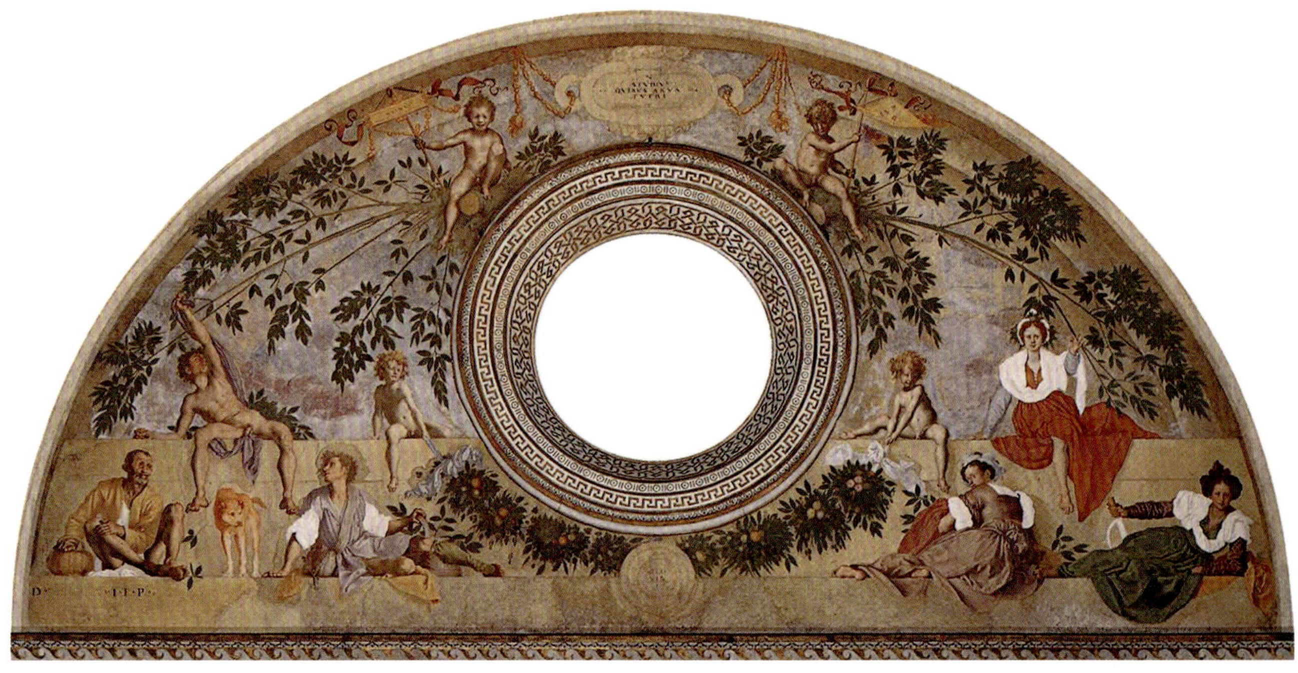

9 Jacopo Pontormo, *Vertumnus and Pomona*, 1519–21, fresco, 461 × 990 cm (181 ½ × 389 ¾ in), Villa Medici, Poggio a Caiano

10 (BELOW LEFT) Michelangelo, *Ignudi* framing the *Separation of Light from Darkness*, Sistine Chapel ceiling, fresco, 180 x 260 cm (70 9/10 × 102 2/5 in), Vatican, Rome

11 (BELOW RIGHT) Filippino Lippi, *Triumph of St Thomas Aquinas over the Heretics*, detail, 1489–93, fresco, Carafa Chapel, Santa Maria sopra Minerva, Rome

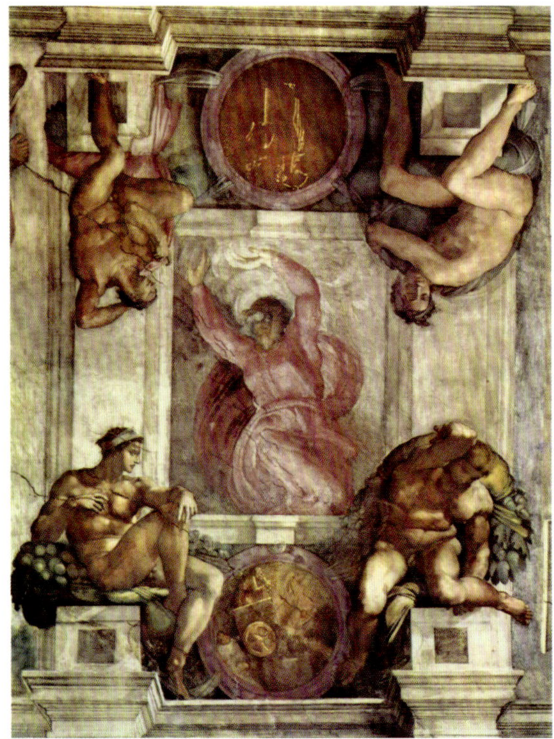

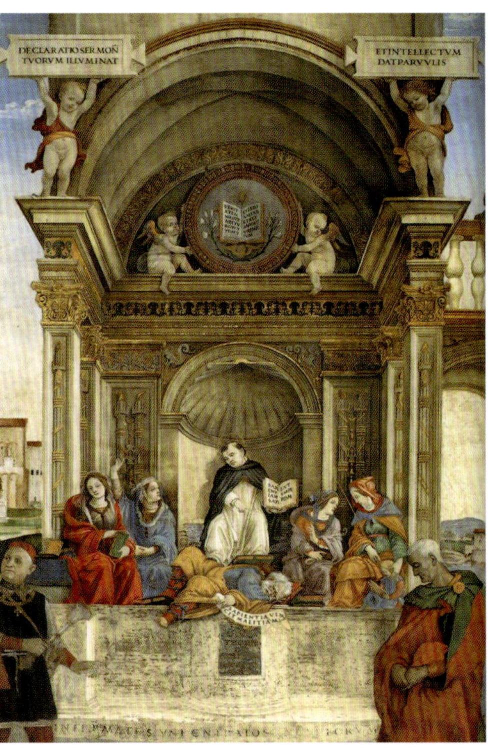

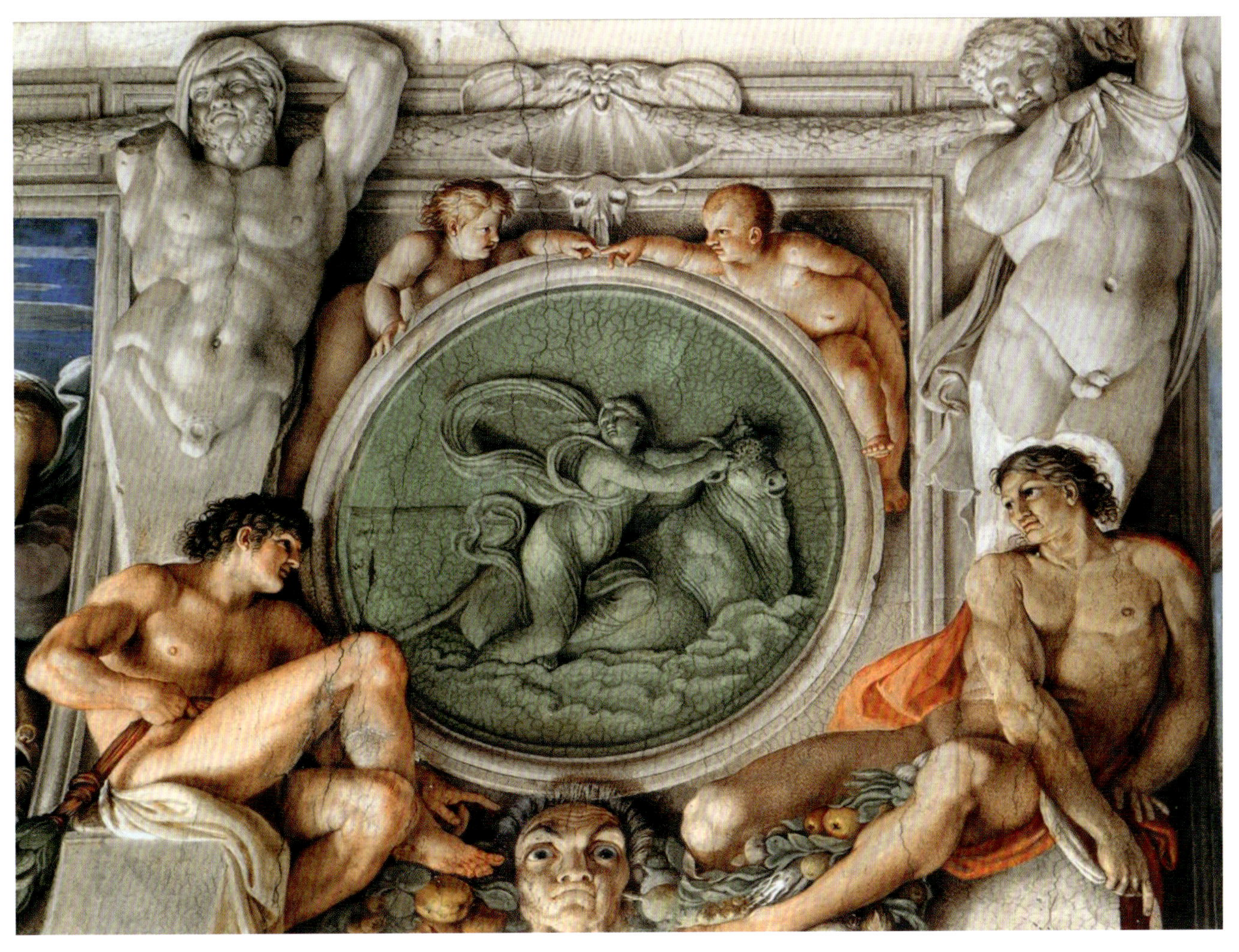

12 Annibale Carracci, *Loves of the Gods*, detail, 1597–1602, fresco, 2450 x 1430 cm (964 9/16 x 562 99/100 in), Galleria Farnese, Palazzo Farnese, Rome

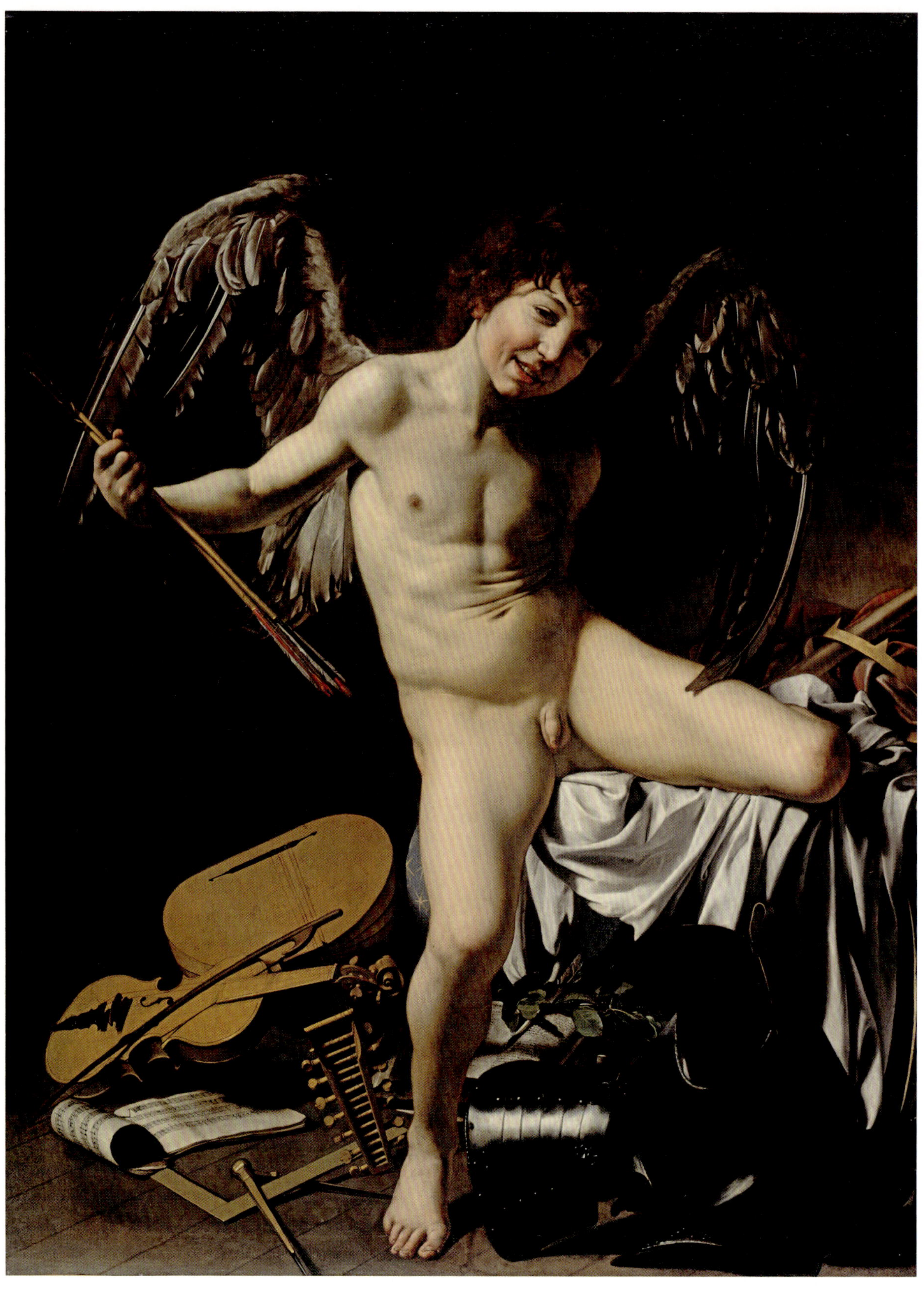

13 Caravaggio, *Amor Vincit Omnia*, 1602, oil on canvas, 156 × 113 cm (61 7/16 × 44 1/2 in), Gemäldegalerie, Staatliche Museen, Berlin

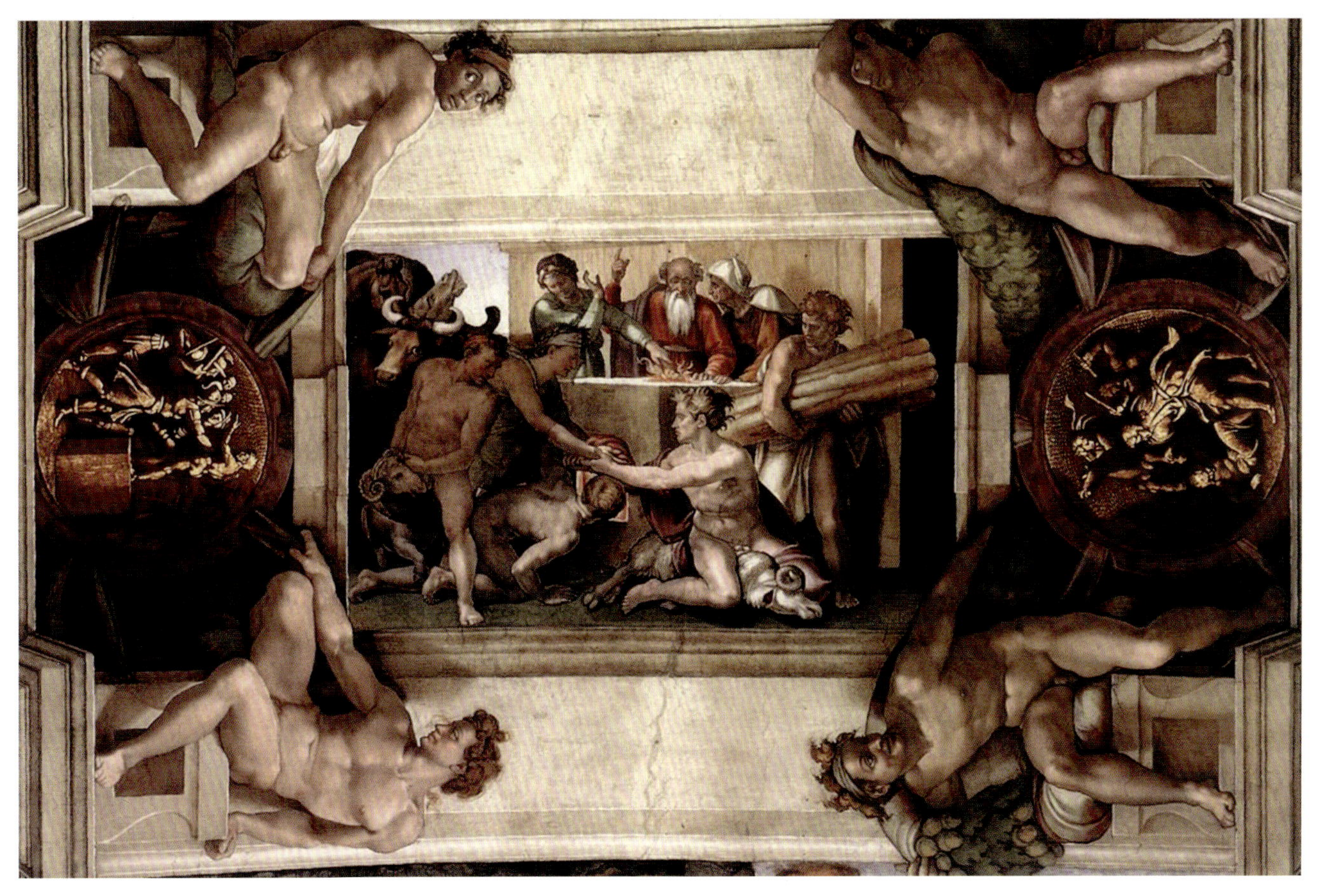

14 Michelangelo, *Scene of Sacrifice*, 1509, fresco, 170 × 260 cm (66 15/16 × 102 3/8 in), Sistine Chapel, Vatican, Rome

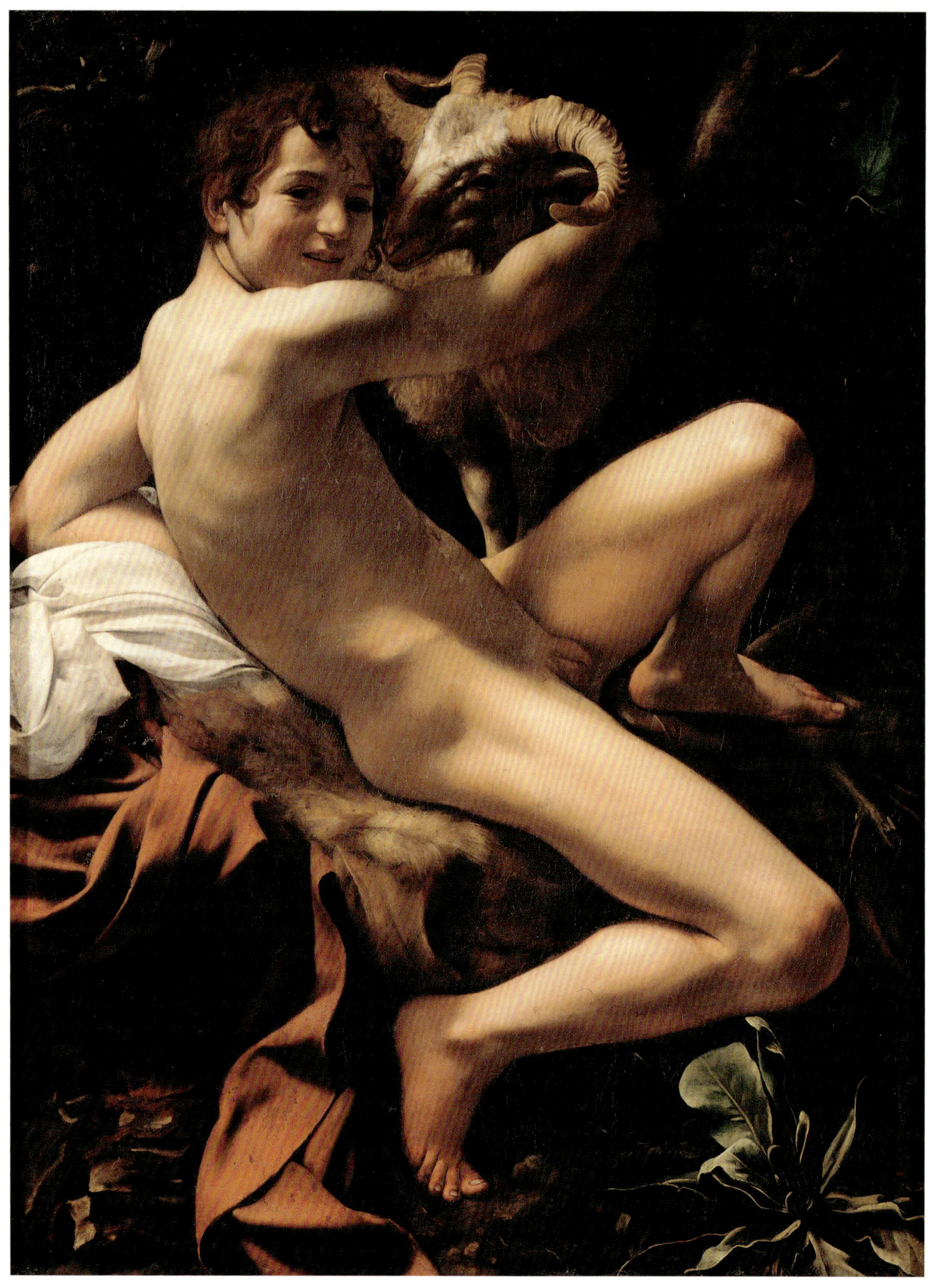

15 Caravaggio, *Saint John the Baptist*, 1601–2, oil on canvas, 129 × 94 cm (50 13/16 × 37 in), Pinacoteca, Musei Capitolini, Rome

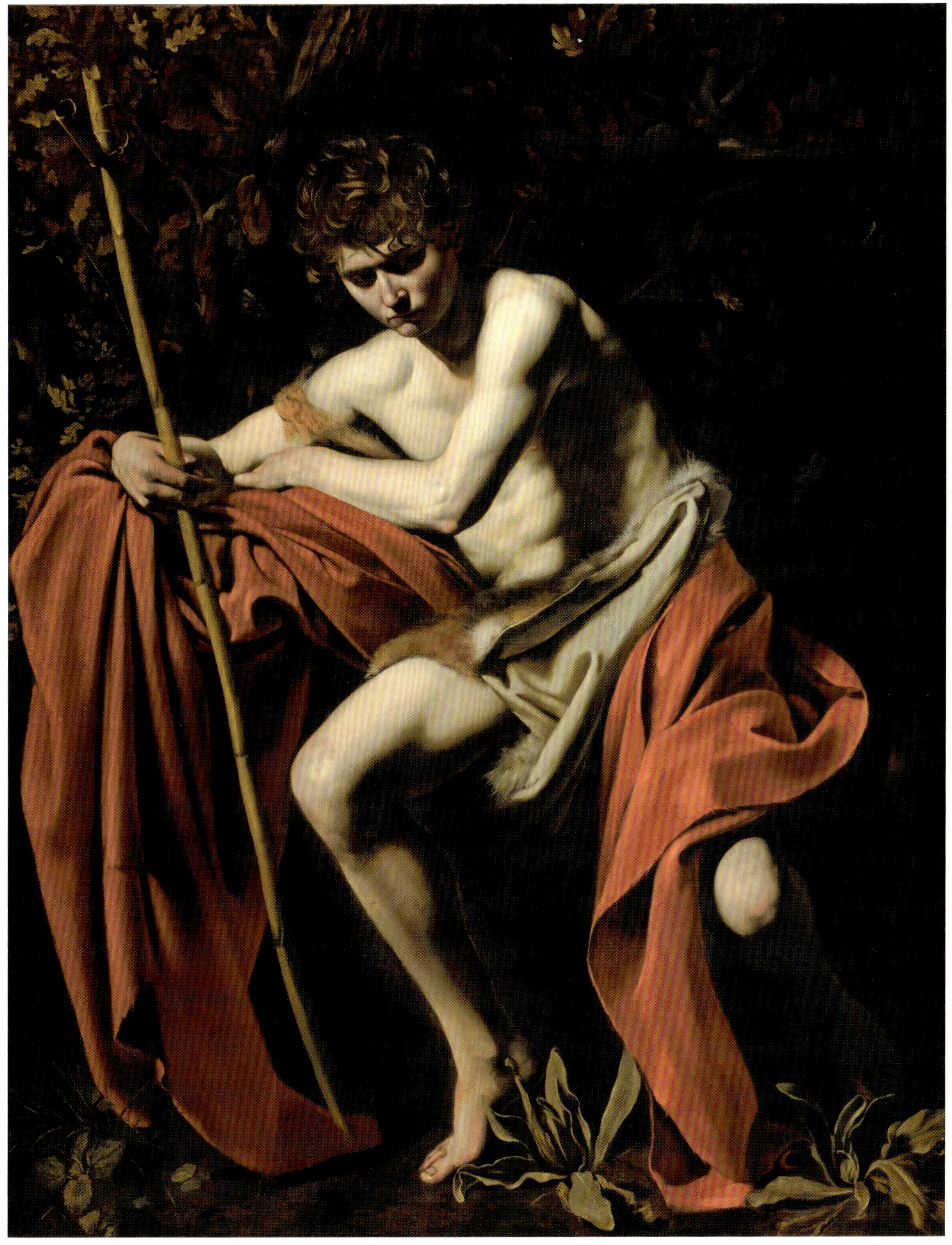

16 Caravaggio, *Saint John the Baptist in the Wilderness*, 1604, oil on canvas, 172.7 × 132 cm (68 × 51 15/16 in), The Nelson-Atkins Museum of Art, Kansas City

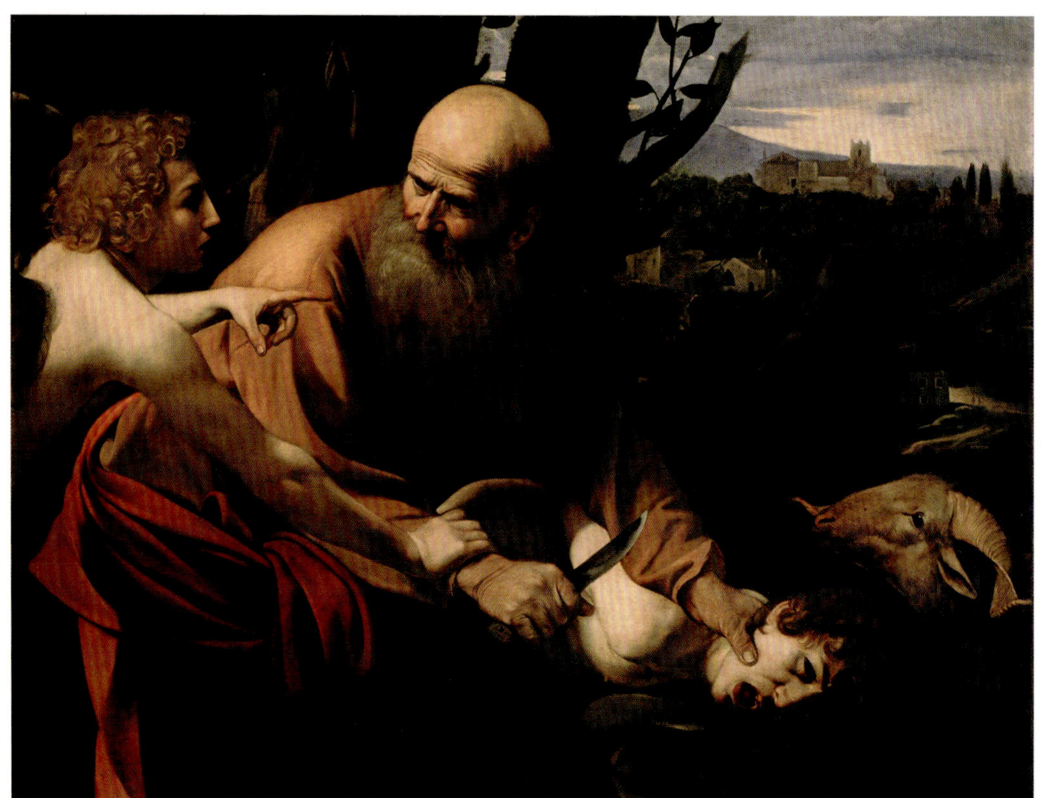

17 Caravaggio, *The Sacrifice of Isaac*, *c.*1603, oil on canvas, 104 × 135 cm (40 15/16 × 53 1/8 in), Uffizi Galleries, Florence

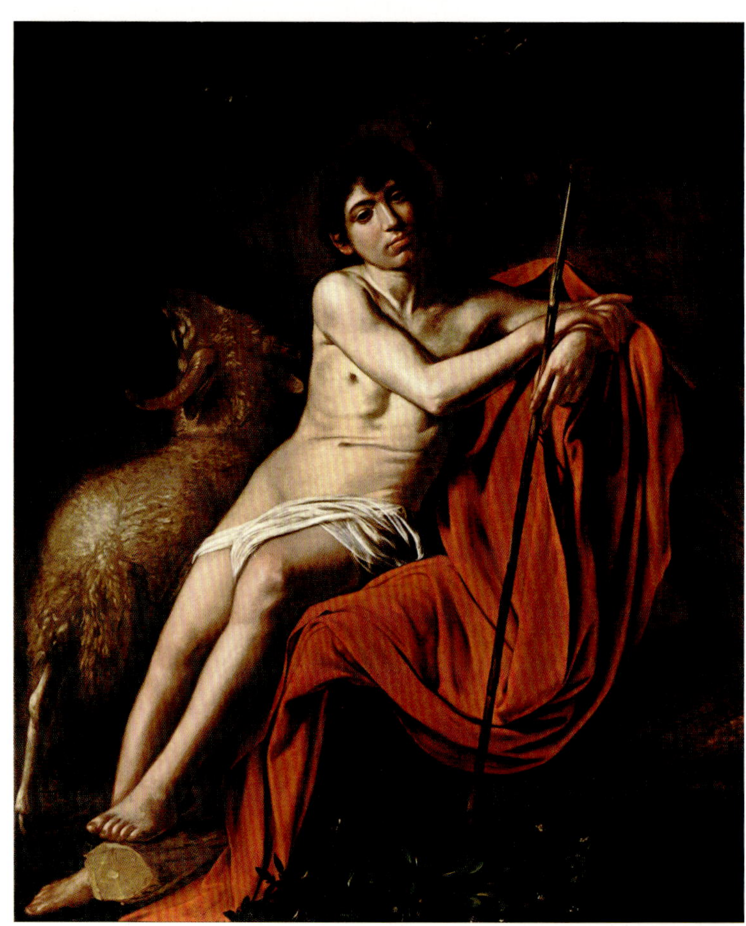

18 Caravaggio, *Saint John the Baptist*, 1610, oil on canvas, 159 × 124.5 cm (62 5/8 × 49 in), Borghese Gallery, Rome

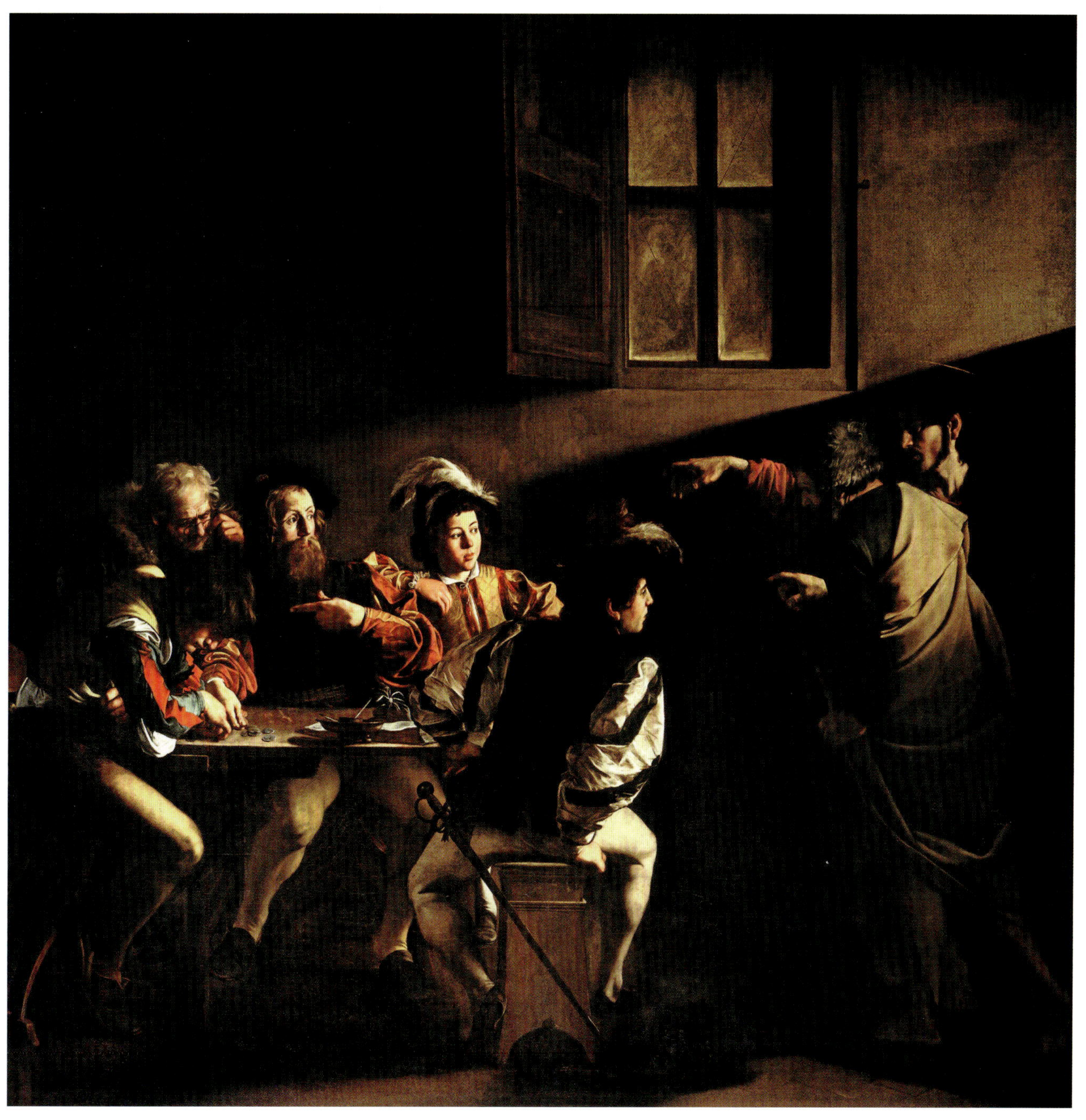

19 Caravaggio, *The Calling of Saint Matthew*, 1599–1600, oil on canvas, 322 × 340 (126 ¾ × 133 ⅞ in), Contarelli Chapel, San Luigi dei Francesi, Rome

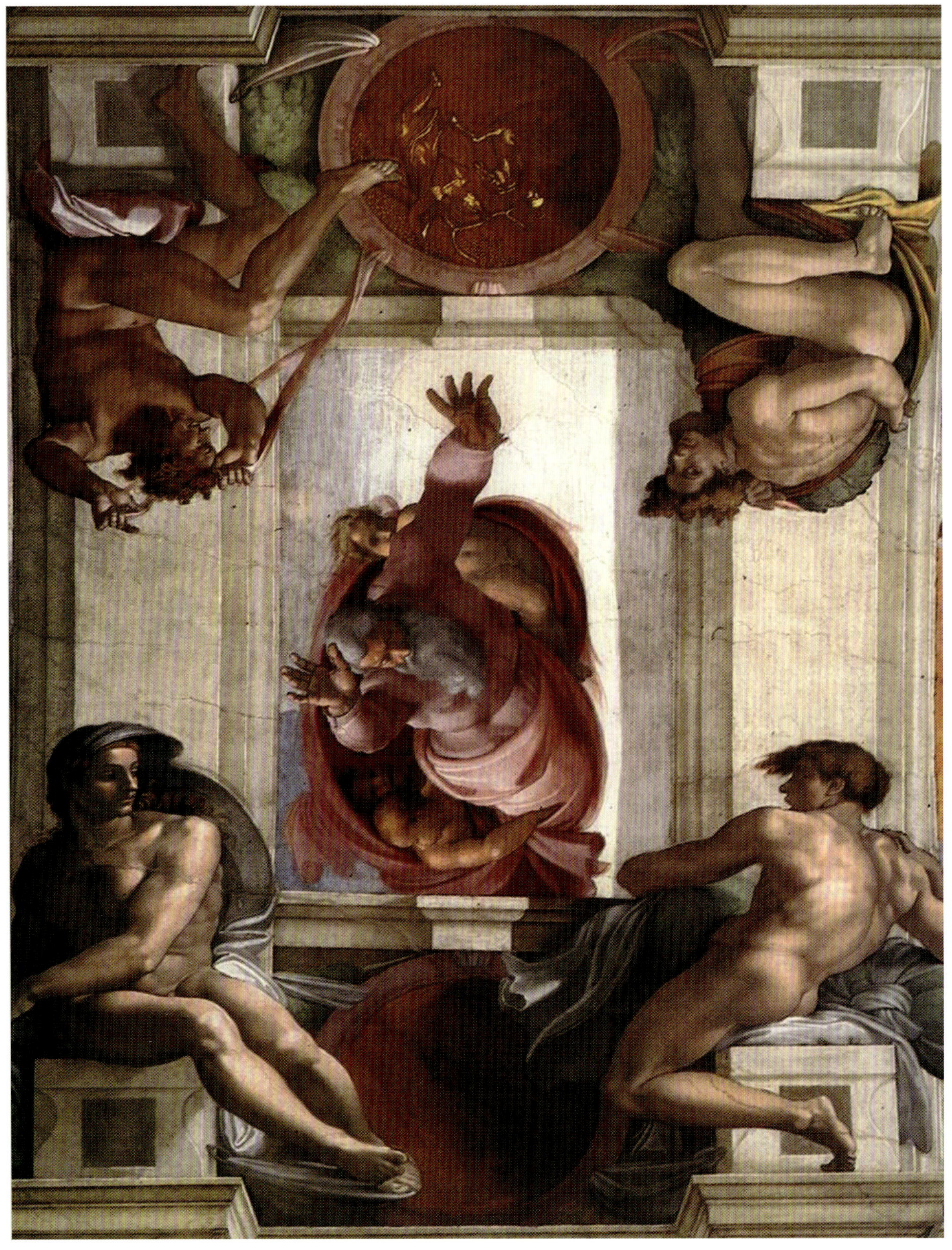

20 Michelangelo, *The Separation of Land from Water*, 1511, fresco, 155 × 270 cm (61 × 106 5/16 in), Sistine Chapel, Vatican, Rome

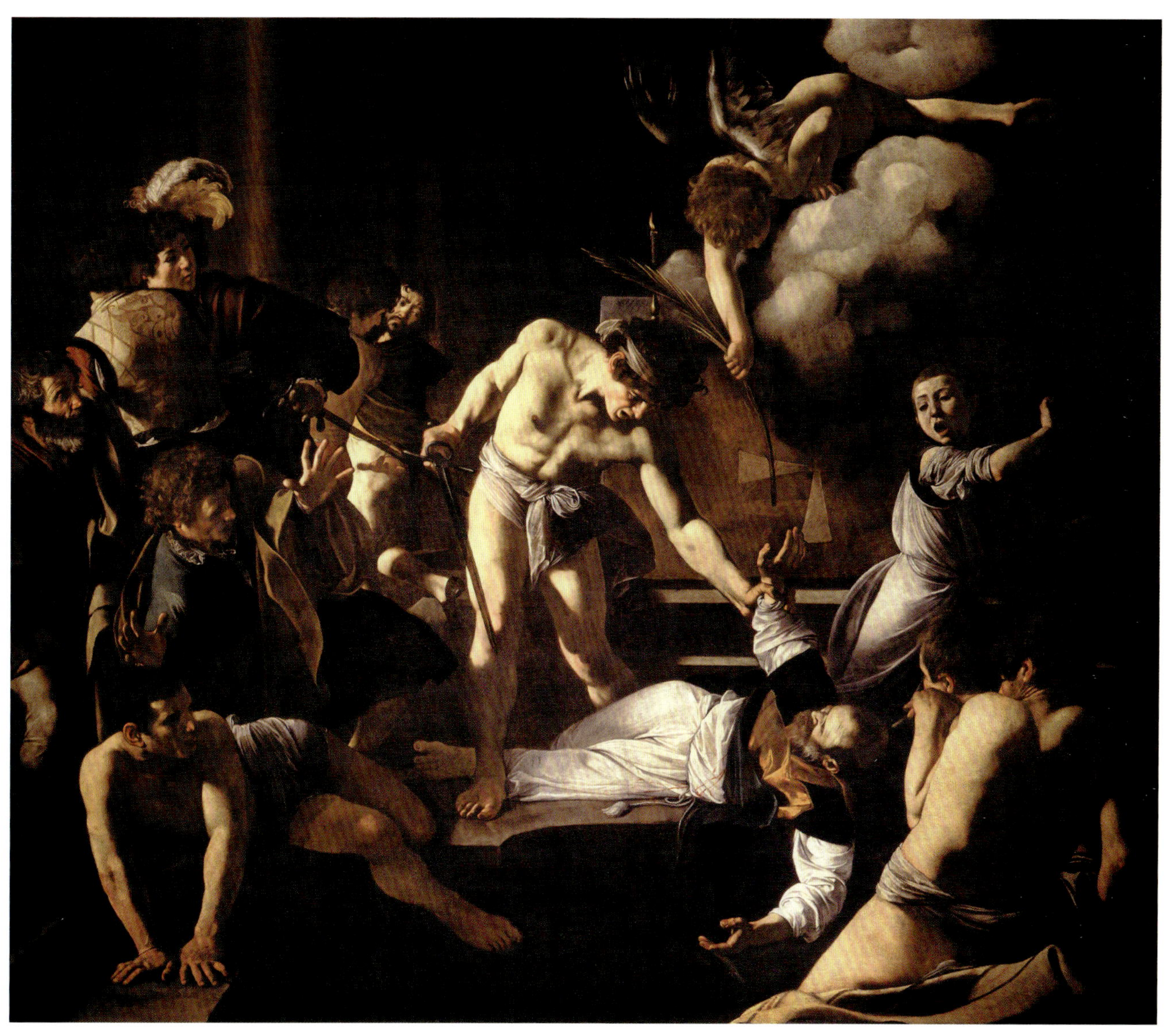

21 Caravaggio, *The Martyrdom of Saint Matthew*, 1599–1600, oil on canvas, 323 × 343 cm (127 3/16 × 135 1/16 in), Contarelli Chapel, San Luigi dei Francesi, Rome

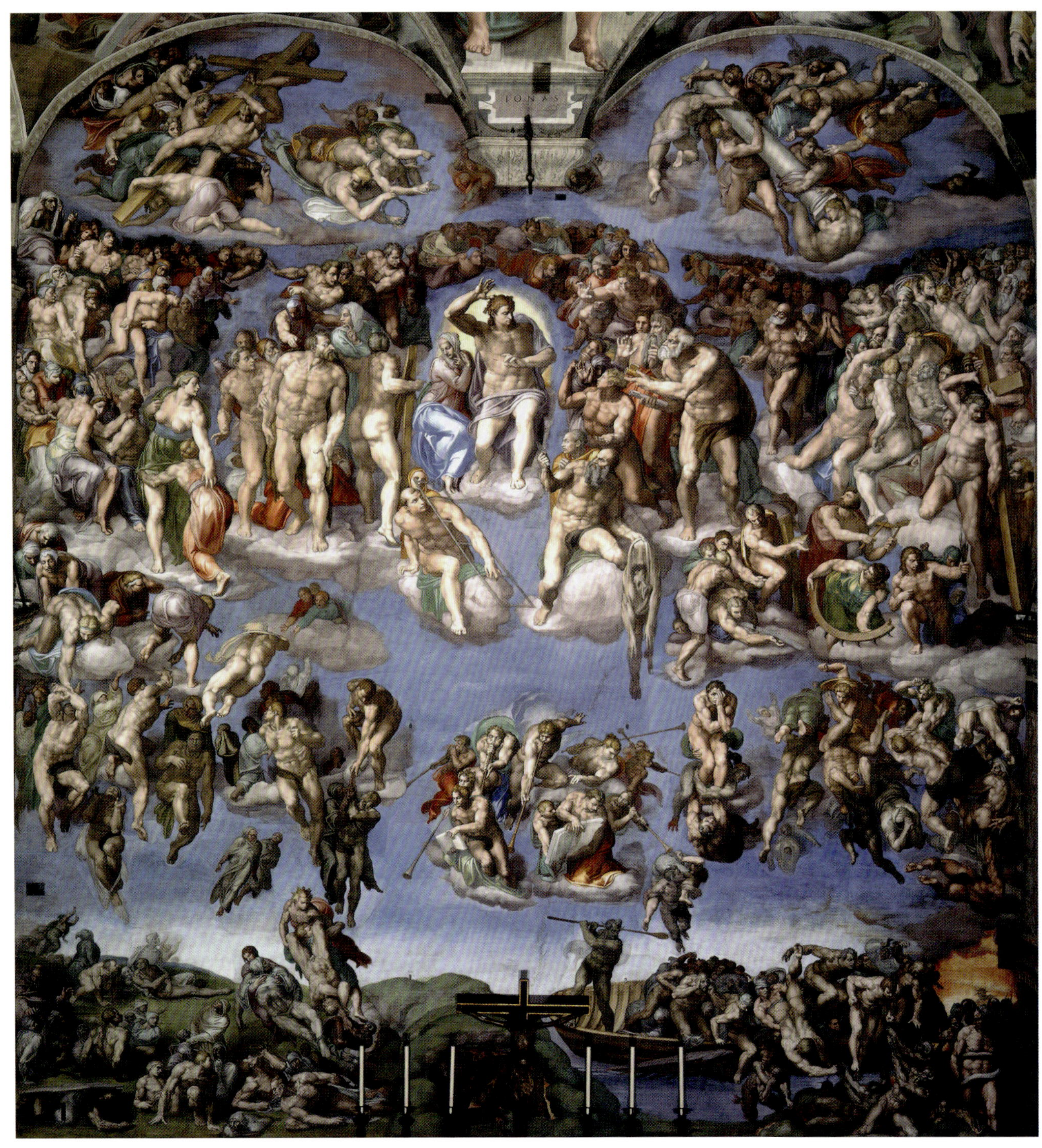

22 Michelangelo, *The Last Judgment*, 1536–41, fresco, 1370 × 1220 cm (539 3/8 × 480 5/16 in), Sistine Chapel, Vatican, Rome

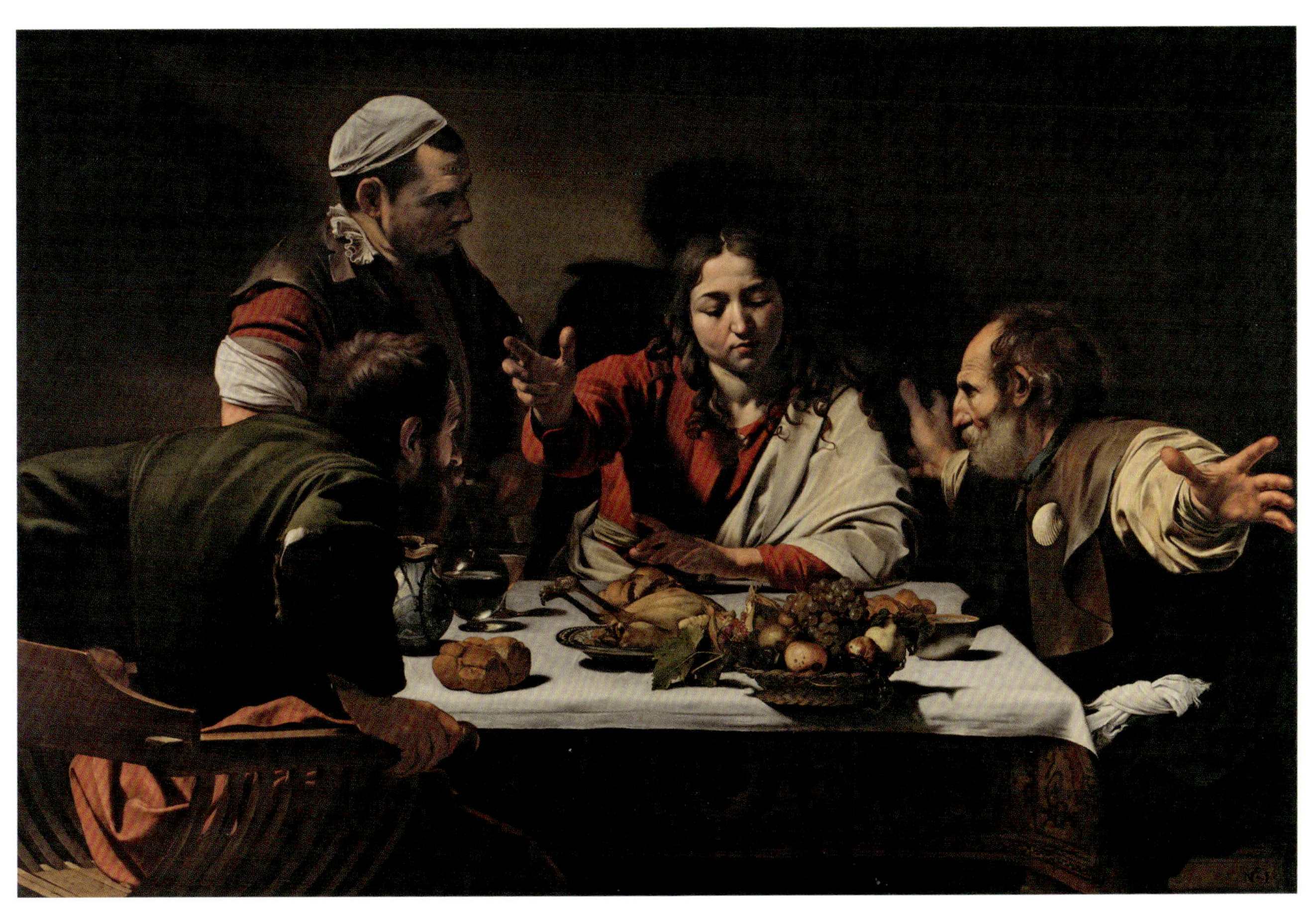

23 Caravaggio, *The Supper at Emmaus*, 1601, oil on canvas, 141 × 196.2 cm (55 ½ × 77 ¼ in), National Gallery, London

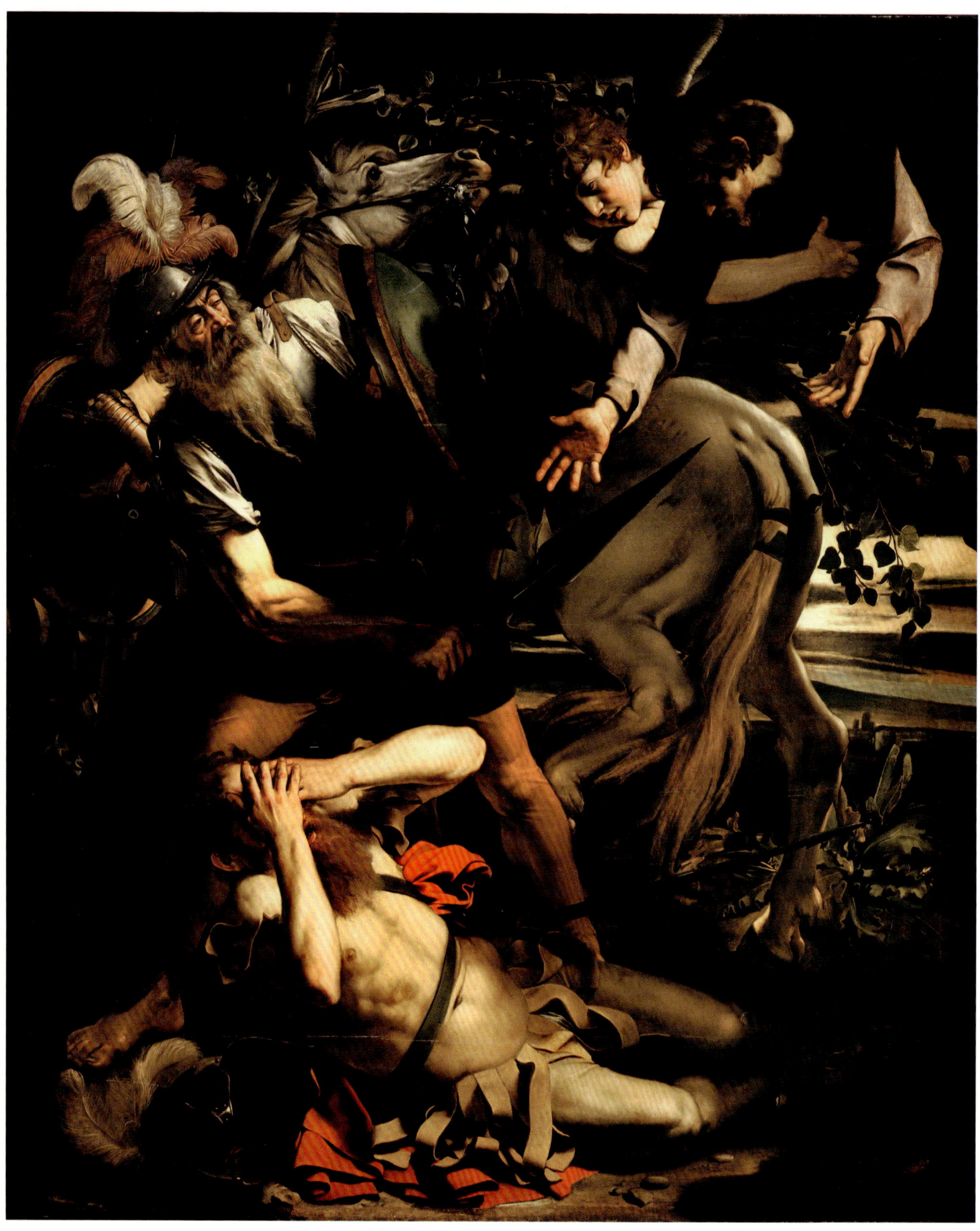

24 Caravaggio, *The Conversion of Saint Paul*, 1600, oil on panel, 237 × 189 cm (93 5/16 × 74 7/16 in), Odescalchi Collection, Rome

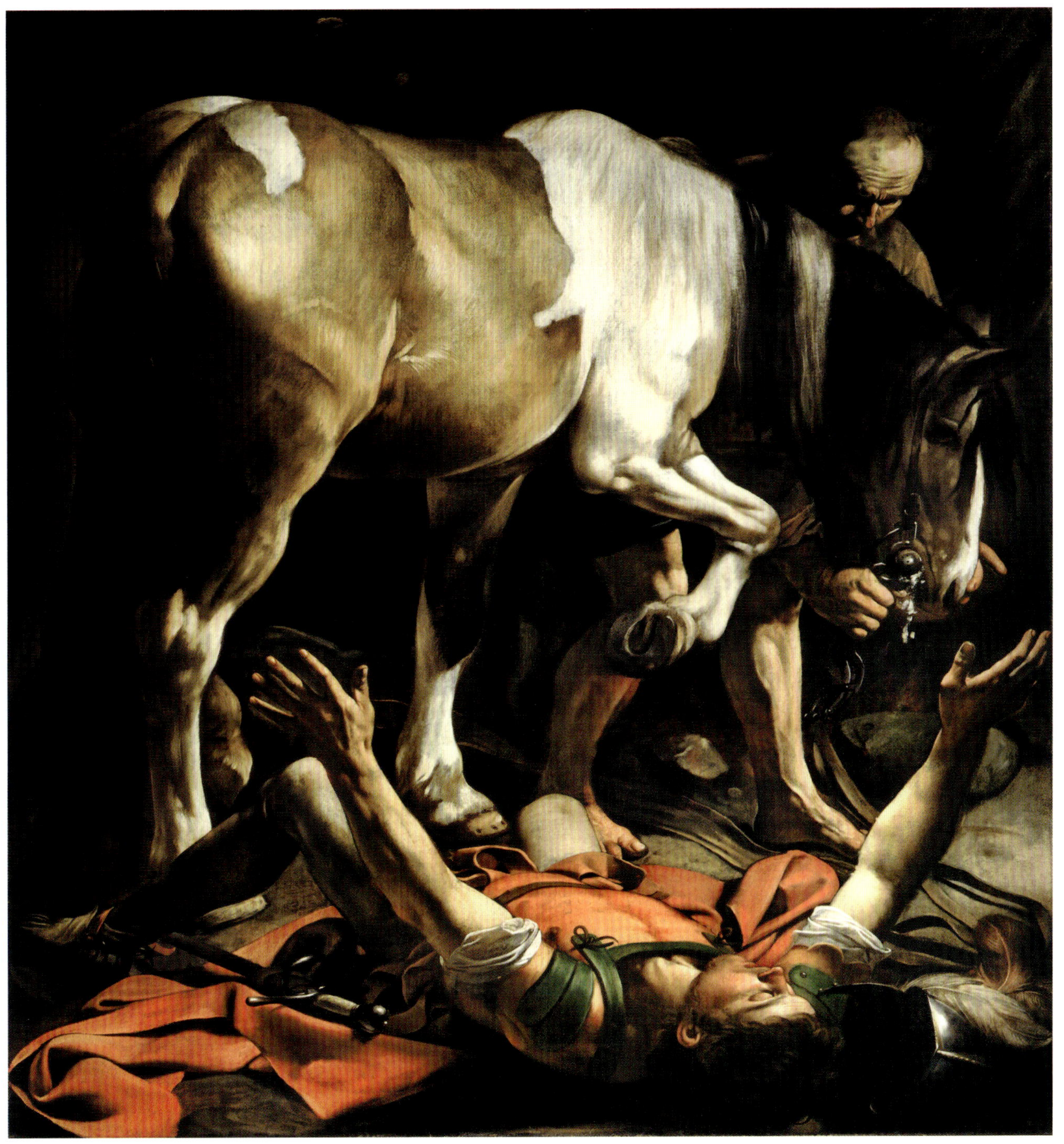

25 Caravaggio, *The Conversion of Saint Paul*, 1604–5, oil on canvas, 230 × 175 cm (90 9/16 × 68 7/8 in), Cerasi Chapel, Santa Maria del Popolo, Rome

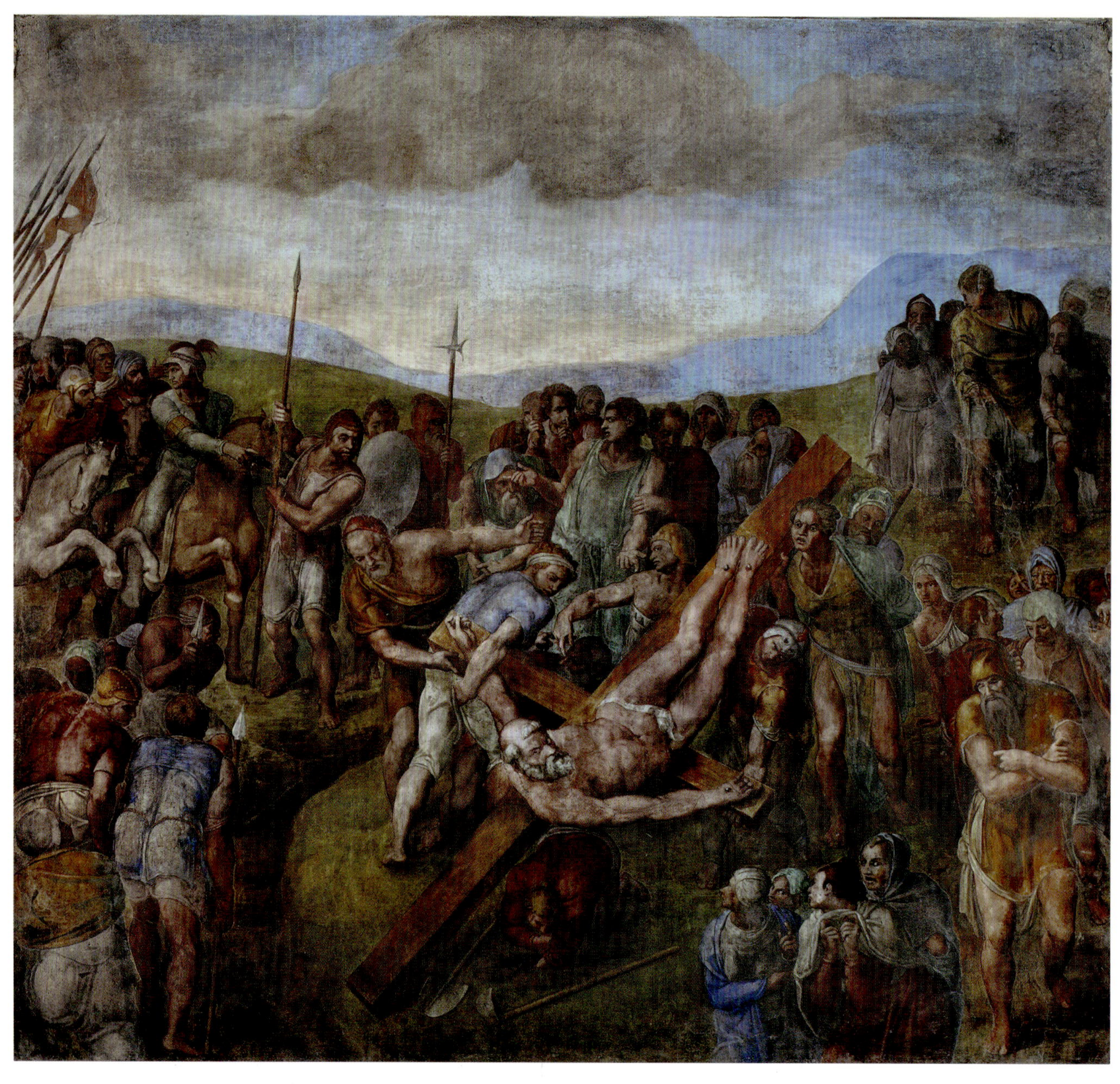

26 Michelangelo, *The Crucifixion of Saint Peter*, 1546–50, fresco, 625 × 662 cm (246 1/16 × 260 5/8 in), Pauline Chapel, Vatican, Rome

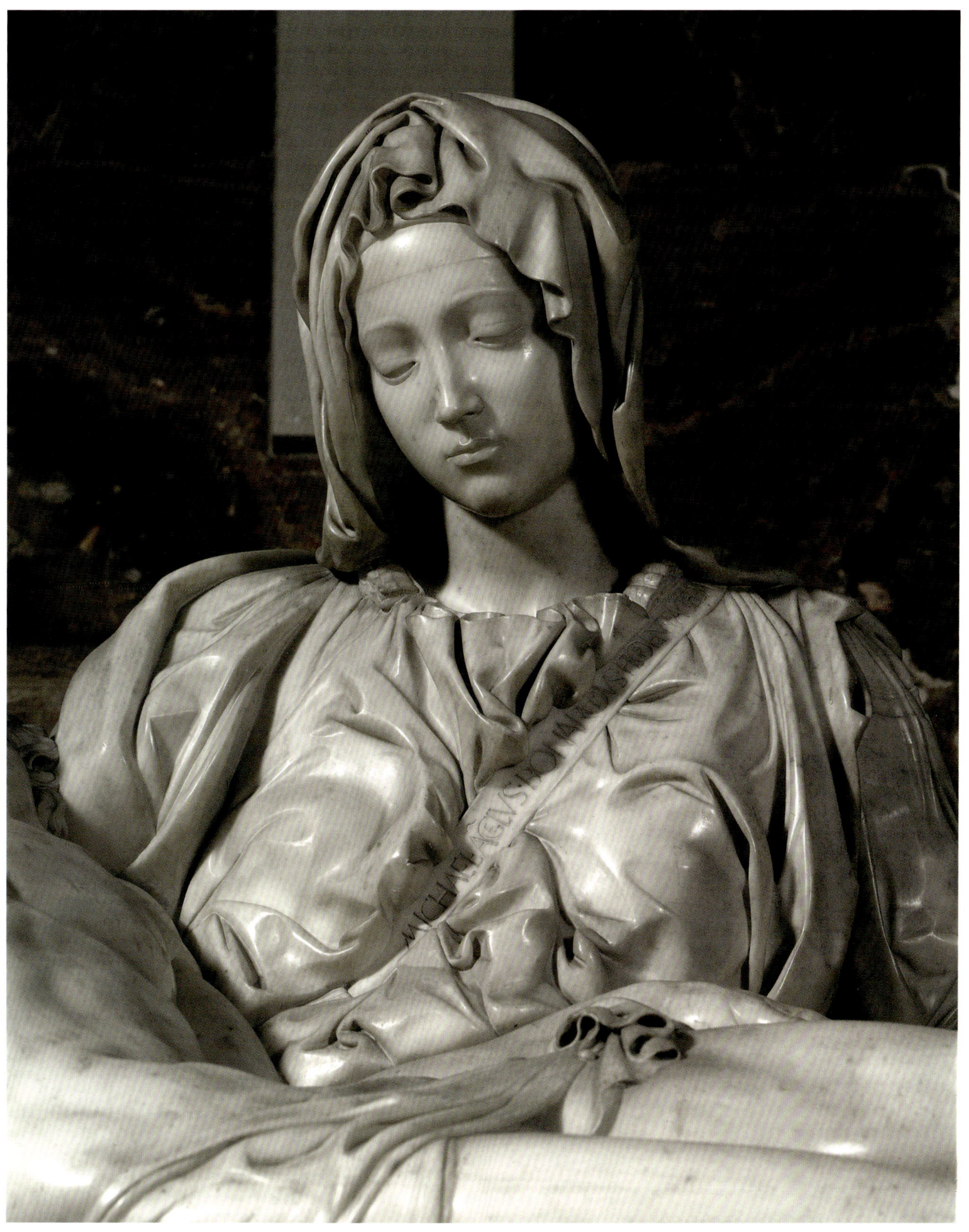

27 Michelangelo, *Pietà*, 1498 (detail of signature), marble, height 174 cm (68 ½ in), Saint Peter's Basilica, Vatican, Rome

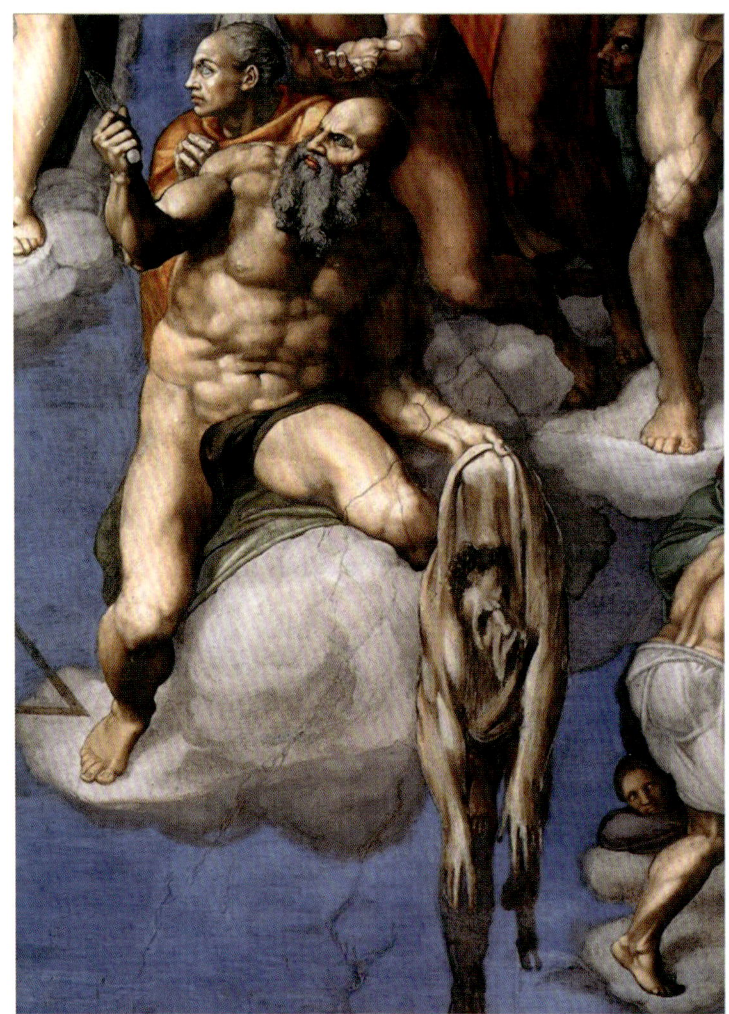

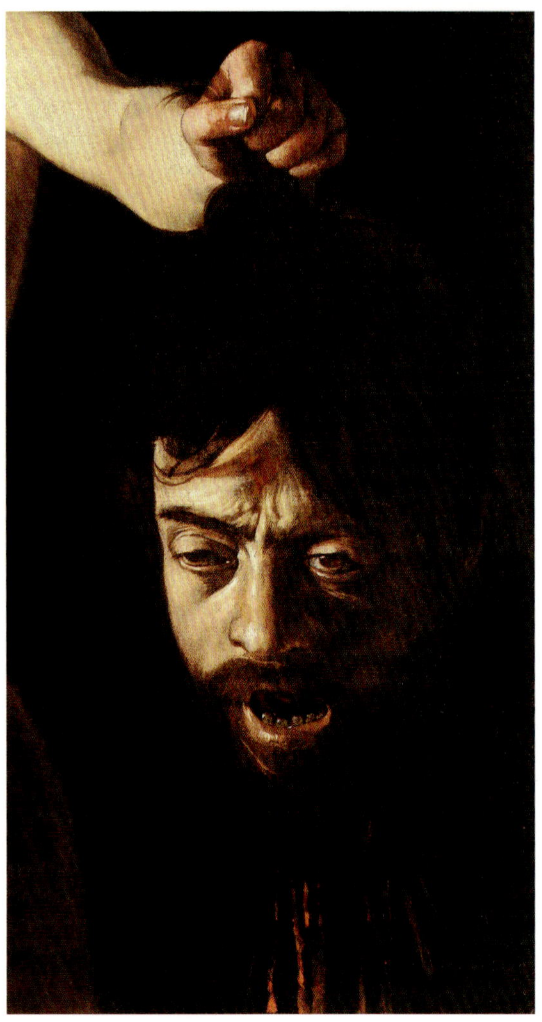

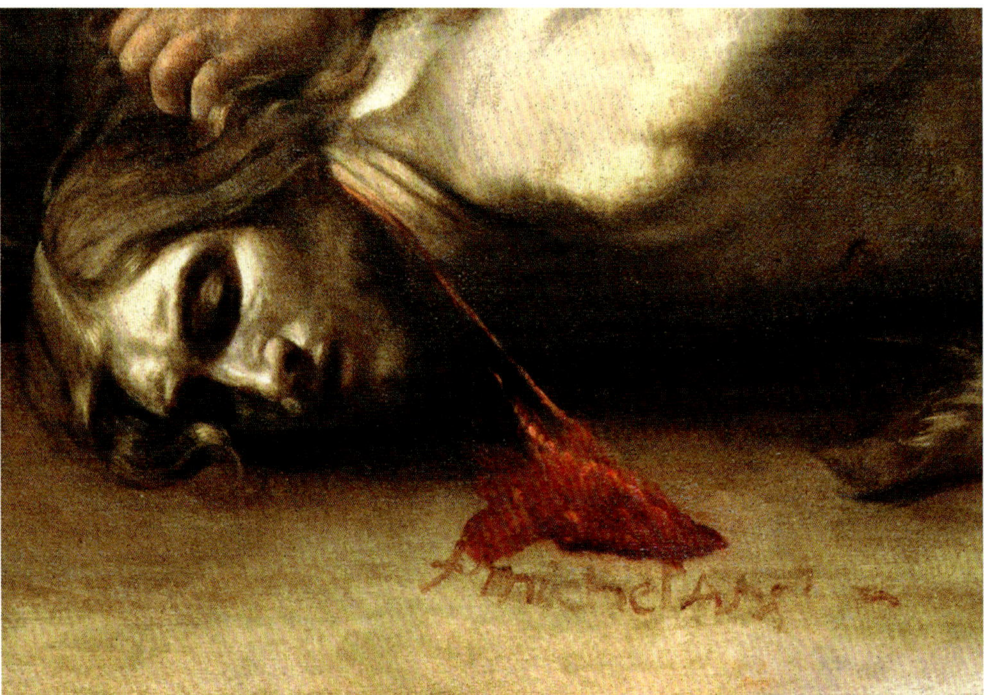

28 (ABOVE LEFT) Michelangelo, Self-portrait on flayed skin, detail, *The Last Judgment*, 1536–41, fresco, 1370 x 1220 cm (539 3/8 x 480 5/16 in), Sistine Chapel, Vatican, Rome

29 (ABOVE RIGHT) Caravaggio, Self-portrait as head of Goliath, detail, *David with the Head of Goliath*, 1609–10, oil on canvas, 125 × 101 cm (46 3/16 × 39 3/4 in) Borghese Gallery, Rome

30 Caravaggio, signature in blood, detail, *Beheading of Saint John the Baptist*, 1608, oil on canvas, 361 x 520 cm (142 1/8 x 204 7/10 in), Oratory of Saint John's Cathedral, Valletta, Malta

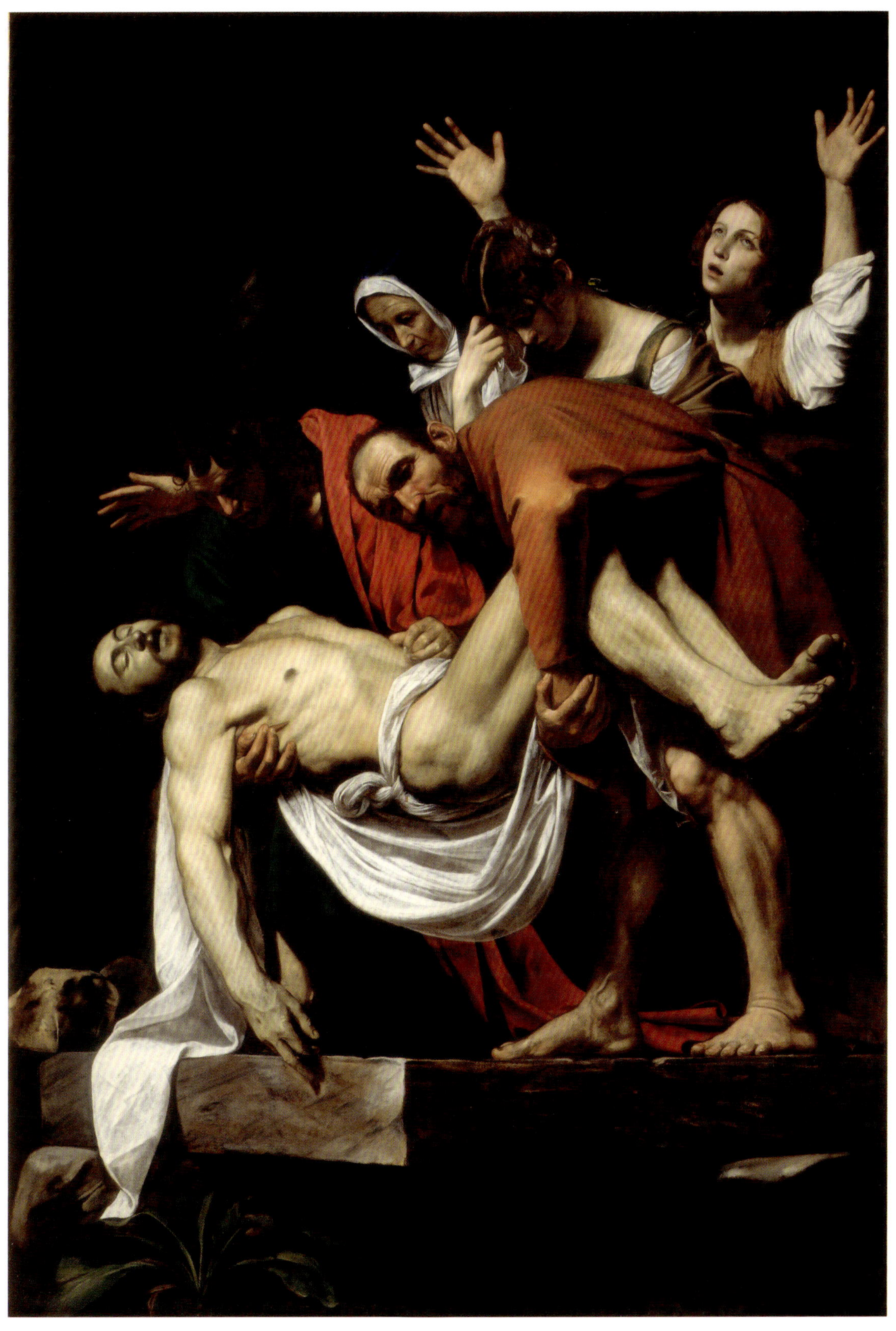

31 Caravaggio, *The Deposition*, *c.*1602–4, oil on canvas, 300 × 203 cm (118 ⅛ × 79 15/16 in), Pinacoteca Vaticana, Vatican, Rome

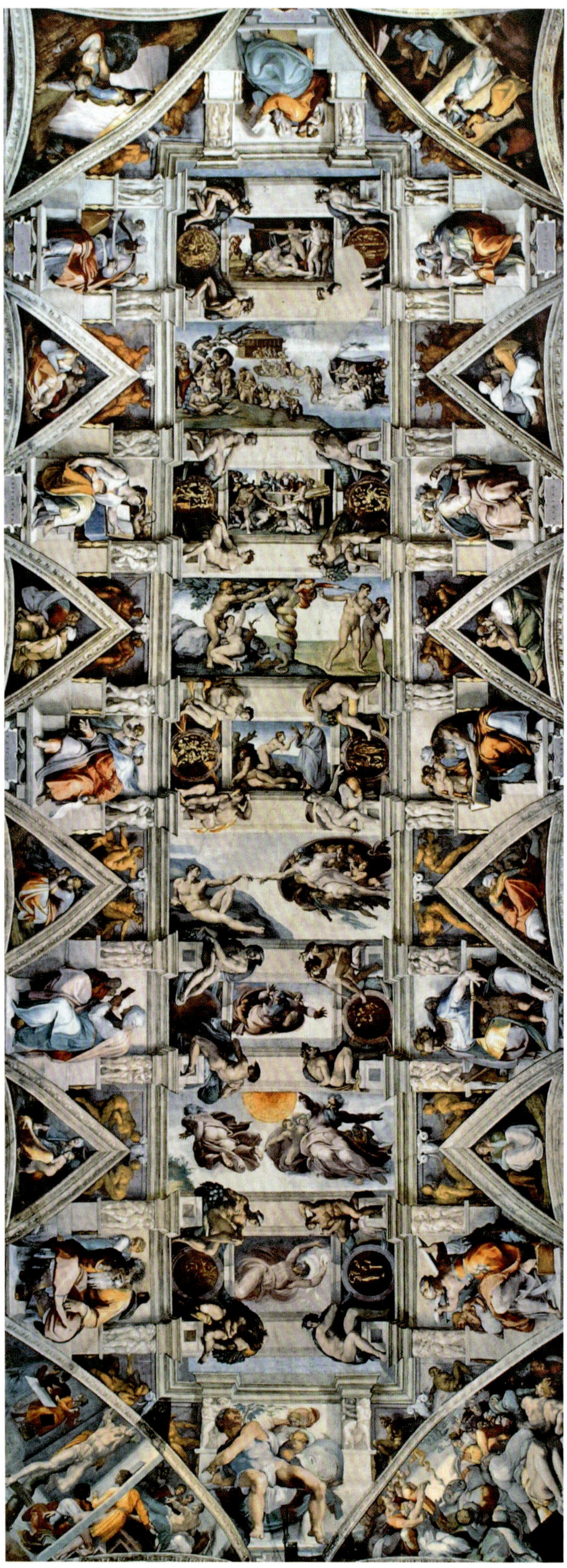

32 View of the Sistine Chapel, ceiling fresco, 1508–12, fresco, 4050 × 1340 cm (1594 ½ × 527 ⅗ in), Vatican, Rome

3

Michelangelo's *Ignudi* of the Sistine Chapel, their Ancestors, Descendants and Caravaggio's Shocking Responses

Caravaggio's most direct, provocative and daring interaction with Michelangelo's art was a result of his study of the *ignudi*, the athletic male nudes ranged along the central section of the Sistine ceiling, which comprise a serial motif with startling visual impact (Plate 32). Their appearance within the chapel's carefully constructed sequences of biblical stories and papal symbols is so unexpected that they have been generally referred to by remarking upon their nudity – the *ignudi* – a description coming from the artist himself by way of Condivi's biography.[1] Caravaggio's responses to the *ignudi* matched his models in boldness and symbolic complexity and represent particularly intense examples of 'talking back' to his namesake. Caravaggio manipulated the *ignudi* in such a way as to copy their form but invert their meaning, producing figures that cite Michelangelo's compositions but tear down his very philosophy of art. To fully appreciate Caravaggio's mastery in accomplishing this feat of subversion, we have first to see how richly conceived Michelangelo's *ignudi* are, with their own derivation from and innovation upon a conspicuous tradition developed primarily in 15th-century Florentine art.

Michelangelo's monumental nude figures puzzle modern scholarship, although their inescapable power compels attention and elicits wide-ranging reactions. The diversity of interpretations about their meaning leads to a fear that we have lost the basic key that could unlock their true meaning. The unashamed, unselfconscious nudity of the figures, surprising in the sacred space of the chapel, yet moderated by the great height at which they are situated, is in emphatic contrast to modern religious sensibility. Their nudity has often created a stumbling block that prevents a dispassionate viewing, which demands contextualization within the boundaries of how art functioned in the early 16th century. By thinking about the marvelous *ignudi* in relation to their immediate artistic precedents, we can arrive at a lucid perception of their core significance. An understanding of the profoundly spiritual meanings embodied by the *ignudi* and awareness of the sources of their symbolism are crucial to an appreciation of how outrageous some of Caravaggio's appropriations would have been to the eyes of his contemporaries. Although extraordinarily inventive and undoubtedly unique at the moment of their appearance on the ceiling, Michelangelo's *ignudi* decisively follow a very popular yet sophisticated motif, rooted in antique practice and developed with great verve in Florentine art of the Quattrocento. At the beginning of the following century, Michelangelo's contribution caused a sensation and had extensive repercussions strong enough to attract Caravaggio's attention when he arrived in Rome at the close of the century and grappled with the accomplishments of his forerunner.

What exactly was Michelangelo's extraordinarily original contribution in the creation of the *ignudi*? Nothing less than a transformation of the traditional spritely, rollicking companies of winged *putti* into a squadron of impossibly idealized young men.[2] The absence of wings in Michelangelo's examples has helped to veil the connection to their prototypes, as have their modification from children to young adults with powerful physiques. These figures are so noticeably muscled that they have also been thought of as Christian athletes, akin to the flawless male bodies perfected in classical Greek sculpture.

We can follow Michelangelo's path to these surprising figures by first establishing the purpose of the *ignudi;* and despite the amount of discussion around them, their function is unexpectedly straightforward. They hold in place large medallions that are painted to imitate bronze roundels, threaded with silky ribbons (Plate 10). Because their postures in grasping the ribbons are so extravagant and their musculature so emphatic, it is easy to miss the basic function that underlies their gyrations; it has often been overlooked in discussing them. However, the unassailable fact is on record, found in Condivi's authoritative gloss on the composition of the ceiling. He simply states that *ignudi* are placed on either side of the medallions to hold them up.[3] Careful observation discloses that each one of the figures performs this task; further, many of the *ignudi* carry thick garlands of acorns across their shoulders. The garlands are heraldic, symbolic of the pope's Della Rovere family, whose name refers to an oak tree.

These actions – supporting roundels and bearing garlands – place the *ignudi* in a tradition that flourished in the ancient world and was revived in the early Renaissance. In antique practice the figures were formed as winged children or adolescents referred to as *genii;* Michelangelo's immediate predecessors retained the wings while favoring chubby male babies (*putti*), and gave them a spritely character, which led to the nomenclature of *spiritelli*.[4] Their relation to the variety of Christian angels given the form of infants is clear and provided them easy entry to religious settings. Their nudity was permissible as an extension of belief in the uncorrupted innocence of children; it was also sanctioned by the classical sources of the figures, elevating them to a category that we would call 'high art'. Similar considerations would have protected Michelangelo's adaptations of the shield-bearers from criticism; they were so idealized as to be removed from the circuit of human depravity and they took their place in a symbolic system derived from antiquity, renewed in the 15th century. The capacity of the *ignudi* to carry symbolic meaning is fundamental to their existence in Michelangelo's decoration of the Sistine ceiling. This results not only from their idealization, but also through their absorption of the conventions associated with their prototypes, one of which was intimately linked to Michelangelo's commission.

Naked putti holding a heraldic device appear in the Della Rovere Chapel dedicated to San Girolamo in Santa Maria del Popolo. Commissioned by Cardinal Domenico Della Rovere, the chapel embellishes the church built by his illustrious protector, Pope Sixtus IV; its decoration was carried out around 1479.[5] A striking balustrade at the entry to the chapel features a winged child/angel placed on either side of the patron's coat of arms (Fig. 9), holding it with ribbons that flutter behind them; a pertinent model for Michelangelo's *ignudi*. The decoration of the chapel is an early instance of incorporating ancient motifs from Nero's Golden House buried in the center of Rome and was highly influential. Michelangelo, then, made reference to a current Della Rovere emblem when he designed an aggrandized version of the *all'antica* shield-bearers for

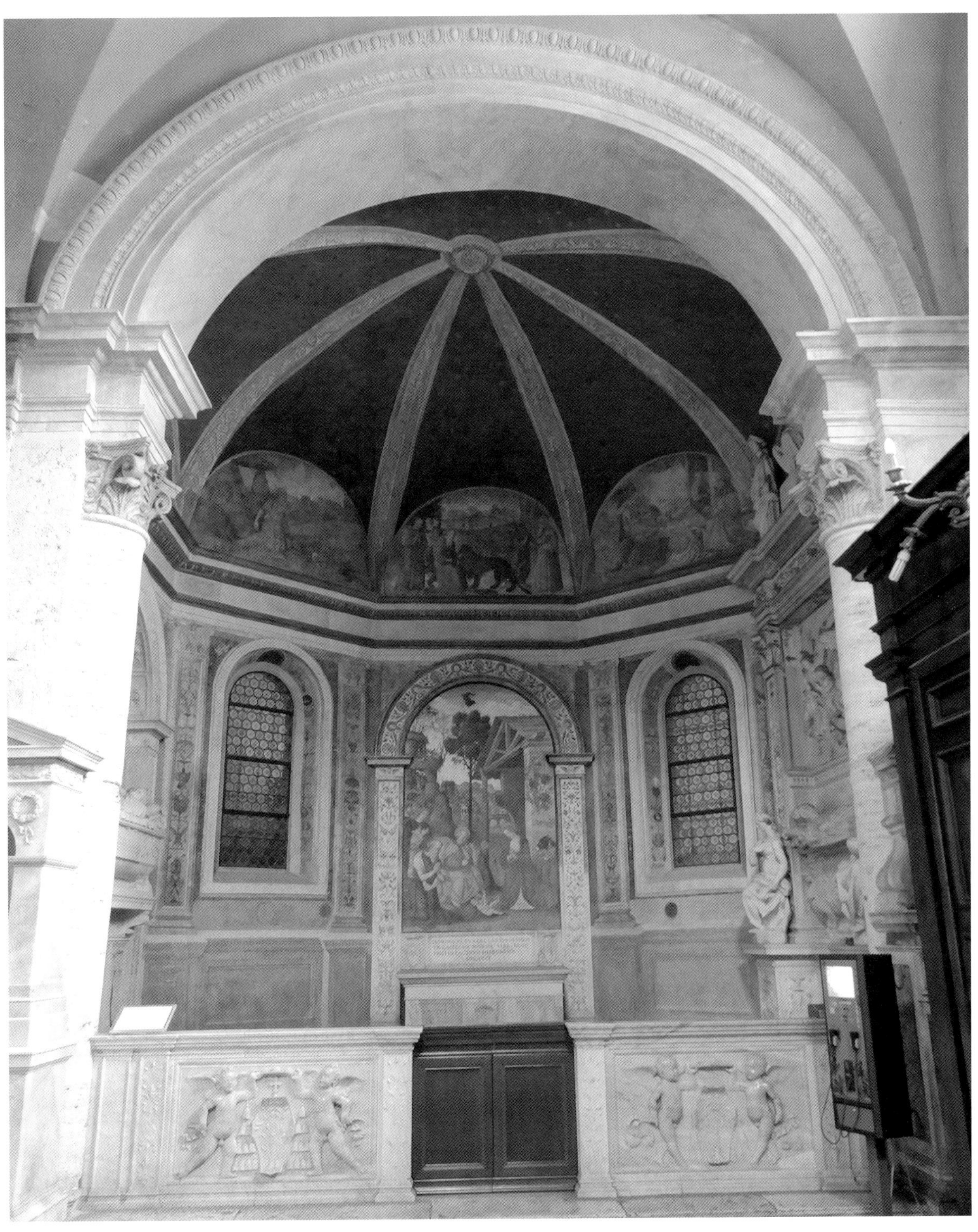

9 Chapel of San Girolamo, acquired by the Della Rovere Family in 1477, Santa Maria del Popolo, Rome

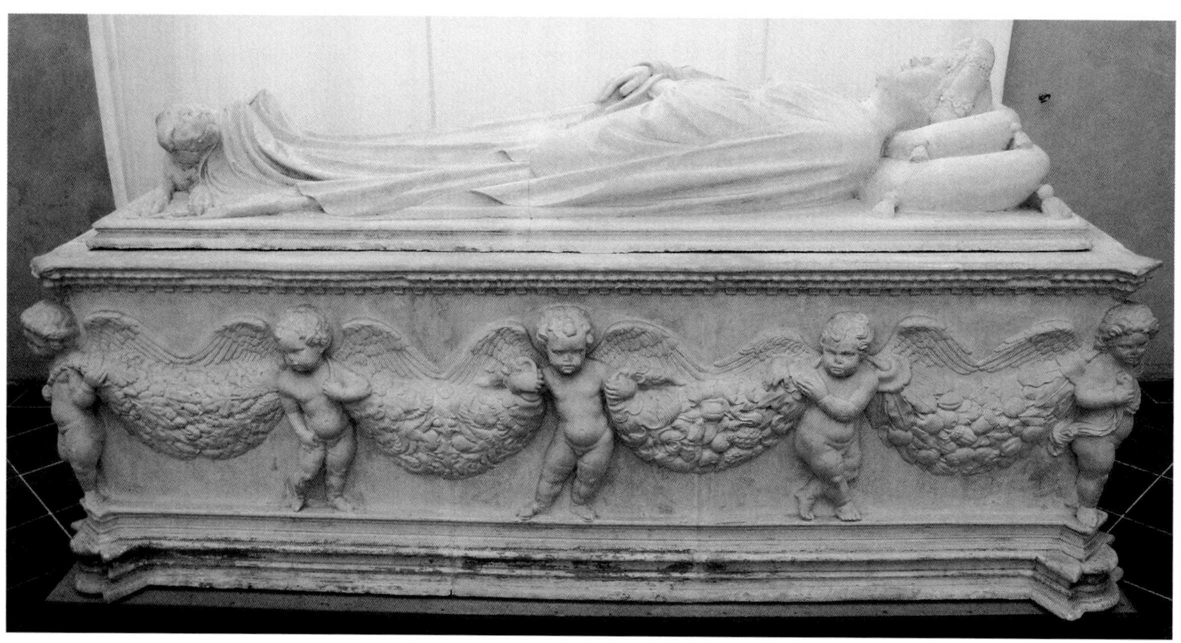

10 Jacopo della Quercia, *Tomb of Ilaria del Carretto*, 1406, marble, 244 × 88 × 66.5 cm (96 1/16 × 34 5/8 × 26 3/16 in), Cathedral of San Martino, Lucca

Pope Julius' ceiling, echoing the ones found in the family church. The balustrade's carvings would have struck a chord with Michelangelo from his Florentine heritage. He devised a new chapter in the history of this legacy, particularly apt for his Della Rovere patron; Michelangelo's Sistine *ignudi* are nothing less than colossal variants of the Tuscan *spiritello*; indeed, they might be thought of as *spiritoni*.[6]

Singling out several examples from the truly staggering number of possibilities will show how rich was the tradition that Michelangelo took on and how unique his modification of it. The tomb that Jacopo della Quercia created for Ilaria del Carretto in the Duomo of Lucca displays the first influential Renaissance transformation of the classical winged spirit into angelic putti carrying festoons (Fig. 10).[7] Jacopo designed the elegant sarcophagus with the gracefully sculpted figure of Ilaria lying in eternal repose along its lid. In contrast, the sides of the coffin are enlivened by a frieze of winged, chubby little boys in a variety of dancing postures, sustaining heavy garlands of fruits and flowers. This must have been an astonishing sight as it emerged during the seven years of its creation, from 1406–13. The tomb's balance of serenity and playfulness, its evocation of the quiet sadness of death and mute celebration of a joyous realm, are still deeply moving today.

The decorative scheme of the nude, garland-bearing angel became immensely popular, even at the most sacred sites. The north sacristy, or vesting room, known as the Sacrestia delle Messe in the Cathedral of Florence, is adorned by a frieze of dancing youths who grasp a continuous chain of lavish garlands above the elaborate intarsia of the walls.[8] They appear in the exact formation of their counterparts on the tomb in Lucca, caught in joyous movement as they sustain the long festoons that sway between them. The Florentine version employs more slender proportions, slim boys rather than chubby babies, yet the exuberant effect is the same. The one significant change in the pattern is that the *spiritelli* in the sacristy have not been provided with wings. Michelangelo followed this option and created wingless angelic figures

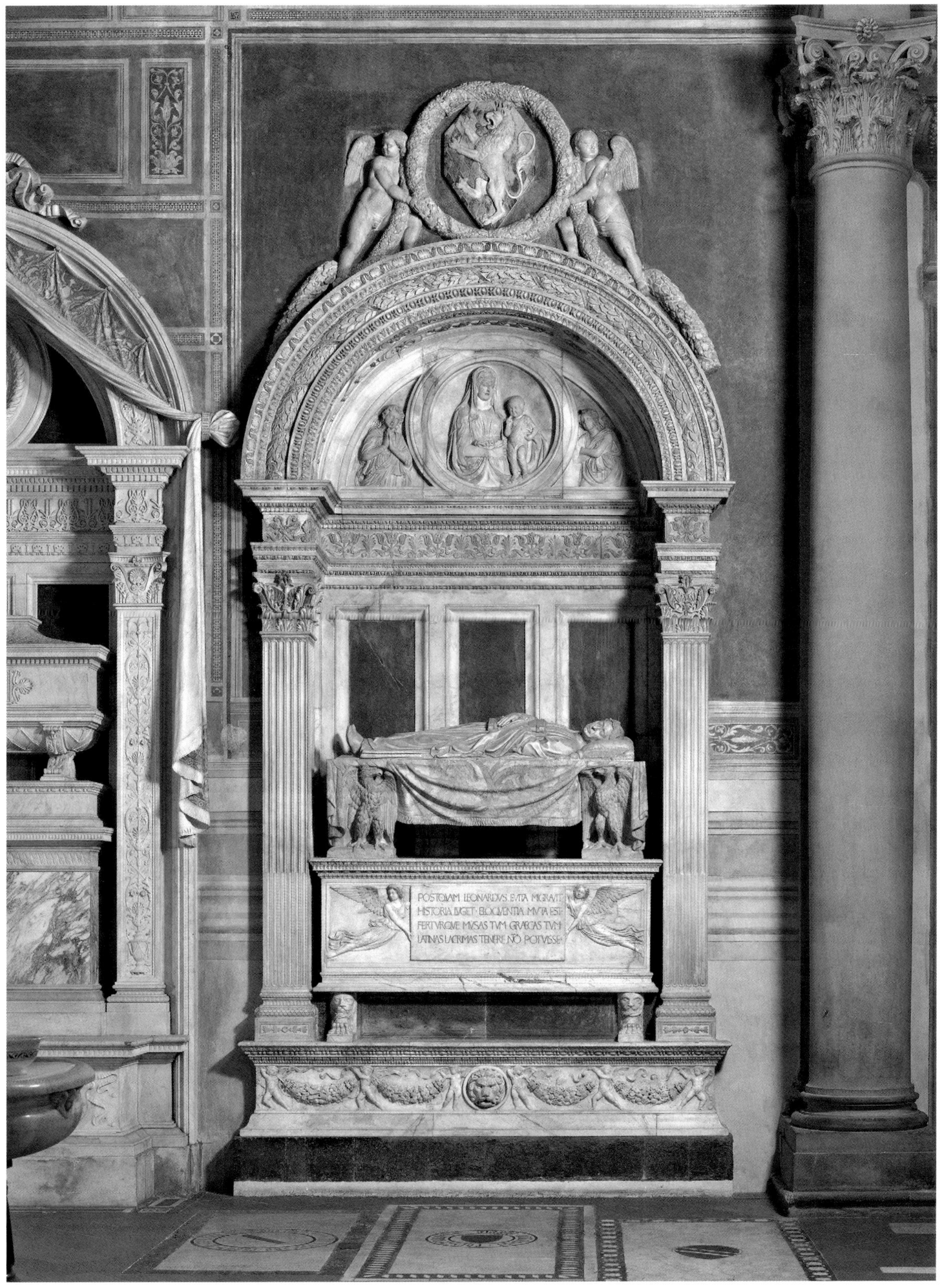

11 Bernardo Rossellino, *Tomb of Leonardo Bruni*, 1444–7, marble, height 610 cm (240 3/16 in), Santa Croce, Florence

to bear the garlands adorning the Sistine ceiling.

The principal monuments of Michelangelo's native city are replete with variations of angelic *putti*. Santa Croce, the Buonarroti family's neighborhood church, houses an example that appears to have been particularly influential on the artist's conception of the *ignudi*. They are a prominent feature of Bernardo Rossellino's tomb for Leonardo Bruni, the Chancellor of Florence who died in 1444 (Fig. 11). The statesman's coat of arms is the crowning feature of the multi-level sculptural ensemble, which soars 20 feet in height. Wreathed in a circular garland, the shield is held in prominent place by two *spiritelli* who additionally carry long festoons draped on their shoulders. They are a variant of the motif found at the base of the monument where a line of *putti* prance along the frieze, in pairs that effortlessly pull heavy swags of festoons along with them. Admiration for this monument may well have come to mind when Michelangelo elaborated his grandiose scheme of decoration for the Sistine Chapel.

Donatello (1386–1466), Michelangelo's forerunner as the most influential Florentine sculptor of his age, was irrevocably seduced by the *spiritelli* and did most to establish their iconography and popularity. The angels/sprites began to appear in his work in the 1420s and proliferated in the following decade. Donatello's corpus was a guide for Michelangelo's formation as a sculptor and the abundance of the *spiritello* in all its expressive potential left its mark. Its function as a decorative figure, capable of signaling the meaning of a larger work by holding symbolic emblems, formed part of Michelangelo's artistic arsenal as he filled the huge space of the Sistine ceiling.

At the end of the 15th century, long after the death of Donatello in 1466, the *spiritello* continued to be a pervasive motif; its function as a bearer of standards and festoons was deeply embedded in Florentine art. It is not surprising that it arrived in Rome at the end of the century as part of the decorative vocabulary of Florentines who came to work in the papal city. The vogue for their creative production ensured that it could be used as collateral in diplomatic exchanges. This was the case when the talented Filippino Lippi (1457–1504) received a noteworthy commission from the Neapolitan Cardinal Oliviero Carafa (1430–1511); his selection was due to the intervention of Lorenzo de' Medici himself.

Lippi interrupted his painting of an equally important chapel in Santa Maria Novella to comply with Lorenzo's wish, transferred to Rome and completed the Carafa Chapel in 1491. Constructed within the church of Santa Maria sopra Minerva, it is located in a zone of outstanding ancient sites not far from the Pantheon, where Lippi's blend of classical motifs and Florentine modernism was perfect for the venue. The chapel is dedicated to Saint Thomas Aquinas, with its altar wall honoring the theologian's triumph in his disputation with heretics. Above this scene, a book of Thomas's writings is encircled by a fictive, gilt stucco molding held by a chubby *putto* on either side (Plate 11). They twist in their seated positions to grasp the roundel with both hands, which is much larger in scale than themselves. In this scene, the Florentine *spiritelli* are transformed from sculpture into paint and transplanted to the papal city. Frescoed *spiritelli* were otherwise rare, with only one prominent mid-century precedent by Andrea del Castagno (before 1419–1457). They appear in a decorative frieze above Castagno's series of *Famous Men and Women*, originally painted for the Villa Carducci, shouldering garlands and holding ribbons, with some placed adjacent to roundels with coats of arms.[9] Following the lead of his countrymen, another ambitious Florentine followed this pattern. Tasked with a huge fresco commission – and protesting that painting was not his true profession – Michelangelo converted his own sculptural ideas into frescoed, festoon-bearing figures. The visual evidence attests to Michelangelo's appreciation of his predecessors' masterstroke in recalibrating the *spiritelli* from three to two dimensions, while retaining their function as bearers of garlands and ornamental disks.[10]

The derivation of the *ignudi* from the *spiritelli* explains their true ancestry. Michelangelo's recasting of the childish sprites into heroically muscled young men was both a daring, unexpected innovation after one hundred years of tradition and an obvious development in his emergent painting style. His preference for creation in three dimensions and his attraction to monumental scale endowed Michelangelo's two-dimensional work with a pronounced effect of volume and mass. The sequence of the *ignudi*, along with the plethora of other characters filling the ceiling, swelled to a remarkable level of gigantism and abstraction as the figures advanced toward the altar wall. The first pairs of *ignudi* seated closest to the chapel's entrance are weighty and muscled, yet their pronounced movements are comfortably contained within their marble thrones. When they appear at the altar, to frame a minimalist scene of the Prime Mover separating light from darkness, the immensity of the *ignudi* surges to near abstraction, hefting their now ponderous freight of garlands bearing the emblematic Della Rovere acorns.

The urge toward monumentality is a constant in Michelangelo's expression, whether narrating Genesis or ordering household supplies. A delightful accident of history has preserved a draft of Michelangelo's domestic repasts, jotted down in the empty space of a used sheet of paper (Fig. 12). It has been called a grocery list, but since it refers to combinations of main courses, bread and wine, each group separated by a line, it is clearly a plan for several meals. The components surge as they cascade downward, giving rise to teasing (yet telling) interpretations of the humble list as typifying Michelangelo's heroic style and the innate expansiveness of his artistic conceptions.[11]

The illustration of the provisions is usually discussed as an aid to an illiterate servant. But surely the sketches, buoyant and lighthearted in effect rather than detailed, are due to the master's constant, almost reflexive habit of translating thoughts into drawings with pen in hand. Before our eyes the simple iteration of the makings of a meal grows in size as it descends the sheet, eventually filling all available space the corner

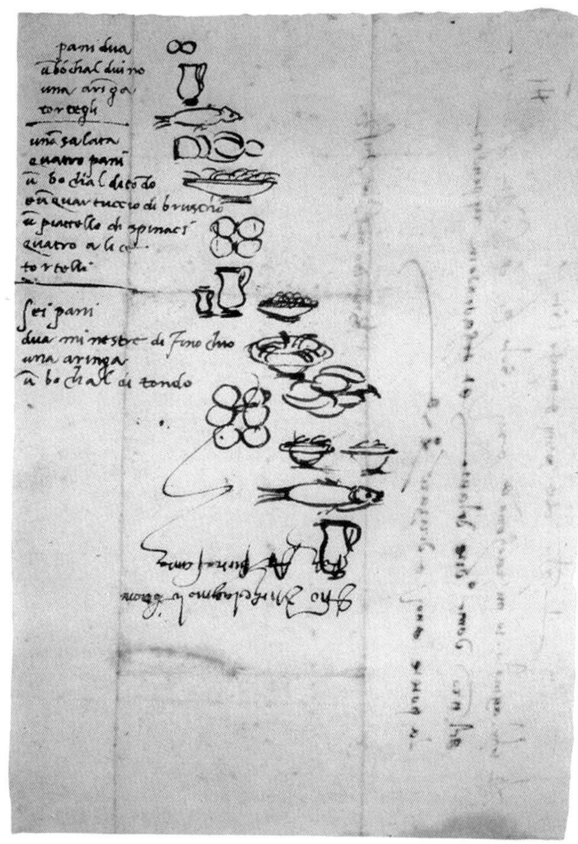

12 Michelangelo, Sketches of food and drink, 1517, drawing, 21.2 × 14.5 cm (8 3/8 × 5 11/16 in), Archivio Buonarroti, Casa Buonarroti, Florence

allows. The modest supper becomes a veritable feast as its components swell to an exuberant finale above the upturned address to Michelangelo in Florence.

The visual information contained in the rapid sketches of this appealing document echoes the stately progress of the biblical personages and their attendants along the expanse of the Sistine ceiling, eventually overlapping the design of boundaries no longer sufficient for their distending presence. Michelangelo's refashioning of the traditional child-like winged sprites into heroic, young adult *ignudi*, culminating in their truly remarkable enlargement as the campaign of the ceiling came to a close, had enormous influence on later 16th-century art. Full of visual impact, the muscular *ignudi* were codified and widely copied and imitated, commencing with work by Michelangelo's younger contemporaries.

The *ignudi* engendered respectful progeny throughout the 16th century, primarily as part of elaborate fresco programs. It is fascinating to consider how these figures spoke so individually to the artists who incorporated them into their own visual language, in some instances directly in the path of Michelangelo's view and influence. As has been noted, skillful imitation was never servile and had an exceptionally high cultural standing during the Renaissance. The goal was to meet and then outdo the prototypes and this, by definition, involved a type of imitation where a given model was used as a stepping stone to an even higher level of achievement. The Renaissance favored competition within restrictive formal and iconographic boundaries as a measure of talent; the challenge was to create distinctive modifications of the norm. Outright copying was the desperate tactic of lesser talents, while the realization of surprising variations on the best models was the mark of brilliance in Renaissance practice. It was understood as a valid, self-imposed challenge resulting in a measurable display of virtuosity.

Michelangelo's dazzling *ignudi* were a magnet for imitation and notable adaptations soon appeared. Between 1519–21 Jacopo Pontormo (1494–1556), a close Florentine collaborator of the older artist, devised a fresco cycle for the Medici villa at Poggio a Caiano, which featured adroit acknowledgments of the *ignudi*, attaining a cunning balance of quotation and variation (Plate 9). Placed high in a lunette around a circular window, the composition features a youth, two little boys and a young woman astride a low wall extending the length of the pictorial space. The young man and woman reach out to grasp branches of laurel that flow down from the perch of two nude children in the manner of *spiritelli*, vaunting tablets decorated with flowing ribbon. The postures of all the half-dozen figures recall those of their Sistine prototypes and their ancestry is reinforced by their functions. They proudly display laurel, the favored emblem of Lorenzo de' Medici who first began construction of the villa, and extend a garland dotted with clusters of spherical fruit and flowers that evoke *palle* [balls], the ubiquitous emblem of the Medici family.

The woman in this grouping is modestly dressed, with an artfully draped, voluminous skirt that does, however, reveal one bare leg hanging casually over the wall in her relaxed posture. In contrast, the nudity of her male counterpart on the other end of the wall is accentuated by his splayed legs, dangling on the viewer's side of the masonry. His lack of clothing is further insisted upon by a swathe of violet fabric which, instead of covering him, gathers in a bunch underneath his exposed penis. The ineffectual drapery, related in color to the ribbons of his brother *ignudi*, is pulled upward by Pontormo's young man, as his muscled arm reaches for the laurel branch. The inflated gesture for a small task also comes from the postures of the *ignudi*, as does the youth's placement outside the structure of the narrative scene below. These details, resonant in their rapport with Michelangelo's creations, validated Pontormo's skill and paid tribute to both the master and the Medici, acting as references to their history of patronage.

The egregious nudity of the stretching young man was acceptable because of its derivation, a quotation that would have been glossed to delight important guests of the household. Pontormo's carefully nuanced pictorial strategy deserves careful consideration for its sustained variation on its model. The postural derivations are immediately apparent, but the entire composition is a finely wrought improvisation. Just as the large size and energetic motions of the *ignudi* may at first glance disguise their function as standard bearers, Pontormo's figures are similar in scale to the personages placed below the wall they straddle. Part of the scene yet not part of the narrative, these descendants of the original *ignudi* similarly defy comprehension until their role as emblem bearers is understood. This is *imitatio* at its most creative level.

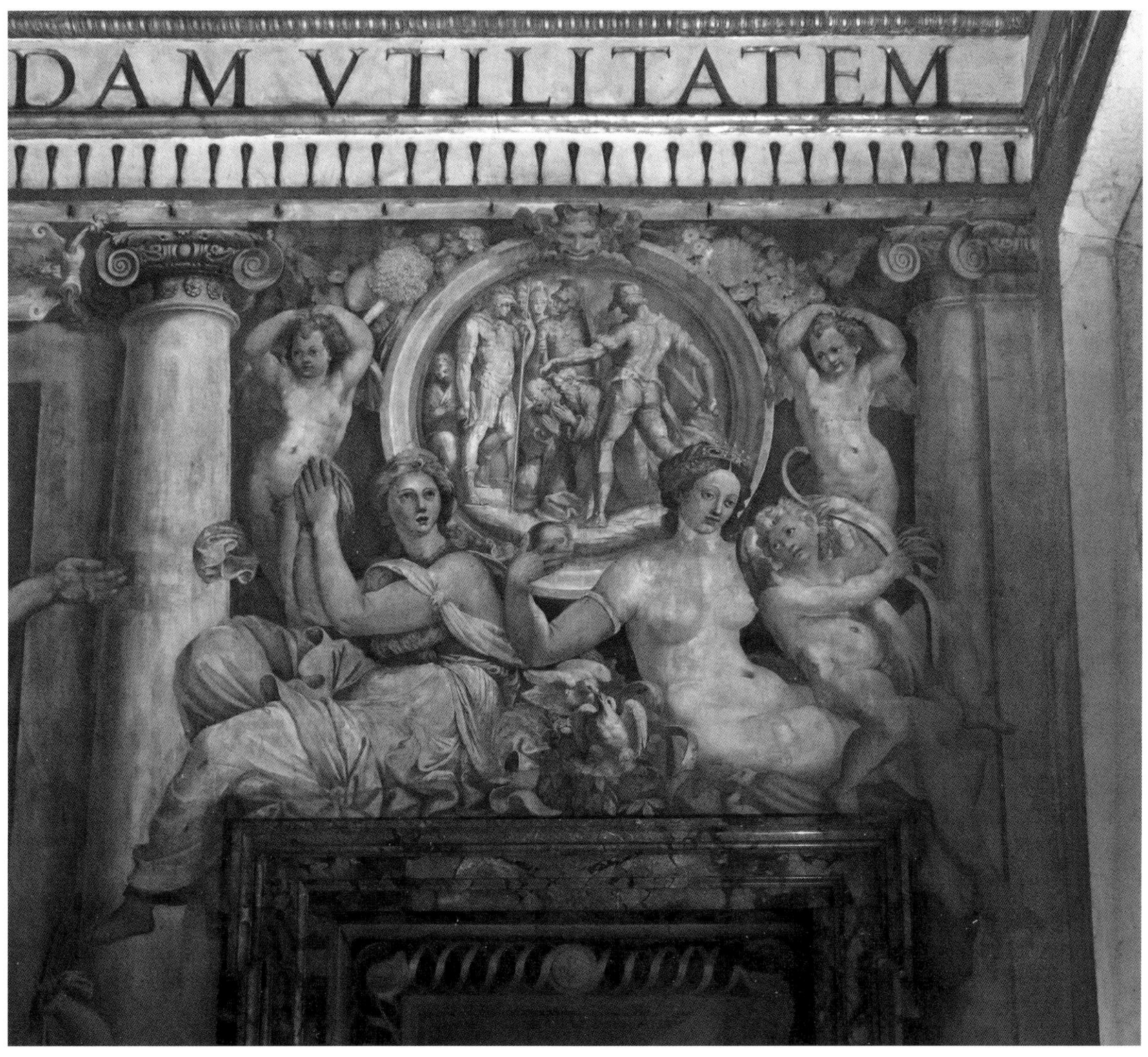

13 Perino del Vaga, View of entrance wall, detail, 1545–7, fresco, Sala Paolina, Castel Sant'Angelo, Rome

The quotation of the *ignudi* was most obvious when they were placed in the surrounds of the main narrative event following more traditional practice. A spectacular instance of this approach appears in the grand fresco program that Perino del Vaga (1501–1547) carried out for Pope Paul III (Farnese), in the Castel Sant'Angelo toward the middle of the 16th century (Fig. 13). The walls and ceiling of the principal reception hall, the Sala Paolina, are dazzlingly filled with figures of both genders, many levels of fiction and all sizes, set within an imposing architectural framework with a complex spatial construction – very like a description of the Sistine ceiling. Whether requested specifically by the pope or personally suggested by Perino, the repetition of many motifs from the Sistine, reimagined in a secular vein for Pope Paul's residence, pays as much homage to the dominance of Michelangelo's style as to the pontiff's sovereign majesty.

Pellegrino Tibaldi (1527–1596), one of Perino's assistants in the Sala Paolina, drew from the expressive possibilities of the *ignudi* throughout his career. Scholars have specifically assigned him the nude youths who hold the ribbons laced through escutcheons below fictive reliefs along the walls of the Sala Paolina, in close analogy to their forebears in the Sistine Chapel, but more languid and with wings appended. Building upon this motif first executed under Perino's direction, Pellegrino continued to devise figures faithfully derived from the *ignudi*. They had clearly become a fashionable element, requested or expected, in high-profile fresco decoration in Rome by mid-century. Tibaldi was to do his part in spreading the new convention to northern Italy.

His jubilant Bolognese fresco cycle in the Palazzo Poggi, the most significant work of Tibaldi's career, incorporates an impressive tribute to the visual power of the *ignudi* which dominates the central room narrating the history of Ulysses. The four corner sections of the ceiling contrive the powerful illusion of a colonnade ascending skyward, each surmounted by an immense *ignudo*. The vertiginous composition, with its breathtaking sensation of soaring space enlivened by the billowing drapery maneuvered by the nude young men, pays open tribute to Michelangelo's figural invention, yet outshines him in illusionistic virtuosity. This is a fine example of the way later 16th-century artists competed with their paradigms, paying reverence with a quotation, then asserting their mastery with an elaboration that aspires to the level of the original.[12] Eventually, Caravaggio's art dared to keep the reference but eliminate the reverence and in a few instances, concentrated on the annihilation of its models. Prior to Caravaggio's audacity, emulation had reigned.

The trend sanctioned by the monumental *ignudi*, installed in the most important site of Christendom, allowed them to inhabit both secular and religious settings. The examples discussed so far all appear in non-religious, private residential sites, where successors to the *ignudi* flourished. However, they also materialize in sacred spaces. Painted by Agnolo Bronzino (1503–1572), the private chapel of Eleonora of Toledo, wife of Duke Cosimo I de' Medici, situated in the Palazzo Vecchio of Florence, contains ingenious variants of the *ignudi*, specifically citing them as well as transforming them, in a refined and entertaining practice of *imitatio* (Fig. 14).[13] Bronzino's *imitatio* is at its most clever and revealing in the ceiling designed for Eleonora's chapel. Appearing as if open to the sky, it is graced by festoons of vegetables, fruits and flowers. At the base of each garland a *spiritello* crouches, bends, strides or spins, in gleeful imitation of his older and more massive prototypes in the Sistine. The nudity so startling in the athletes of the pope's chapel here takes on the innocence of unselfconscious children.

In addition to adapting Michelangelo's figures, Bronzino also followed his prototype by placing the *spiritelli* within the decorative framework of his frescoes, separated from the main subjects. Condivi makes it clear that the Sistine *ignudi* were conceived as existing outside the ceiling's narrative components – the scenes from Genesis – and were part of the ornamental structure, displaying the requisite virtues of beauty and variety.[14] They were ancillary features, yet carried conceptual weight. Even within a summary discussion of the Sistine program, Condivi (speaking for Michelangelo), insists on singling out the *ignudi* for attention, attesting to their importance.[15] As we will see, one aspect of Caravaggio's provocative transformation of his model was to move his appropriated *ignudi* out of the periphery and the realm of the symbolic, making them the focus of his paintings.

Michelangelo's *ignudi* were auspicious models for imitation, ripe for straightforward emulation and inspirational for the daunting contest of generating competitive variations. Bronzino met the challenge by reverting Michelangelo's colossal *spiritoni* to their traditional sprightly dimensions and character, while

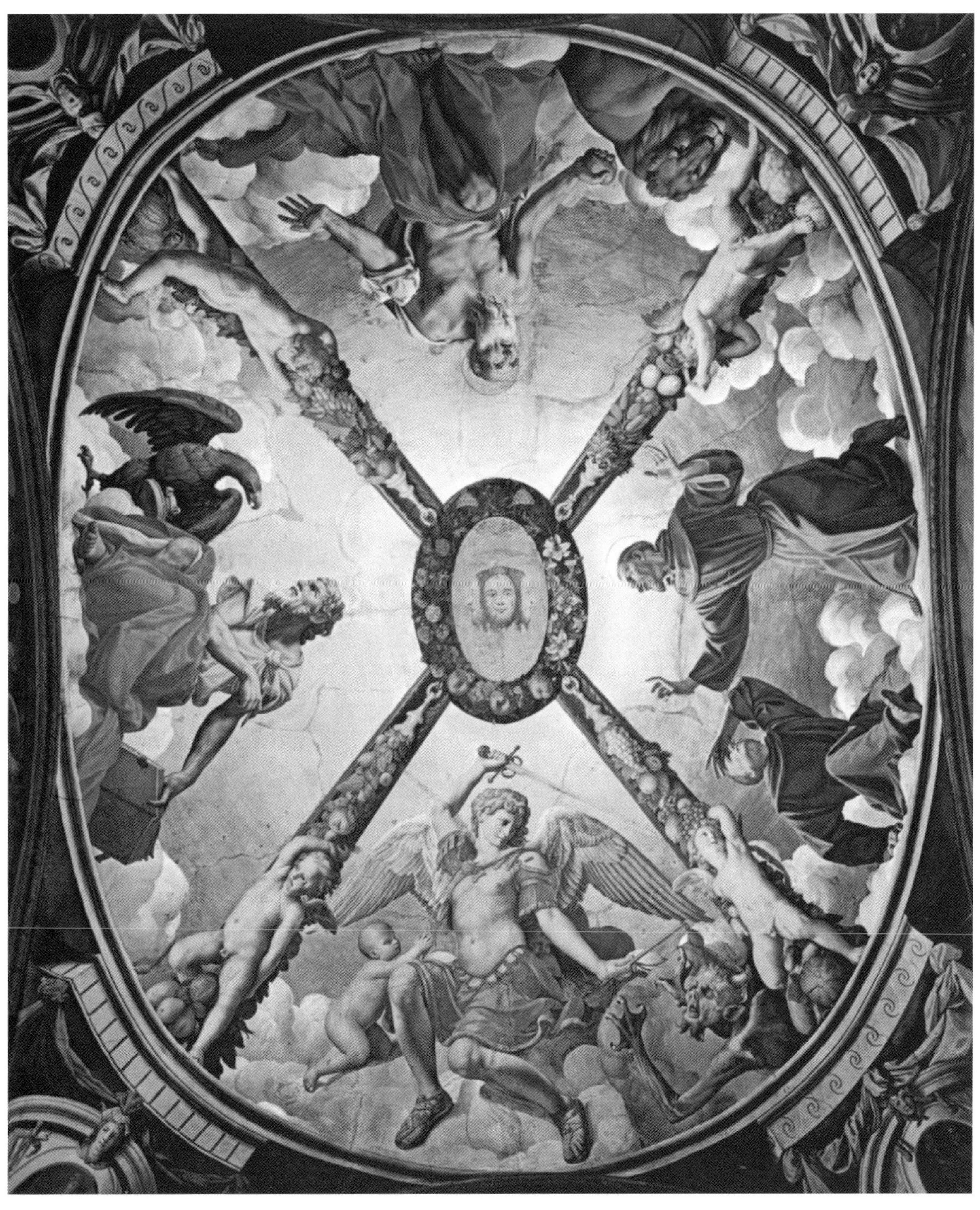

14 Agnolo Bronzino, Vault decoration, 1540–41, fresco, 490 × 385 cm (192 15/16 × 151 9/16 in), Chapel of Eleonora, Palazzo Vecchio, Florence

retaining the inescapable identification with the *ignudi*'s dynamic postures. Bronzino's scaled-down adaptation of the decorative figures was in keeping with the minute scale of Eleonora's private chapel in comparison to the grandeur of the pope's chapel. Their derivation and function, however, paid the highest honor both to Michelangelo's supreme creativity as well as to the younger artist's ability to progress beyond it.

The inevitable influence of Michelangelo's work continued to dominate painting throughout the second half of the 16th century, especially in Rome, covering the spectrum from overinflated copies to ingenious variations. Invariably, the impulse was to compete with the most lauded achievement painting had to offer and to produce stylish works that would attract the most conspicuous patronage. During the first decade of the 17th century, the *ignudi* continued to command the attention of the most resourceful painters. Most were conceived in an adulatory manner, some more imaginative than others, but all encompassed within the positive values of *imitatio*.

Given the overwhelming influence of the *ignudi* and their rich history as prototypes, it is not at all surprising that Caravaggio singled them out for contemplation and fashioned imaginative, commanding art in response to them. He closely studied these figures and stunningly changed their function from noble symbolism to ironic, sophisticated wit. Caravaggio removed the *ignudi* from their 'marginal', ornamental position and imposed an inescapable confrontation on the viewer. Two works painted by Caravaggio just after 1600 were among the last major responses to the *ignudi*; they were destined to be the least flattering and most ingenious in the history of their reception. Caravaggio retained the competitive aspect inherent in imitation, but exchanged reverence for them with a scoffing rebuke.

As styles of painting evolved at the start of the 17th century, the terms of praise for the art of the Renaissance masters began to change and new approaches were developed that distanced themselves from overt dependence on 'michelangelism'. In particular, a renewed focus on close study from live models helped to lessen the authority of unmediated quotations from earlier art. However, even as altered tastes and divergent artistic goals and methods prevailed, the power of the Sistine Chapel ceiling and its figural language continued to be felt. In designing the grand fresco cycle for the Farnese Palace, Annibale Carracci (1560–1609), whose authoritative style set the standard for significant developments in Baroque art, looked to Michelangelo's paradigm as a point of departure. The building's history certainly encouraged a connection to Michelangelo, who had been one of its architects under the original patron, Pope Paul III. In 1597, Cardinal Odoardo Farnese (1612–46) appointed Annibale to decorate a main hall in the palace with stories divulging the amorous entanglements of the pagan gods. It was a momentous commission; the assignment to paint *The Loves of the Gods* was also a perfect proving ground for competition with the 'divine' Michelangelo, who had been dead for only a generation.

Annibale's fresco is a virtuoso display of skill, combining multiple levels of illusion, fictional materials, trompe l'oeil treatments and convincing roles for figures of every possible description (Plate 13). Many are recognizable progeny of the Sistine's population, among which the *ignudi* are given prominence. The formidable derivations flank historiated roundels in pairs, retaining their predecessors' monumental scale and task of bearing garlands, attached to the mauve sashes that faithfully repeat their prototypes. The younger artist adhered diligently to the master's terrain, meeting him on established territory with panache. Annibale further developed the established conventions by achieving a fuller integration of the figures into a complex, almost dizzying, spatial illusion and by an increased emphasis on virtuoso technique. The artist also introduced a cunning variation as the twist to his *imitatio*; while producing an erudite version of Michelangelo's form (blending study from life with the study of art), he skillfully replaced biblical content with classical mythology. The narration in the Sistine Chapel of Divine *agape* through creation was transformed into the very worldly love of the Greek and Roman gods, often with touches of droll comedy.[16] The fact that such a witty ensemble is presented in a heroic style calls attention to the artist's ingenuity and compliments the connoisseurship of viewers who are knowledgeable enough to enjoy the transpositions fully.

Annibale's challenge to Michelangelo, taken up and successfully met in the Farnese Gallery, would not have been lost on Caravaggio. When Annibale began his prestigious project for the powerful Farnese family, Caravaggio had been in Rome for about five years and had not yet attained conspicuous success. After having practiced under several different masters in unsatisfactory situations, by the mid-1590s Caravaggio was finally acknowledged as a painter in his own right, brought to the attention of a circle of patronage around Cardinal Francesco Del Monte, in whose household he would reside from 1595 to 1601. His easel paintings were admired and acquired by this influential group, but his first large public commissions arrived only in the summer of 1599. Caravaggio's main interest and technical dexterity, whether in the service of public or private commissions, would always be tied to the medium of oil on canvas, with figures that did not exceed life size, even when the canvasses had huge dimensions. It was only his determination and the extraordinary results wrested from the medium of oil paint that put his canvasses on a par with the traditionally more prestigious fresco cycles.

In 1601, a close friend of Cardinal Del Monte, the Marchese Vincenzo Giustiniani (1564–1637), provided Caravaggio with an opportunity to create a private work that would allow the artist to engage all his creativity and indulge his ambitions in collaboration with an impressively accomplished and discerning patron.[17] Upon completion, the commissioned painting would be seen and discussed by a wide slice of Rome's cultural elite. Caravaggio embraced the opportunity with élan, ultimately delivering a masterwork in a genre that best suited his artistic temperament and radical style. He used this occasion to 'talk back' at full volume to the accomplishment of his immediate rival's *Loves of the Gods*, as well as to his august predecessor and namesake's invincible Sistine ceiling. Vincenzo Giustiniani exulted in the result. Part of his unbounded delight in the painting without doubt came from the audaciousness of the concept and the triumph of the execution, with Caravaggio in absolute control of his pictorial language.

The painting, completed by 1602, is generally referred to as *Amor Vincit Omnia*, retaining the Latin from its source in a poem by Virgil (Plate 13). The passage, from *Eclogue* IX, line 69, proclaims 'Love conquers all; let us surrender to it.' Submission to the sway of love, which can defeat rational thought; be more alluring than the call of duty; and cause even the most powerful to act under its command, is also the *concetto* underlying the Farnese decorations. If, however, the Farnese program derived its share of waggishness from the Virgilian theme, its ribald details are politely discreet, eliciting an educated chuckle in comparison to Caravaggio's strategy of bold laughter.

In adapting the subject of the supremacy of Eros for Giustiniani's painting, Caravaggio fearlessly condensed Carracci's multifaceted fresco cycle into a single figure. The decision required the fashioning of an individual protagonist extraordinary enough to contain the complexity required to sustain a variety of learned readings. In facing this contest, Caravaggio turned to Michelangelo's *ignudi*, exceptional and compelling figures, which as we have seen, were endlessly celebrated and quoted by artists for almost a century. In an accomplished game of *imitatio*, Caravaggio did not produce a perfect copy of a specific figure, but appropriated particular details from several figures, each adaptation purposefully copied or modified according to the artist's desired result. Caravaggio's Cupid is most closely related to the *ignudi* framing the scene of sacrifice in the third bay from the entrance door (Plate 14 and Fig. 15). Cupid's left thigh, however, is pushed back further

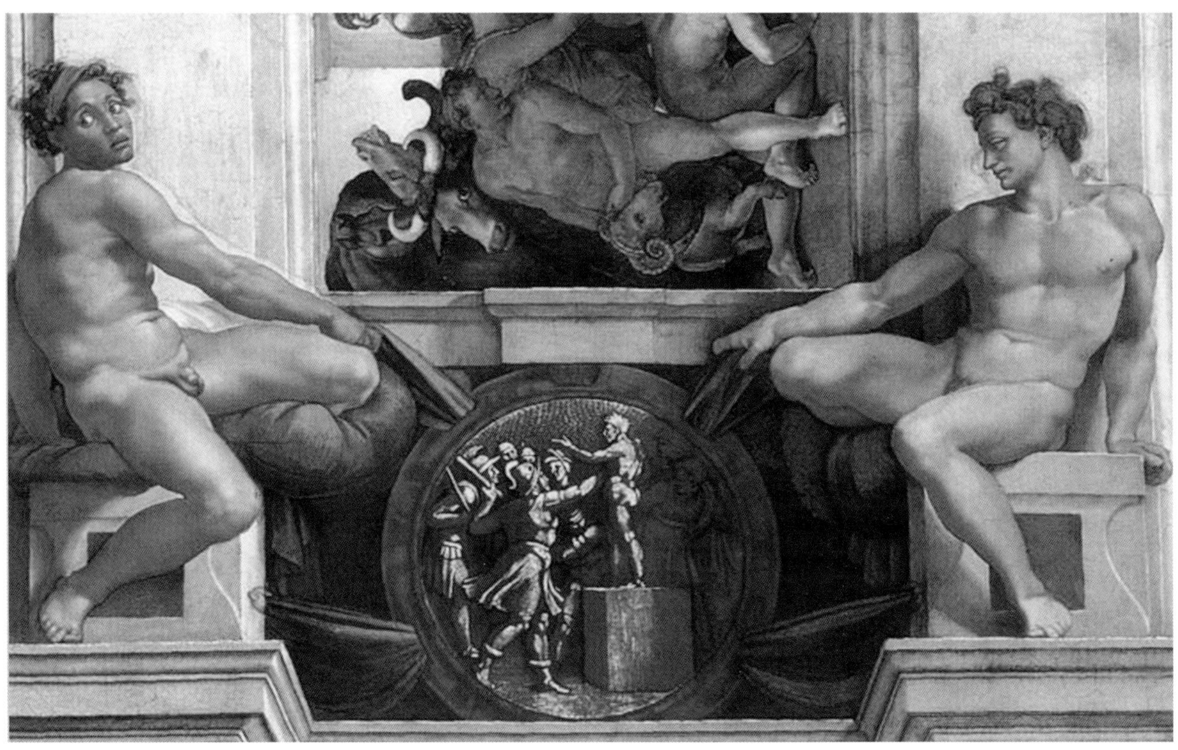

15 Michelangelo, Pair of *ignudi*, detail, *Scene of Sacrifice*, 1509, fresco, 190 × 390 cm (74 13/16 × 153 9/16 in), Sistine Chapel, Vatican, Rome

than any of his models and the entire calf and foot disappear behind the bent knee. The placement of the thigh adds to the graphic sexuality of Caravaggio's figure, exposing the boy's genitalia completely; the surrounding white fabric magnifies the effect of the light shining upon the entire anatomical area.

The splayed legs combined with a twisting torso are a recurrent motif in Michelangelo's repertoire, which he combined in a variety of poses throughout the Sistine frescoes. The arrangement is strongly evocative of the *ignudi*, several of which are composed with one leg tensed to support the figure's weight and projecting slightly forward, while the other is bent backwards to varying degrees. Michelangelo continued to paint variants of the position throughout his career; Saint Bartholomew stands in this manner in *The Last Judgment*, completed on the altar wall around thirty years after the ceiling (see Chapter 4 and Plate 22).

The *Amor Vincit Omnia* measures approximately 156 × 113 cm (61 × 44 in), which is to say just about the minimum requirements for presenting a life-size figure. While the artist's insistence on life-size rather than monumental scale has been interpreted as a limitation of technique, the artist's record of painterly virtuosity signals instead that it was a carefully chosen value, a coherent element in a style calculated for an effect of realism. Michelangelo's contemporaries make it clear they understood perfectly well how the artist manipulated his drive toward the monumental and his comfort with the colossal in such a way as to inspire awestruck wonderment in those viewing his art.[18] In contrast, Caravaggio took the opposite approach and fabricated his own brand of amazement by respecting realistic proportions and naturalistic elements, yet commingling them to conjure up visions not to be found in nature. Caravaggio sought a different sort of astonishment than that induced by Michelangelo, yet his work shows that the younger artist would have valued the strong visual impact attained by his predecessor. The effect Caravaggio consistently achieves is perhaps less cerebral, certainly more physical. Always devised with a forceful intellect, Caravaggio's images were often calculated to elicit vehement emotion, or at least discomfiture, from the observer.

The *Amor Vincit Omnia* abundantly succeeds in disquieting the viewer, in part through its clashing combinations. The adolescent playing the title role of Cupid was painted from a live model, as contemporary sources specify, and was probably a friend of the artist. However, the enormous wings sprouting from the youth's shoulders falsify his everyday appearance and negate our impulse to perceive this particularized representation of a young man as a portrait. Those same wings, whose colors comprise a shabby palette ranging from dusty taupe to deeper browns, whose feathers appear to be a little worse for wear, might have been an enlarged study from the remains of a bird of prey. Less fancifully, we know for certain that the wings were a studio prop borrowed from his friend, Orazio Gentileschi.[19] With the attachment of 'real' wings (which instead are an artist's confection) to a body apparently studied from life yet posed to quote a legendary work of art, Caravaggio employs high-level artifice to unsettle the viewer, requiring mental gyrations before a balance can be regained. This perturbing dislocation of the viewer between what is shown to be tangible versus what is known to be possible is at the base of Caravaggio's style of realism; it is part of what makes his achievement so extraordinary.

In this instance, the brash nudity of the Cupid provides the greatest shock to the observer; the fact that the figure is unmistakably derived from one of the *ignudi* does not mitigate the impact. Caravaggio has undermined the respected tradition of imitation by presenting a recognizable quotation that manages to say the complete opposite of its model. While the colossal size of the *ignudi*, their magnificent idealization and their remove from the immediate physical space of the spectator allow for a symbolic and contemplative reading, the naked Cupid thrusts forward aggressively into the foreground of a canvas that can be encountered at close range.

The constructed realism of Caravaggio's style, including the unattractive folds on the boy's twisting torso, demands exclusion of the image from an idealized realm. But above all, it is Cupid's expression that unnerves the viewer. Head cocked sideways, his mouth emerges from shadow slightly opened, as if he is beginning to chuckle at the observer. The brightly lit, deep dimple amplifies the effect, as do the heavy-lidded eyes that narrow their gaze towards the world. Enthroned on a pile of objects that symbolizes all that is noble, beautiful and powerful on earth, Cupid clutches arrows brandished in the place of a scepter. To qualify his characterization as 'mischievous' is to use the most anodyne adjective possible. Yet Caravaggio's Cupid does manage to convey an amusing impudence as well as disturbing self-assertion.

Cupid's total subjugation of all other systems of authority is evidenced by the disarray of their collective attributes, portrayed with detailed fidelity to visual experience. Close looking is rewarded; for example, the lute and *viola da gamba* lack several strings, rendering them useless. In the midst of this sophisticated composition, Caravaggio insists on his prowess as a painter of still life, which he famously declared to be as difficult as painting a figure. This is another front on which Caravaggio could outdo his rival, for Michelangelo was just as famous for privileging the human form as the exclusive expression of his art.

The idealized formal perfection and classical pedigree of Michelangelo's *ignudi* make them vehicles for concepts related to the sublimation of desire and spiritual love. In a few words, beauty is equated with goodness and becomes its symbol; its contemplation initiates a journey that leads to the spiritual realm. Caravaggio negates that reference, visually evoking the *ignudi* only to present his Cupid as an image of carnal love, an earthy deity, whose lineaments are taken from a living model. With no improvements upon nature apparent, there is a decided lack of signposts towards a heavenly destination. To emphasize his deviation from the meaning of Michelangelo's paradigm, Caravaggio has removed his terrestrial *ignudo* from the original context of borders and embellishment – so closely adhered to in late 16th-century citations – and he has placed Cupid's flagrantly undraped figure front and center, the sole subject of the painting. If Michelangelo rerouted the eroticism of nudity toward the transcendence of flesh, Caravaggio rejected this philosophy and embodied the sensual as a purely earth-bound impulse.

In one of the contradictions that emerge from the symbolic systems adhered to in Renaissance art, Michelangelo removed the wings from his adult *spiritelli* to insist that human forms convey spiritual beauty, while the 'realist' Caravaggio appended feathers to depict his model's role as a mythological character. The wings also create a visual reference to the vast race of little Cupids, or *amorini*, that populate art in the classical tradition. Part of Caravaggio's triumph in the *Amor Vincit Omnia* is to include knowledgeable references to classical practices, both ancient and modern, while he unabashedly overturns them. The implied erudition in matters of art complimented the patron and challenged sophisticated viewers.

Access to the *Amor Vincit Omnia* was carefully controlled, granted only to select guests in a dramatic procedure of unveiling. Theatricality was well suited to the vivid setting Caravaggio had created within the painting; the Marchese's decision to conceal it behind a silk drapery, uncovered as the 'grand finale' to the tour of his collection, set the stage for the strongest possible effect. Joachim von Sandrart (1606–88), a widely traveled German artist who had resided in the Giustiniani palace during a stay in Italy, takes credit for the scenario. Allowing for the inevitable bragging, Sandrart's residency gives particular authority to the account published in his *Book of Biographies* (1675):

> This piece was publicly exhibited in a room with another hundred and twenty made by the most prominent artists; however on my advice it was covered with a dark green silk curtain, and only when all the other paintings had been seen to satisfaction, was it finally uncovered, for otherwise it would have made the other curiosities insignificant; not without reason may this painting be called 'the eclipse of all paintings'.[20]

If, as recorded, Giustiniani had the painting overhung with a concealing curtain, the jolt upon its removal would have been as much in response to the revolutionary style of the work as to its eroticism, both in terms of its formal qualities and its iconoclasm. Sandrart's concern about the potency of Caravaggio's painting is one that artists today continue to voice: the fear that one work will 'blow the others off the wall'. The life-size Cupid's brazen countenance makes his confrontation with those who look at him all the more riveting.

Caravaggio's *Amor* smirks not only at the viewer, but also at the convention of *imitatio*, teasing his model, whose achievement makes him important enough both to copy and to dismantle. Raillery is a proven strategy for grappling with a rival who deserves credit and demands to be vanquished. A pioneering study of Caravaggio's rivalry with the heritage of his namesake characterized the Lombard artist's response to the *ignudi* as 'persiflage'.[21] This term, indicating 'light and slightly contemptuous mockery or banter', has fallen from use since publication of that study; the impoverishment is unfortunate, since persiflage admirably evokes Caravaggio's stance. He acknowledges the power of what he copies, but expresses it in a style so opposed to the values inherent in his model that the citation becomes derisive. Caravaggio's *imitatio* is delivered in a quip rather than a quotation. He is bantering with his rival; his visual comments inject a considerable amount of play into the conversation.

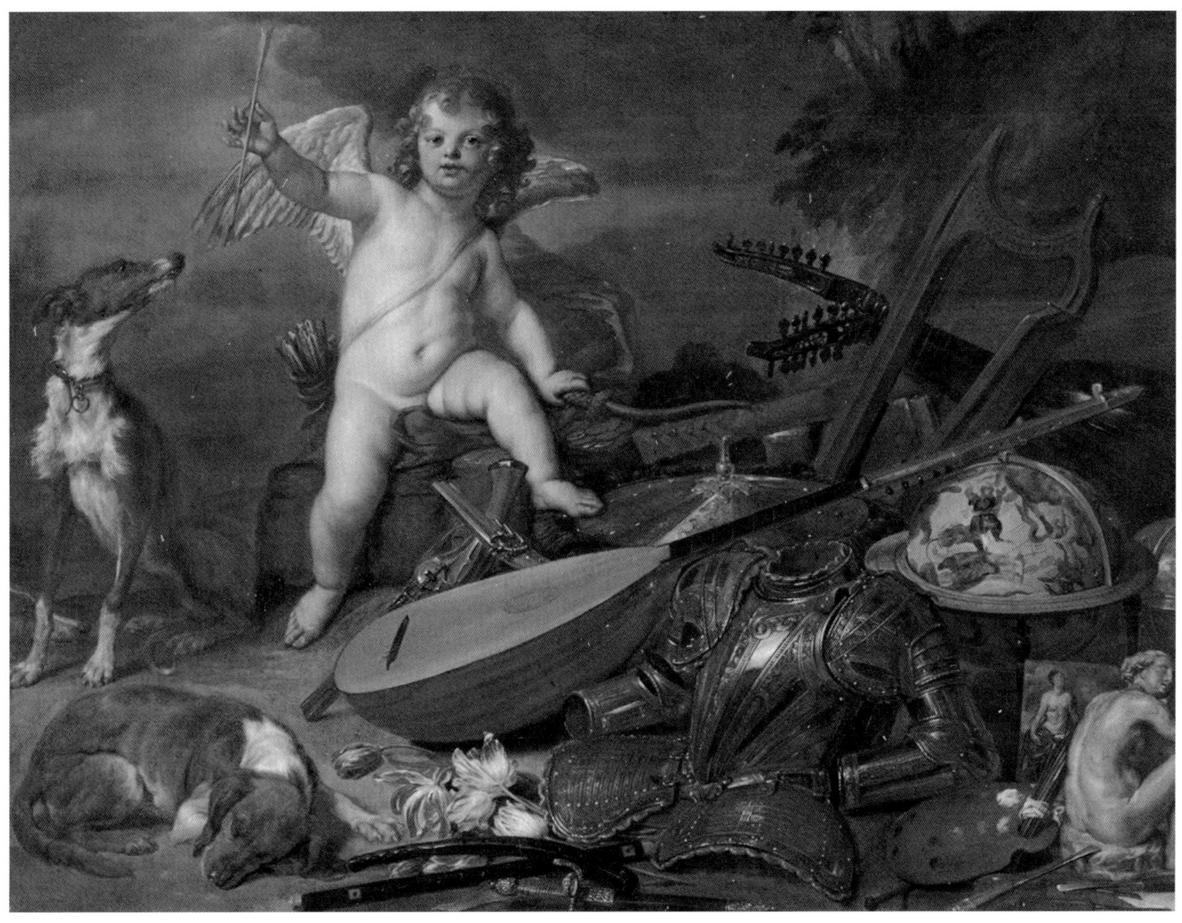

16 Jan van den Hoecke and Paul de Vos, *Amor Vincit Omnia*, 1640s, oil on canvas, 152 × 193 (59 13/16 × 76 in), Kunsthistorisches Museum, Vienna

Playfulness was a powerful ingredient in Caravaggio's art in the early stages of his career, which we now tend to overlook because of our exclusive insistence on the violence of his personality, which is transferred as an overlay to his paintings. His work is more complex than is often allowed by critics, as is the relation between his temperament and his artistic output.

Artists closer to Caravaggio's time were well aware of what was subtle and what was scandalous in his art, a fact made evident when his work, in its turn, provided the paradigms for imitation. Two Flemish artists working in Rome in the 1640s, Jan van den Hoecke (1611–51) and Paul de Vos (*c.*1595–1678), collaborated on an amusing variation of the subject of *Amor Vincit Omnia* (Fig. 16), the former painting the figure, while the latter supplied the multitude of still life elements. Following his model, van den Hoecke seats Cupid presiding over a mound of objects referring to the realms he has vanquished and has him hold aloft his arrow with two colors displayed in its feathers. The Flemish artist returns Cupid to childhood and golden curls and bequeaths the basic pose of Caravaggio's adolescent, altering only the chubby left leg so that it extends to rest on a shield. The little Cupid's genitalia are covered by a fold of red drapery, his fluffy white wings are petite and angelic and his forthright gaze innocently meets the viewer. All of the most provocative details of Caravaggio's *Amor* have been adjusted and 'corrected' in this miniaturized adaptation. The benign result receives an added touch of humor through the presence of a dog, almost as large as the *Amorino*, which looks toward the unthreatening arrow flaunted by the child, while another dog snoozes obliviously, comfortably curled-up in the foreground. Rather than dominating the space, this Cupid is almost overwhelmed by the abundant still life composition which cascades toward the viewer, expertly painted by de Vos. Not only has Caravaggio's insolent god of love been tamed, but the artist's famous mastery of still life components has been challenged and defeated by abundance, if not quality. No impertinent victor, this Cupid is a captive of the emerging still life genre that had begun to conquer an increasing audience in Italy, supplanting the market of mythological subjects in the 17th century.

The *Amor Vincit Omnia*, which gained such notoriety and engendered all manner of reaction, was not Caravaggio's only rejoinder to the *ignudi*. In the same years he was carrying out the commission for the Marchese Giustiniani, Caravaggio confronted his namesake by once more incorporating a borrowed pose from the Sistine Chapel in the composition of *Saint John the Baptist* (Plate 15).[22] With further variations on the *ignudi*, particularly one of the figures surrounding the *Scene of Sacrifice* (Fig. 19), Caravaggio produced another remarkable painting. It was commissioned by Ciriaco Mattei (1545–1614), whose professional credits include a little-noted qualification that makes his patronage of Caravaggio's art particularly significant. From 1576, Mattei oversaw the completion of Michelangelo's Campidoglio plaza; his daily responsibilities would have kept the legacy of the Renaissance master a vivid reality. Once again, an implicit *paragone* is inescapable. Mattei was also an intimate of Caravaggio's circle of patrons, whose family benefited from close ties to Pope Clement VIII. Papal concessions ennobled Ciriaco's brothers, creating Girolamo a cardinal and Asdrubale a marchese. The Mattei collection, as we will see, eventually boasted three paintings commissioned from Caravaggio.[23] The *Saint John* was painted during the same two-year period as the *Amor Vincit Omnia*; together these paintings inescapably show how deeply Caravaggio had immersed himself in Michelangelo's art at the time, as well as how unexpected were the results he wrested from his model.

Artists were allowed entry to the Sistine Chapel and could experience the power of Michelangelo's inventions directly, albeit at some distance and with some limitations. The availability of prints, however, permitted prolonged study of individual figures and groupings in a much more focused manner. It is likely that Caravaggio availed himself of engravings of the *ignudi* by Cherubino Alberti (1553–1615), a colleague in Rome, in order to devise his variations. Two prints in particular are germane to his compositions in the Giustiniani and Mattei paintings (Figs 17 and 18), and their study may well have been part of Caravaggio's creative process, as a vehicle for close study of single figures, without access to scaffolding.[24] Many details of his quotations of the *ignudi* come from the four individual figures copied by Alberti, dated 1577, which argues for his specific use of the prints to hone ideas gathered from the entire ceiling.[25] After coming to terms with what he wanted from the engravings, Caravaggio would have then posed his models with the deliberate discrepancies that served his own pictorial needs. Each is an easily recognizable variant blending the two models.

While the formal source of *Saint John* is apparent, the significance of the painting is elusive. The image is so perplexing that existing documentation compounds rather than clarifies its mysteries, chief of which is how to identify the central figure. Although the identification of Saint John is generally accepted,

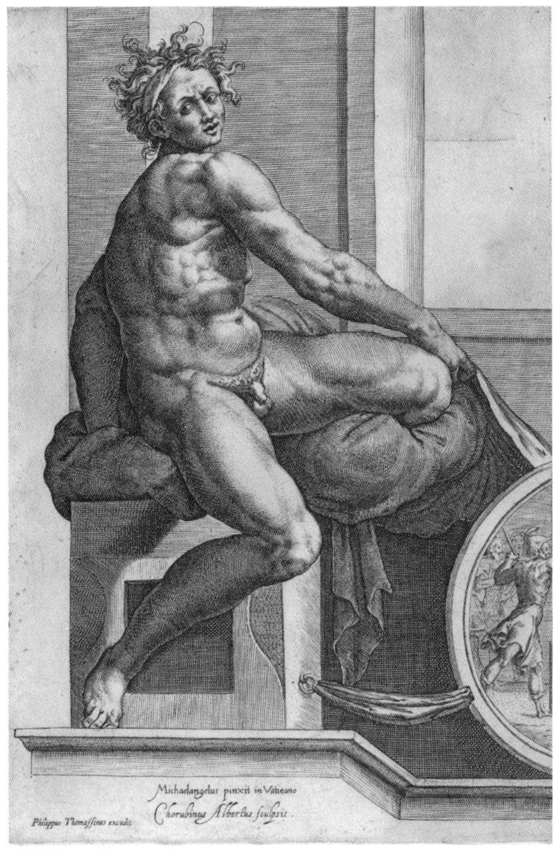

17 Cherubino Alberti, *A naked man (Ignudo), twisting towards the right, holding drapery, after Michelangelo's fresco in the Sistine Chapel*, 1580–90, engraving, 31.6 × 20.5 cm (12 7/16 × 8 1/16 in), Metropolitan Museum of Art, New York

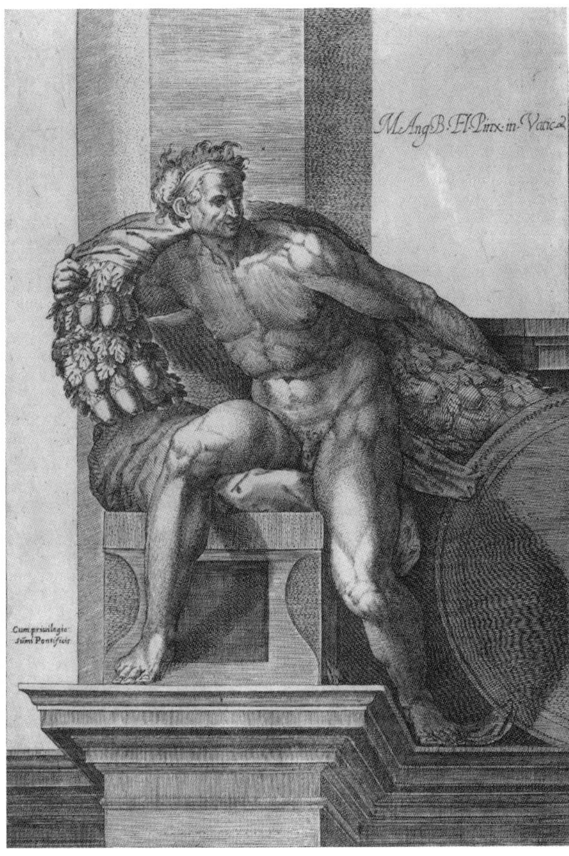

18 Cherubino Alberti, *A naked man (Ignudo) with a garland with acorns over his shoulders, after Michelangelo's fresco in the Sistine Chapel*, 1580–90, engraving, 28.7 × 19.5 cm (11 5/16 × 7 11/16 in), Metropolitan Museum of Art, New York

several other names have been advanced. However, no matter how the young man with the ram is identified, the salient fact remains that his pose was based on a specific *ignudo* from the Sistine ceiling. As mentioned, it corresponds closely to the painted and engraved model, copying the general configuration, including the turn of the head over the right shoulder, the extended right leg and the pivot of the torso that exposes chest and abdomen, as well as the back (Fig. 18). While the angles of the arms and left thigh are modified, the sideways glance of the eyes and the unusual, slightly opened mouth revealing the upper row of teeth are repeated. Caravaggio evidently wanted the derivation of the striking figure, based in art and then painted from a posed model, to be unmistakable for all informed viewers; the slight alterations, calculated for increased audacity, would also be patent.

Today, Mattei's *Saint John the Baptist* is in the collection of the Capitoline Museum in Rome (Plate 15). Its authenticity, now widely accepted, is complicated

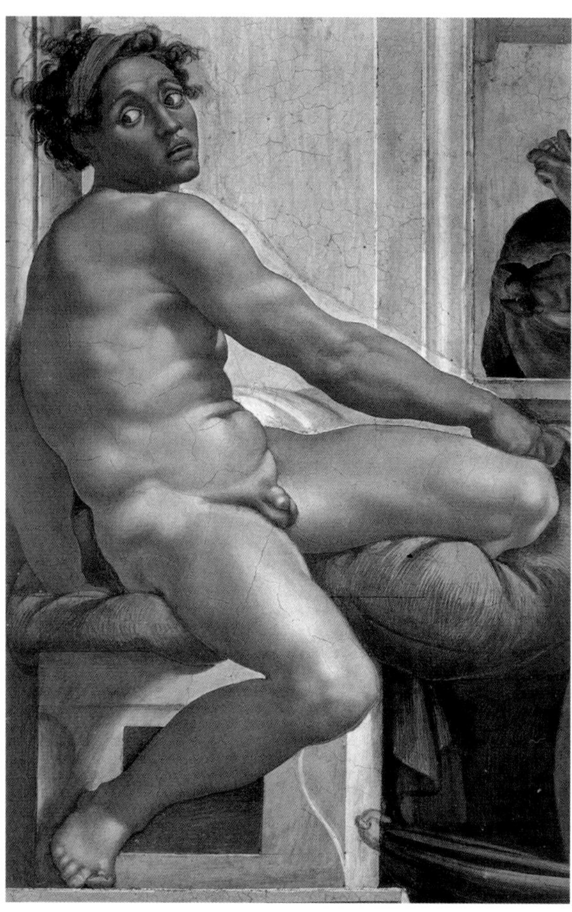

19 Michelangelo, *Ignudo*, detail, as above fig. 15, fresco, Sistine Chapel, Vatican, Rome

by a high-quality contemporary replica in the Doria Pamphilij Gallery, perhaps by Caravaggio himself or a member of his circle. Mattei made documented payments for a commission in 1602, which provides us the date but not the subject. A 1620 catalogue of paintings in Rome compiled by Gaspare Celio, lists the painting as a *Pastor Friso* [Phrygian Shepherd], a title that has confused everyone and was never repeated in contemporary or later documents. Several interpretations of the name have been put forward, none with an airtight conclusion.[26]

The one incontestable fact regarding the ascribed subject is that the iconography of the painting was so unusual that it immediately caused bewilderment. Caravaggio's feat in this image is precisely that it can be read, with tenable justifications, both as a sacred subject and a secular one, which is a display of sheer virtuosity that threatens to defeat the viewer's desire for clarity. Is it a literary figure of a shepherd boy, or does it represent the precursor of Christ in the wilderness, based on religious texts? The dilemma is woven deep within Caravaggio's imagery and was recognized by his contemporaries. In a famous passage from a letter written in 1603, Cardinal Ottavio Paravicino (1552–1611) applied a pithy observation to Caravaggio's work, which has not been bettered for precision or accuracy: Caravaggio created art '*in quel mezzo tra il devoto et profano*'.[27] It is challenging to render a translation equally compact and rich in nuance, especially taking into account the overall teasing tone of the letter. A literal rendering is: 'halfway between the devout and profane', that is, on a scale ranging from a devotional image to one of profanity. In a context specifically alluding to painting, it can be thought of as indicating religious or sacrilegious images, whose terrains are usually quite distinct. The contradiction perfectly applies to the characterization Caravaggio gave to his purported Saint John, which had been painted shortly before Paravicino wrote his letter. Many points can be iterated in favor of another identification for the boy with a ram and demand our attention; yet they still must contend with the strong visual connections to traditional presentations of the Baptist. The contradictory elements that continue to cause perplexity in our readings of the figure could not have been accidental in Caravaggio's conception, given his proven mastery in constructing innovative representations of traditional subjects, both sacred and secular. An iconographical challenge, whose terms we cannot yet reconstruct, may have motivated the artist to invent a composite figure, existing somewhere 'between the devout and the profane'.

The wide acceptance of the figure as Saint John has convincing external arguments, beginning with a connection to the name of the patron's son, Giovanni Battista, who inherited the painting on his father's death in 1614. The reference to a *Saint John* appears for the first time in the 1616 inventory of Giovanni Battista's property; the unqualified identification at that point was likely influenced by its connection to the owner's name. Honoring the son's name-saint may have been a deciding factor in the original commission, or it might have been only part of a larger context for the painting's meaning. The painting had exceptional significance for the owners, demonstrated by the fact that the father bequeathed it specifically to his son and the son, in his turn, carefully stipulated in a codicil to his own will that the painting be inherited by Cardinal Del Monte. Kept within the extended family of Caravaggio's early patrons, the *Saint John* was a potentially incendiary painting, one whose unconventional imagery was best kept among connoisseurs who understood its import and appreciated its guile.

The young Saint John's meditative time in the wilderness before taking up his mission was a popular topic, taken from the saint's hagiography. His abstention from worldly comforts was routinely conveyed by his near nudity, covered only by animal skins; some type of red mantle was traditionally added. As an individual touch, Caravaggio always adjoined a smaller area of white drapery to the more abundant folds of the red cloth in his extant paintings of the saint. Saint John's defining attributes in the wilderness setting are a staff with a cross at its apex and a lamb symbolizing Christ as the sacrificial 'Lamb of God'. Oddly, neither of these is present in the Capitoline painting.

However, Caravaggio hints at all these elements without actually showing them. Despite the wooded area, a cruciform staff is not in evidence; the lamb is evoked through an ostensible mistake, for John reaches to embrace an adult horned ram rather than a young lamb. The adolescent boy sits on a camel skin (as specified in the Bible), and leans back on the abundant folds of bright white and red drapery, but these fabrics do not conceal his nudity; rather they are ostentatiously discarded as the youth twists and propels himself toward the viewer. It is, in fact, the boy's mien and posture that make him such a baffling portrayal – indeed almost an impossible one – much more worrisome than a lack of traditional attributes.

It is instructive that variations on Caravaggio's Capitoline *Saint John* invariably 'correct' the iconography with traditional attributes, even when the figure is closely copied.[28] They also change the position of the figure's left leg. The angle of its upward bending, hoisted by the pressure of the foot's tensed placement, pushing toward the viewer and radiantly lit, was apparently too risqué to follow. Amusement and sensuousness have no place in characterizing John's seriousness of purpose in his retreat to the desert between Jerusalem and the Red Sea, as described in the biblical text. The eroticism and lack of solemnity pose challenging questions about the painting's subject and purpose.

Caravaggio gives us much to ponder. His variations on the depiction of Saint John in the Capitoline/Doria Pamphilij examples were deliberate, as attested by several surviving paintings of the subject where purely conventional iconography is included. This is true of *Saint John the Baptist in the Wilderness*, held in the Nelson-Atkins Museum of Art, Kansas City (Plate 16). Although John is seated in a posture that references an *ignudo* engraved by Alberti (Fig. 18), he is presented modestly this time, with an animal skin and abundant folds of a mantle and drapery that cover his groin and left thigh. It is a vivid interpretation of the saint as a brooding young man, which has him blazingly lit amid dark foliage, prominently holding a cruciform staff. The devotional image is composed with more conventional elements, but its innovative style of intense visual dramatization is dazzling. The artist painted this version for a wealthy Ligurian banker, Ottavio Costa, who made an advance payment in the spring of 1602. Costa had originally intended to donate the painting to the Oratory of Saint John in Albenga (a small city near

Genoa), but upon seeing the remarkable result, held back the original and sent a copy. It is easy to sympathize with Costa's compromised generosity; withholding the masterpiece notably augmented his collection of Caravaggio's religious paintings, which included *Saint Francis in Ecstasy* (held by the Wadsworth Atheneum, Hartford, Connecticut), and *Judith and Holofernes*, now in the collection of the Palazzo Barberini.

In another of his paintings of Saint John, a work long part of the Corsini Collection (Fig. 20) dating from around the same time as the example in Plate 16, Caravaggio produced a moving and less controversial representation. He repeats the forceful lighting on the bare flesh of the figure, which projects outwards from the dark background. A swathe of white drapery and a brilliant red mantle, a consistent part of Caravaggio's imagery for Saint John, cover the adolescent's groin and all that is visible of his left thigh and leg. Saint John's staff protrudes into the viewer's space, yet the lower bar forming the cross is strangely cut off, encouraging a focus on the simple still life objects that accompany the saint's rustic existence. The bowl in the arrangement can also be viewed as a symbolic reference to its function in baptismal rites, that is, the pouring of water over the head of the initiate. X-rays of the underpainting reveal that Caravaggio had originally included a lamb behind the saint's left shoulder and had placed the cruciform staff in his left hand, prominently displayed in its entirety. The artist's decision to remove and truncate two of the main attributes associated with Saint John tells us that the artist preferred to leave room for ambiguity, or at least to restrict some factors that would rigidly determine the reading of the painting.

In comparison to the strict cohesiveness of the *Saint John the Baptist in the Wilderness* (Plate 16) and the Corsini representations (Fig. 20), the anomalies of the Capitoline *Saint John* (Plate 15) become even more apparent. The troubling details underscore the painting's exceptionality as a treatment of the subject and have elicited alternative interpretations in attempts to account for them. For example, a strong alternative posits the figure to be Isaac saved through divine intervention just before his father, Abraham, was to sacrifice him on an altar.[29] This identification provides an explanation for the presence of the ram, prominent in the iconography of Isaac; according to these readings, he rejoices that the animal will replace him on the sacrificial altar. This narrative also explains his 'laughing' countenance, if that is not too strong a characterization of the boy's slightly opened mouth; his lips have broken into a smile as he turns his head to appraise the viewer's reaction to his strange performance. The very bright light shining on his face adds effervescence to his expression, as do the 'laugh lines' under his eye.

Another point in favor of a connection to the story of Isaac is that the young boy sits atop a stack of wood, difficult to discern in the dark palette, but visible in a close viewing. There even appear to be touches of red paint within the woodpile that approximate burning embers.[30] These could certainly allude to the sacrificial fire Isaac escaped, accentuating a fundamental point made in the biblical text: The God of the Israelites did not require human sacrifice. The inclusion of the altar wood, the disrobing of the figure, the replacement of the lamb with a ram and the lack of Saint John's cruciform staff are all details making the story of Isaac a reference too strong to ignore.

The search for meaning must turn back to the figure's derivation from the *ignudi*, since its genesis is unquestionably manifest. Is there any way in which Caravaggio alluded to his model's context and incorporated its memory into his painting? The figure attentively studied by Caravaggio is one of a pair of mirror-image *ignudi* surrounding a scene of sacrifice (Fig. 19). Although the scene is usually referred to as *The Sacrifice of Noah*, Condivi describes it as 'the sacrifice of Abel and Cain' (Plate 14).[31] This is supported by the visual evidence of the two young men in the foreground, one leading a ram toward the altar and one proceeding with the ritual dissection of another ram. The importance of this sacrificial

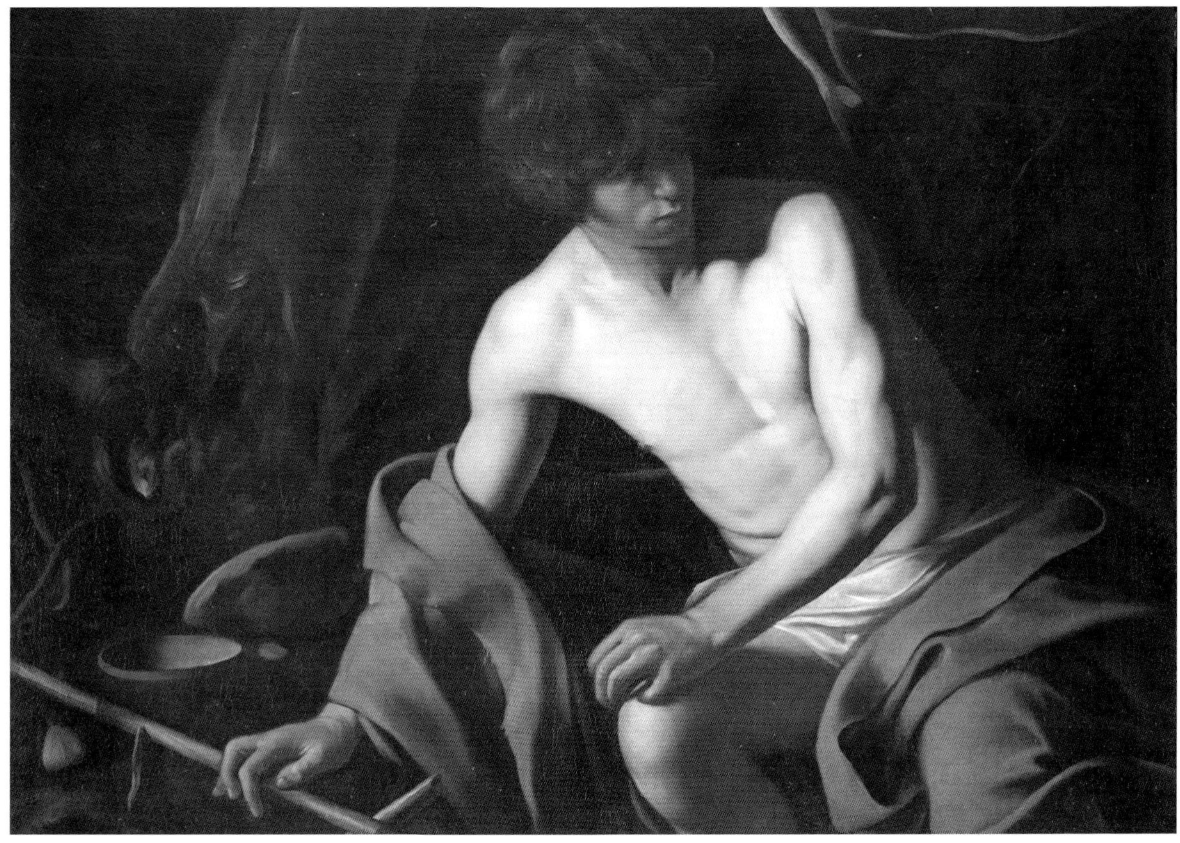

20 Caravaggio, *Saint John the Baptist*, 1604–6, oil on canvas, 94 × 131 cm (37 × 51 ⁹⁄₁₆ in), Palazzo Corsini, Galleria Nazionale d'Arte Antica, Rome

animal in Michelangelo's visual narrative resonates with Caravaggio's imagery in the Capitoline painting.

The proximity of Michelangelo's *ignudi* to the rams within a scene of sacrifice may well have determined Caravaggio's choice of their particular pose as a basis for his unconventional *Boy with a Ram/Saint John*. Or, at the least, having chosen the figure for formal reasons, he welcomed the contextual connection into the range of allusions encompassed by his image. Although Michelangelo's exact subject from the book of Genesis is open to different interpretations, including the sacrifices of Noah, Cain and Abel and also Jacob and Esau, all the suggested scenarios treat ritual sacrifices from the Old Testament, a fact that is arguably linked to Caravaggio's exploitation of his exemplum. It is worth recalling that subsequent to the completion of the *Saint John*, Caravaggio painted a straightforward treatment of the *Sacrifice of Isaac* (Plate 17) for Maffeo Barberini (later Pope Urban VIII), another in his circle of high-ranking clerical patrons.

Caravaggio's rendition stresses the violence of the story and the frightening, last-minute nature of divine intervention, as the angel must seize Abraham's wrist to halt the imminent execution. The startled Abraham has had no time to react; his other hand continues to force down the head of his son, who screams in fright as the knife approaches. The victim's features show us the same model for the Capitoline *Saint John the Baptist,* which was completed sometime shortly before the first payment for this commission in May 1603. In the Barberini painting (now in the Uffizi collection), Caravaggio has juxtaposed the child's head with that of the soon to be slaughtered ram; the curve of the ram's neck stretches just above the boy's curly hair and this virtual embrace inescapably calls to mind the young Saint John's enfolding of the ram with his arm, tugging its head close to his own in the Capitoline painting (Plate 15). It is a further indication that the artist perceived (or was encouraged to render) a link between the two protagonists: Isaac as a symbolic precursor of Christ being offered as a sacrifice and John the Baptist, who linked the eras of the Old and New Testaments as he prepared the way for Christ's ministry and ultimate death.

The ram as a sacrificial animal and Isaac as a portent of Christ's death are established iconography; the reasons why Caravaggio merged them with images of John the Baptist are not clear. It has been suggested that the substitution of the ram for the lamb may allude to the birth date of Giovanni Battista Mattei and allowed Caravaggio to overlay the child's astrological sign with his heavenly patron. This mixture of worldly and devout motifs would certainly have been welcomed by the artist and have a strong appeal to his patrons in an era that continued to value art for its ability to encompass multiple, and even contradictory, meanings. Yet this cannot be the determining explanation; Caravaggio repeated the non-standard pairing of Saint John with a ram in a later painting, under totally different circumstances, for another patron.

Toward the end of his troubled life, when Caravaggio was frantically trying to return to Rome, he called upon the support of Cardinal Scipione Borghese (1577–1633). It is thought that Caravaggio painted the *Saint John the Baptist* in the collection of the Borghese Gallery (Plate 18), one of his final works, as a payment in kind for the goodwill of the formidable cardinal, who was also a voracious art collector. The cardinal satisfied his appetite by any means available. In 1607, on the pretext of penalizing the Cavaliere d'Arpino for an unpaid tax, paintings from his collection were confiscated by papal order and the contents turned over to Scipione, nephew of the pontiff. The contents included several of Caravaggio's early works, which remain among the most valuable holdings of the Borghese Gallery.

The Borghese *Saint John the Baptist* shares several motifs with its Capitoline counterpart, most notably the ram and the conspicuous nudity of the luminous figure, although in the later instance a narrow band of white fabric maintains the boy's modesty as he leans upon the abundant drapes of a red mantle. Saint John is no longer seated on an altar of wood, yet his right foot rests noticeably on a log that projects toward the viewer's space. While the cruciform staff is absent, John holds a long reed prominently placed to his left. The iconography of the Baptist is intertwined with sacrificial symbols, adding a reference to the passion of Christ.

A recent study of the Borghese *Saint John* focuses attention on the reed, pointing out the unusual position of the hands, one crossing over the other at the wrist, with the reed held lightly between thumb and the first two fingers of the left hand.[32] Here the configuration is slightly awkward, given the pose; yet in depictions of the Passion, Christ's hands are often bound one atop the other enclosing a reed, an impoverished symbol of rule, mocking claims to a kingdom. This observation supports the theory of an iconography that assimilates symbols of Christ's passion and sacrifice with those of the Baptist. It is further strengthened by a detail from Caravaggio's *The Crowning with Thorns,* one of several works commissioned by Vincenzo Giustiniani (Fig. 21). Although partially hidden by Christ's red mantle (similar to those found in the paintings of Saint John), the Savior's hands are tied by a leather strap, clearly visible; a worthless reed lightly held by his right index finger, replaces a ruler's scepter.

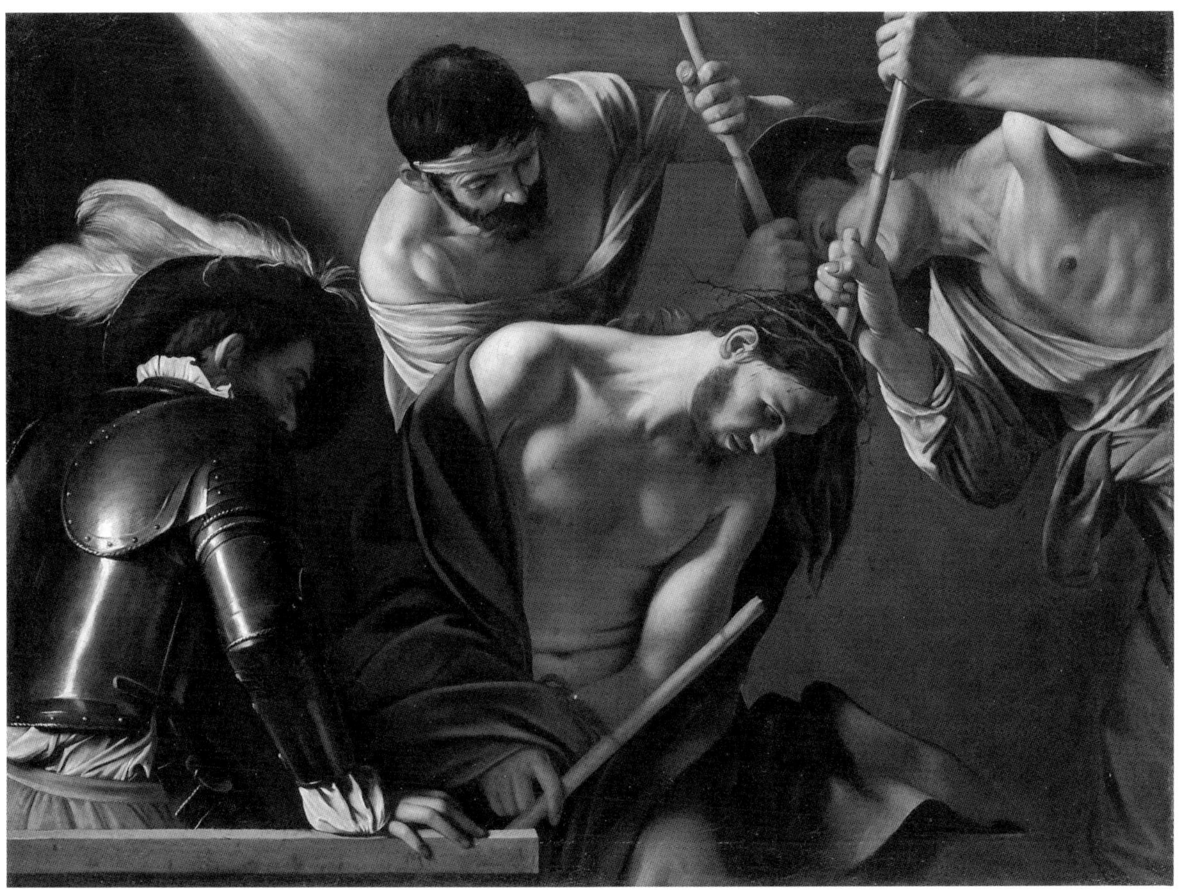

21 Caravaggio, *The Crowning with Thorns*, 1602–4, oil on canvas, 127 × 165.5 cm (50 × 65 3/16 in), Kunsthistorisches Museum, Vienna

It is tempting to understand the reed in the Borghese painting to be a poignant repetition of this motif of humiliation and suffering. It matches the gloom of the depiction in which the ram turns away from his companion to nibble on a vine, emblematic of Eucharistic wine, a symbol of the blood of Christ. The pointed detachment of the ram from Saint John stands in glaring contrast to the tender clasping of the animal in the exuberant Capitoline painting. The Borghese example is suffused with melancholy and sacrificial symbolism. Once again, it becomes evident that the vagaries of Caravaggio's imagery are puzzling because they are unique to the artist. Yet they were strictly controlled within a system of his own devising, one which was accepted by his patrons.

In the early part of his career, Caravaggio was doing nothing less than trying to establish a new visual language, attracting the most adventurous patrons who encouraged this pursuit. Vincenzo Giustiniani and Ciriaco Mattei were categorized in this way by at least one contemporary. Giovanni Baglione, the embittered rival painter and unfriendly biographer, coupled the two collectors in their desire for sensationalism in succumbing to the 'trend' set by Caravaggio. According to Baglione's report, Caravaggio's works caused a commotion; Giustiniani was 'besotted beyond all reason' and Mattei was 'soaked for many hundreds of scudi'.[33]

The maliciousness of Baglione's words shows just how much reaction and controversy Caravaggio's innovations evoked. Caravaggio succeeded in his quest for notoriety through inflammatory art; he used his study of Michelangelo, another artist of great reputation and fiery imagination, to achieve this. The pictorial elements introduced by Caravaggio demand an updated reading of the figures, supplanting the original model while referring to it. In the *Amor Vincit Omnia* and the Capitoline *Saint John the Baptist*, Caravaggio looked to Michelangelo's idealized, heroic bodies and his high-minded concept of sublimating desire only to negate them.

Caravaggio called upon the Renaissance master's work as a reference throughout his career, although with time his reaction to it became less contentious. The *Amor Vincit Omnia* and the Capitoline *Saint John* are the two works in which Caravaggio's idiosyncratic practice of *imitatio* is most blatant, where he both borrows from and conducts a dialogue with the content (or the meaning) of his models. Caravaggio's youthful commentary was provocative as well as witty, badinage with a finely honed edge; it is not coincidental that the two argumentative descendants of the *ignudi* are depicted as smiling. Their imagery is complex, ambitious and shocking, supported by the erudition and indulgence of his knowledgeable patrons. Caravaggio took to heart the significance of the sublime *ignudi*, glorious incarnations of a spiritual impulse and slyly converted them into earthy renditions oscillating 'between the religious and the sacrilegious'. Yet Caravaggio was not destined to remain in this indeterminate realm; we will see in the next chapter how the art of both Michelangelos came to focus on profoundly religious imagery.

4

Religious Messages Conveyed through Body Language, from Impeccable Heroes to Imperfect Humans

Michelangelo's sculpture is based on his belief in the eloquence of the perfected human form as the absolute vehicle of communication in art and his paintings follow suit. His surviving corpus is almost devoid of portraits and landscapes. Michelangelo Merisi on the other hand, was admired for his telling portraiture, while his genre and narrative paintings were valued for their persuasive rendition of the human condition. Each artist was an epoch-making interpreter of a major spiritual path followed in his lifetime: Renaissance Christian neoplatonism cultivated in Florence, as opposed to the popular, pietistic movements of the Counter-Reformation disseminated in early 17th-century Rome. The term 'Counter-Reformation' characterizes the response of the Catholic Church to the revolutionary challenges with regard to its authority, doctrine and practices as amended by the creeds of Protestant Christianity. The Counter-Reformation was embodied institutionally by the Council of Trent, a conference whose sessions took place between 1545 and 1563, with the task of reaffirming the truth of contested Catholic dogma and pronouncing on the correct performance of its practices.[1]

The 'Catholic Reformation' is another term applied to the Church's attempts at amelioration. The nuances between the two characterizations are subtle, but important. In general, speaking of the Catholic Reformation slightly alters the perspective, with emphasis on self-reflective approaches from within Catholicism to address and correct weaknesses that had developed over the centuries. It implies a long-term struggle for rectification on the part of tangents within Catholicism and independent explorations by individual believers to find effective paths for living their beliefs. As we will see, the impulse toward interiorized self-reform eventually directed Michelangelo's spiritual probing and his art in later life. The attitudes that pervade his sacred art through the first three decades of the 16th century, however, were those of an optimism that encouraged the absorption and Christianization of all available sources, an approach that accompanies unquestioned hegemony. This helps to bring into focus the clear-cut differences between how the human body looks and behaves in sacred histories as imagined by the two Michelangelos at the outset of their mature works.

Where Michelangelo's figure style is idealized and heroic, using beauty as a symbol of goodness, Caravaggio expresses religious yearning through figures whose details are observed and transmitted without enhancement, whose unadorned, imperfect features convey spirituality connected to 'pauperism'. Each artist developed a visual system that codified and deepened options within the current teachings of the Catholic Church and each accomplished this through compelling expressions of the human form. Michelangelo's hyper-perfect nudes in religious settings can be understood as stemming from the doctrine of Incarnation – the legacy of divinity clothed in humanity – while Caravaggio's personages, whether rough or attractive, with dirty feet or properly clothed in elegant contemporary fashions, stress the incorporation of all classes into a process of redemption. The various strains of Early Modern symbolism are not automatically compatible with today's systems of visual meaning and must be unlocked by reintegration into their historical contexts.

For example, Michelangelo's armies of nude figures painted in the most sacred of Christian spaces cause some consternation, even among today's observers, who wonder how it was acceptable to adorn churches in this manner. First, it is crucial to remember that the popes who commissioned his fresco cycles in the Sistine Chapel, where unclothed figures abound, were complicit in the imagery and proud of the results. Complaints followed later and from other sources.[2] Our classification of Michelangelo's work as 'high art' with the attendant license granted to this category, along with the fact that we distance his sacred art by approaching it with the behavior and responses calibrated for secular, museum settings, allows us to side-step the important question of propriety. This quality, codified as 'decorum', was the single most significant factor in establishing the acceptability or censure of a work of art in the Early Modern period; it is made all the more elusive by the fact that its definition changes from one time period to another and even at the same moment, differs in various locations.

With regard to the nudity contained in Michelangelo's art, however, the core of the historical answer is not difficult to grasp. Simply put, if Christ clothed himself in human flesh through his Incarnation, the body can encompass divinity and is therefore an exalted means of artistic expression. With the humanity of Christ as a model, the innocent, virtuous, or saintly human body is morally good and its goodness can be symbolically expressed through beauty. If the body is the most noble form in nature, having shared the divinity of Christ, its representation in art is the most exalted vehicle of expression. According to this view, human fabrication comes closest to divine creation when it imitates the making of a human form. This is another reason why reference to the 'divine Michelangelo' was such a telling, and apt, epithet.

Michelangelo's philosophy of art, as expressed in his poetry, is anchored in this understanding of the symbolic potential and dominance, of beauty. It is movingly expressed in a madrigal most likely written to honor Tommaso Cavalieri, a young man whom the artist loved. In the eyes of Michelangelo, his beloved was a paragon of physical comeliness combined with spiritual worth:

> My eyes, desirous of beautiful things,
> and my soul, likewise, of its salvation,
> have no other means to rise
> to heaven but to gaze at all such things.[3]

The madrigal is a perfect statement of how sublimated beauty can become a beacon leading to spiritual deliverance. If contemplation of beauty helps the soul to ascend to heaven, then Michelangelo's nudes become a vehicle of prayer. Even after a coherent exegesis, the premise of this symbolic system is hard for many to accept and this extends to current cultural values that equate beautiful bodies, especially if unrobed, solely in connection to eroticism. Nor was there unanimous acceptance among Michelangelo's contemporaries that ideal forms can transcend lust. But there was a strong consensus, especially among the elite viewing public in Italy before the mid-16th century, which approved symbolic and idealized nudity as a heroic Christian expression.[4] For the preponderance of critics and patrons, Michelangelo was the awesome and undisputed master of imitating divine creation. His art stood at the apex of a style whose impossibly valiant humanity was an uplifting source of release for worshipers from all levels of society. By the time Caravaggio rose to distinction half a century later, the former confident majority had withered into a defensive minority and other attitudes took command. Caravaggio's emergent style was in perfect harmony with the evolving requirements of religious narration in paintings at the start of the 17th century.

The Cardinal-Archbishop of Milan, Federico Borromeo (1564–1631), gave authoritative expression to revisionist ideas regarding the painting of religious subjects in his polemical text, *Sacred Painting*, published in 1624. As a compact summary of post-Tridentine attitudes that informed the early 1600s, it has direct relevance for Caravaggio's art, not only because of chronology. Caravaggio's early life and apprenticeship took place in 'Borromean Milan', whose Catholicism was molded by San Carlo Borromeo (1538–84), and further shaped by Federico as heir to his older cousin's legacy. Federico Borromeo's impressive art collection forms the core of today's Ambrosiano Museum, which since 1607 has preserved one of the early independent still life paintings produced in Italy, Caravaggio's *Basket of Fruit*. Caravaggio's great protectors, the Colonna family, were blood relations of the Borromeo clan and other supporters of his art were followers of San Filippo Neri (1515–95), one of Cardinal Borromeo's closest associates and advisors. Neri was the founder of the Congregation of the Oratory in Rome (1575), whose members were bound by dedication to charitable works and to preaching the Catholic faith. Caravaggio's first circle of patrons, including Del Monte, Giustiniani, Mattei and Crescenzi, all held close ties to the Oratorian Congregation and thus to Borromeo.[5] The approach taken by the Oratorians is discernible in some of Caravaggio's religious imagery, influenced by his patrons and his patrimony. It was after all a highly placed Oratorian, Ottavio Paravicino, who decisively described the artist's strategy of disorientation as 'mixing unequal measures of both the devout and profane'.[6]

On the devout side, Caravaggio's stylistic tenets were admirably in step with Borromeo's stricture against nudity. The terse language of the brief section in *Sacred Painting* articulates a closed subject: 'Nudity is of necessity unsuited for the truth of a church teaching; it can also offend the sensibilities of viewers and weaken their religious devotion.'[7] At the basis of the restriction is a pronounced concern with the effect of imagery on the more humble audience, those without the education to apply neoplatonic principles to their experience of art. This new emphasis pervaded the Catholic reformers' desire to use art as an instrument of widespread change, a very different goal from the Renaissance manifestation of spirituality through lofty imaginings of an ideal realm, visually linked to classical culture. Caravaggio's lack of interest in the fashioning of classical nudes was accompanied by his urgent desire to compose figures with the immediacy of direct encounters. His fiction of depicting everyday reality in his paintings admirably suited the desire of the reformers to convey sacred messages to its worshipers in the most accessible terms possible.

The summer of 1599 presented Caravaggio with a first opportunity to prove himself as painter of the new Catholic imperatives. He won the commission to fill the lateral walls of an important chapel in the heart of Rome with scenes from the life of Matthew the Evangelist, depicting the moment Christ calls him to be an Apostle and to his eventual martyrdom. The paintings survive in their original location, the Contarelli Chapel in San Luigi dei Francesi, the French national church in Rome. It is situated in close proximity to the former residences of Cardinal Del Monte and the Marchese Giustiniani, both of whom actively backed Caravaggio's undertaking, as well the Crescenzi family who had been entrusted with overseeing decoration of the chapel. If we add to this grouping the Medici family, proprietors of the

Villa Madama, who had been involved in financing the construction and embellishment of San Luigi, we find the nucleus of Caravaggio's first committed patrons anchored in the immediate neighborhood of the church. The appointment to paint the Contarelli Chapel was a momentous opportunity for the 27-year-old artist, his first institutional rather than private commission, with results that were sure to be broadcast throughout Rome and beyond.

Before Caravaggio's commission there had been a long and tortuous history of failure to complete the decoration of the chapel. Originally envisioned by Cardinal Matthieu Cointerel [Italianized as Matteo Contarelli] (1519–85), work had proceeded only fitfully from 1565, when the original contract was signed. Twenty years later the decorative campaign languished altogether. Ample funding had been bequeathed in the cardinal's will, yet the chapel remained incomplete and boarded up. The priests of San Luigi finally made their complaints heard, accusing the executors of the estate, that is, members of the Crescenzi family, of corruption. In 1597 the matter was placed in the hands of a papal committee, the Fabbrica di San Pietro, whose chief officer happened to be Cardinal Del Monte. Caravaggio was awarded the contract and signed on to the original terms of the commission, as well as agreeing to a delivery date in one year's time. Spurred by this windfall opportunity, Caravaggio carried the day and had the paintings installed by July of 1600, in time for the crowds and celebrations of a Roman Jubilee Year. In retrospect, the Saint Matthew series appears to have ushered in a new epoch of painting, on cue at the start of a new century. The paintings were, indeed, the talk of the town.

Caravaggio's fulfillment of the commission, triumphantly putting an end to almost half a century of waiting, must have had an impact similar to Michelangelo's completion of the *David*, whose gestation also arose from long periods of postponements and false starts. It had been the sculptor's first great Florentine commission and emerged, as the story goes, from an almost completely ruined block of marble which had been abandoned for decades. In each case a promising artist in his twenties was affirmed as a talent to reckon with; his ability to succeed where other more established artists had failed added legendary status to an emerging career, marked him as exceptional and ensured future commissions and patrons of consequence.

For Caravaggio, the decisive contract came during an intensely creative and productive period in his work. His considerable accomplishments, however, did not completely prepare him for the scope of the commission, with many components contractually designated. The artist was called upon to paint two complex narratives based on biblical texts, whose compositions were required to be multi-figured and contained within a monumental format, roughly 10 × 11 ft each. This was a daunting endeavor for which he had no experience; the potential for failure in such a public arena was immense. Caravaggio's success is a testament to his determination and talent, bringing to light the rapidity with which he could absorb lessons and devise innovative responses to pictorial challenges. But the path to the realization of the paintings was fraught rather than smooth and we are fortunate that technical analysis has allowed us to follow that development. An underpainting became evident through X-rays taken in 1966, showing a group of figures and the outline of an architectural setting obliterated by a second layer of painting that produced the final version of the *Martyrdom of Saint Matthew* (Plate 21).[8]

The first attempt at composition reveals an initial miscalculation of the necessary scale, with under life-size figures rendered too small for the considerable dimensions of the canvas. Caravaggio disregarded the contract's specification of frescoes – the only stipulation he ignored – limiting the enormous set of untried challenges imposed by the commission. The fact that the artist was permitted to follow his preferred technique of designing directly on canvas in oil demonstrates the absolute confidence of Caravaggio's patrons. It also reveals the general deployment of his first attack, preserved beneath the overpainting. The reasons for the artist's dissatisfaction and his decision to start over are evinced by the static arrangement of the original figural grouping and the recycled classicism of the outlines for the architectural setting. That Caravaggio, under immense pressure, was able to adjust his design comprehensively and courageously in order to forge an entirely new composition, tells us of his professional discipline and drive.

It is not surprising that when he needed help to re-imagine the scene of Matthew's martyrdom, Caravaggio turned to the most eminent master of monumental decoration for religious sites; yet it has been little remarked upon in the critical literature. Michelangelo Merisi looked once more to Michelangelo Buonarroti's Sistine Chapel ceiling, but this time for an encounter of quiet respect, all persiflage and retorts banished. To form a dramatic punctuation of space that defines the pictorial realm and beckons the viewer toward Matthew's murder, Caravaggio painted a striking variation on a set of *ignudi*. Just as in his predecessor's arrangement, framing *The Separation of Land and Water* (Plate 20) Caravaggio's paired figures act as a bracket to the scene taking place behind them, turning their heads to observe it. The reclining pose of the youth on the left has been elongated and his arms pulled forward to support his torso as he moves toward the viewer, accentuated by strong lighting. The companion figure on the right presents his back to us, as he strains to shift further away from the violence. The exaggerated musculature of Caravaggio's figure is a variant of the emphatically brawny anatomy of the Sistine athlete (another of the four engraved by Cherubino Alberti), and makes an almost abstract impression. Its readability is further complicated by the juxtaposition of the head and arm of another young initiate in the foreground group; a jigsaw arrangement that became a hallmark of Caravaggio's compositional preferences.

The role of these young men in the narrative, as neophyte Christians awaiting baptism by immersion, provides a convincing rationale for their partial nudity. The state of undress is shared by Matthew's assassin, implying that the killer gained access to his target and the advantage of surprise, by feigning conversion to the Christian cult. It is the single example we have of a group of male nudes painted by Caravaggio and the Michelangelesque appropriation is entirely explicable as a perfect compositional solution – one that had to be arrived at quickly and effectively. It is to Caravaggio's great credit that he borrowed astutely, seamlessly transformed the figures into his own style and then entirely discarded the whole gambit in his later narrative works. But in his urgent need for a visual vocabulary suited to dramatic narrative action in the Saint Matthew paintings, Caravaggio resolutely pilfered from his namesake.

The force of the Sistine ceiling remained a powerful draw for artists at the end of the 16th century, reinforced by its diffusion in prints. The figural grouping just discussed in relation to the *Martyrdom of Saint Matthew* proves Caravaggio's continued and varied responses to the *ignudi*, but they were not the only components he studied within the grand decorative program. Vasari had already noted a basic feature of the Genesis panels ranged along the center of the ceiling, remarking on one of Michelangelo's subtle devices: 'In these compartments he used no rule of perspectives in foreshortening, nor is there any fixed point of view, but he accommodated the compartments to the figures, rather than the figures to the compartments.'[9] This pictorial strategy, which places the figures close to the foreground and uses their volume to create space, eschewing complicated perspectival structuring, served Michelangelo well for narrative scenes that loomed far above the viewer below. Simplification and enhanced readability, even for canvasses held comfortably within the faithful's zone of worship, were pictorial goals embraced by Caravaggio in presentation of religious subjects, perfectly attuned to the Counter-Reformation

Church's desire for the straightforward delivery of its doctrine and precepts.

Having struggled with the *Martyrdom*, Caravaggio regained his own pictorial territory in *The Calling of Matthew* (Plate 19), yet was not quite ready to dispense with Michelangelo's aid. The story of Christ's unlikely summons of Matthew, a tax collector by profession, allowed for a mise-en-scène much more closely aligned to Caravaggio's early works. He depicts Matthew at work, interrupted as he tallies his hoard of coins, account books at the ready. As always, the still life elements are arranged with finesse, although here they are given less prominence. Seated at a table, the future apostle is surrounded by companions in contemporary dress, closely related to the cast of young men who appear in the artist's popular secular works of much smaller format. The harmonized cluster is counterbalanced by the two standing figures who enter the nebulous structure of the room from the opposite side of the painting. Christ and Peter, dressed in conventional biblical garb, form a tight twosome, quite distinct in unadorned costume and grave manner from the worldly-wise ensemble seated at the table.

The shared palette of deep reds and a tawny range of yellow, beige and ivory tones, along with carefully controlled lighting, creates an illusion of harmony between the two disparate groups, masking their differences at first glance. Perhaps it was this virtuoso trick of light and color, executed with confidence from the Venetian legacy of Caravaggio's training, which caused many to comment on this aspect of the painting. Baglione snidely records a cutting dismissal of the works by an eminent and distinguished painter:

> But when Federico Zuccari came to look at them he said in my presence, 'What is all the fuss about?' and as he carefully examined the entire work, he added, 'I don't see anything here but the thought (*pensiero*) of Giorgione in the picture of the saint called to the Apostolate by Christ.' Stifling laughter and marveling at all this excitement, he shrugged his shoulders and then turned his back and left.[10]

If Federico Zuccari could disdainfully turn his back on Caravaggio's striking representations of the New Testament, others were mesmerized. As the documentation conveys, the public of artists, connoisseurs, worshipers and the merely curious were all rewarded in their contemplation of Caravaggio's unexpected interpretations of his subject matter. His conflation of the contemporary with the historical has an unexpected cogency that is gradually disclosed. The revered figures of Christ and Peter are unequivocally sacred as they emerge in a glow of light from the shadows; a thin golden halo surmounts the head of God made man. The startled Matthew, characterized as a highly secular individual, questions his fate; he is shown by his garb to be the 17th-century viewer's contemporary, encouraging all who encountered the painting to probe their own responses to their faith. The mirroring is calculated to reflect the spectator unambiguously.

Saint Peter, who walks into the composition with his back toward the viewer, was painted as a second thought, superimposed on the completed figure of Christ (discovered by X-ray analysis). While this partially obscures Christ's body, the placement of Peter adds to the weight of the divine presence. It leads the viewer into the painting toward Christ, emboldening us to follow his steps while focusing our attention toward the movement of Christ's outstretched arm and hand. It is the portent on which the entire narration pivots.

For the central motif in the *Calling of St Matthew*, Caravaggio needed a distinctive and persuasive gesture, one carrying the relentlessness of a heavenly directive, capable of distracting the seated group from its venal interests and commanding the viewer's full attention. Caravaggio's quandary led him once again to the Sistine Chapel. He satisfied his quest by quoting from a passage that remains in constant circulation to this day. Caravaggio studied the barely touching

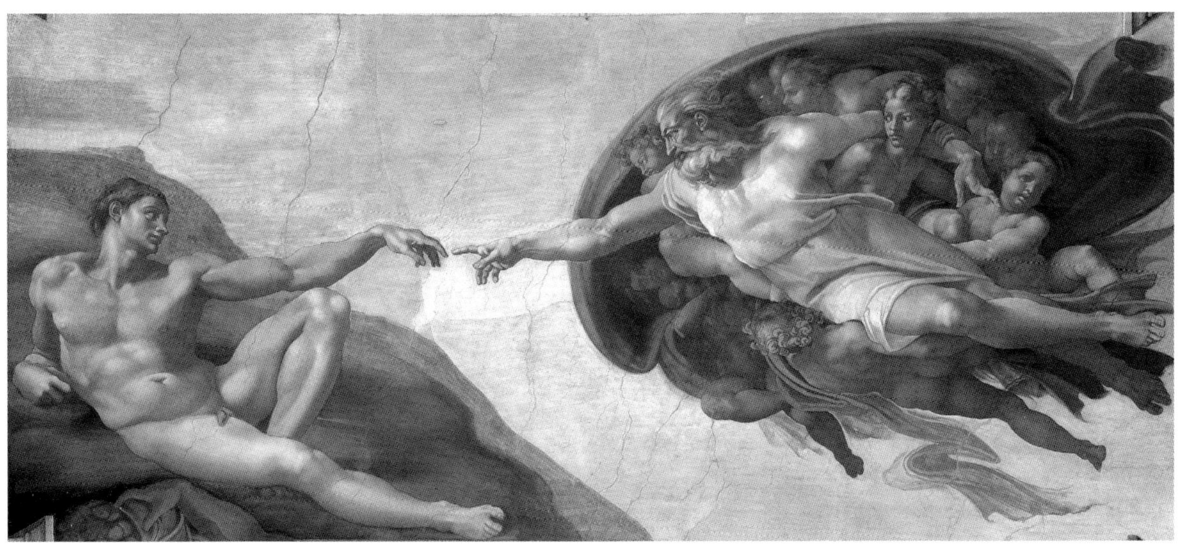

22 Michelangelo, *The Creation of Adam*, 1510, fresco, 280 × 570 cm (110¼ × 224 7/16 in) Sistine Chapel, Vatican, Rome

hands of the Creator and Adam, where the spark of spiritual awakening hovers in the small gap between their fingers (Fig. 22). The X-rays that reveal so much about Caravaggio's process in realizing the Matthew paintings verify that the citation from the Sistine was painted over an initial version showing Christ's hand with fingers tucked downwards in the commonplace motion of beckoning.[11] In his scramble to produce the requisite fireworks necessary for the success of his high-stakes debut, Caravaggio bowed to and borrowed from Michelangelo's stunning invention.

Condivi gives a curious explication of Michelangelo's commanding representation, parsing the scene as follows: 'In the fourth [bay] is the creation of man, where one sees God, with arm and hand outstretched, almost as if giving precepts to Adam regarding what he should and should not do.'[12] This is best understood as an interpretive overlay, with an older Michelangelo adapting his exegesis to the concerns of the Church at mid-century. The *precetti*, or precepts of the Church, are laws that spell out the minimum obligations to be observed by Catholics in good standing, such as attending mass and receiving the sacrament of the Eucharist. They stem from ecclesiastic authorities rather than scripture. There was particular emphasis on their formulation in the second half of the 16th century, with a group of five precepts promulgated in 1555.[13] Imagining God instructing Adam in the precepts of Catholicism at the moment of his spiritual birth is an apt message to ascribe to a scene in the papal chapel and a strong statement of Catholic identity, but it is the product of a later, more contested moment in Church history. It is indicative of Michelangelo's continual meditation on his religion and his participation as a faithful member of the Church, as well as a rethinking of his art and its meaning in the scope of his spiritual well-being.

What we actually see in visual terms, however, presents another point more in harmony with Catholic attitudes current at the start of the 16th century. Adam has been formed with a hyper-perfect, well-muscled corporeality; a body still infused with innocence, a worthy expression of its all-powerful Creator. However, his lethargic posture shows Adam still bound to the earth on which he lies, almost incapable of motion. Adam lifts his potentially mighty hand limply, relying on the support of a bent leg to reach out to the Creator, who soars toward him. God's dynamic touch will convey Adam's soul, instilling a spirituality to invigorate the mortal body of the first human. While without doubt impressive, Adam's physique retains the symbolical import of having been fashioned from a lump of clay; it awaits its spiritual animation.

As we consider closely this stirring passage from the Sistine Chapel ceiling, it is perhaps surprising that Caravaggio should take the hand of Adam as the model rather than that of God the Father. It is so unlikely that many discussions mistakenly refer to the 'hand of God from the Sistine' as the prototype for Christ's gesture in *The Calling of Matthew*. As we have seen, Michelangelo designed Adam's hand to convey a muscular form devoid of energy, awaiting the flash that will fill the body with spirit, triggering a higher form of life. Why is the almost leaden hand of the awakening Adam, all latent power rather than dynamic motion, spotlighted to become the rather flickering beacon that will nevertheless mobilize the hesitant Matthew? Caravaggio, rising to the exigencies of a major religious setting, decided to (or was instructed to) make a specific characterization of Christ implicit in the representation. He presents the figure of Christ as 'the second Adam', one of the many exegetical descriptions of the Savior. The concept alluded to is that just as Adam closed the door to paradise, Christ would become a man in order to re-open the gate of heaven to humanity. As Christ calls his followers to begin his earthly ministry, he takes the first steps on the road that will ineluctably lead to his Passion, death and ultimately, through resurrection, to salvation of the faithful.

This is a conceptually complex elaboration of Michelangelo's Sistine iconography and there is every reason to believe that Caravaggio worked with his patron or was advised by someone in Del Monte's circle to arrive at its expression in the Contarelli canvas. The artist, however, would have been solely responsible for its integration into the composition. That the motif was meaningful to Caravaggio is apparent in his reuse of a closely related gesture in a towering work from the last years of his life, when in 1608–9 he took temporary refuge with associates in Sicily. As usual, important commissions quickly followed his arrival in each successive venue as he moved from one location to another seeking safe haven. The *Raising of Lazarus* was painted for Giovanni Battista de' Lazzari, a rich Genoese merchant living in Messina; the patron's name (Lazzari) provided the motivation for the subject, which had been memorably treated in Renaissance art. On an expanse of canvas measuring 380 × 275 cm (149 ⅝ × 108¼ in), it provided Caravaggio with an opportunity to further his mastery of presenting a stirring sacred subject within a monumental format (Fig. 23). His approach was highly personal, suited both to his skills and also his limitations. Continuing to avoid enlargement of the figures much beyond life size, he apportions emptiness to almost half the pictorial space, obtaining through this strategy a surprisingly poignant and affecting result. Giving the impression of a rather large number of onlookers through a staccato pattern of light across a tightly pressed series of faces, full illumination is allocated only to the haunting corpse of Lazarus, absolutely dominating the composition. His life appears to be returning by degrees as the flesh of Lazarus takes on the warmth of the light, emitting from no earthly source.

Even the figure of Christ, entering almost imperceptibly from the left to conduct the miracle, remains in shadow; indeed, his face is completely obscured by darkness. Yet his extended arm is subtly backlit so that it is possible to discern Christ's gesture, which will reclaim Lazarus from the dead. In this instance, as in *The Calling of Matthew*, Caravaggio's composition demands a commanding gesture, one on which a miracle of enormous magnitude depends. Caravaggio imagines Christ calling to Lazarus as he had beckoned Matthew, with the same impact of Michelangelo's gesture from the Sistine. It is now, however, closer in appearance to God the Father's dynamic hand; the Son revitalizes Lazarus just as the Father invigorated Adam. The imposing gesture,

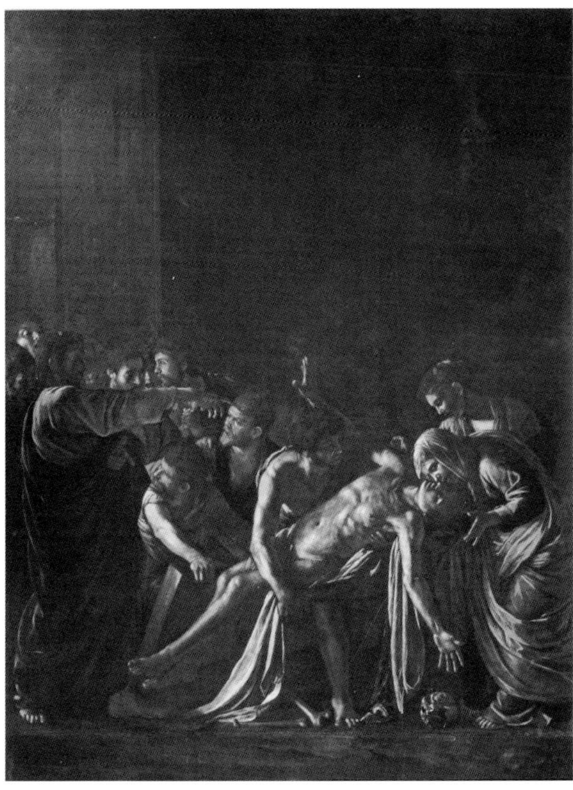

23 Caravaggio, *The Raising of Lazarus*, 1608–9, oil on canvas, 380 × 275 (149 ⅝ × 108 ¼ in), Museo Regionale, Messina

recalled from Caravaggio's acute visual memory, comes into service even as the artist wishes desperately to return to Rome. Caravaggio's proficiency in creating majestic scenes of sacred narration progressed, although he languished under the ban from the Eternal City. The continuity of his iconographic solutions is attested by the Messina canvas, even if Christ's gesture is not featured as prominently, nor is its meaning as layered, as in its precocious appearance within the walls of San Luigi dei Francesi at a time when Caravaggio was flush with ambition and greeted by applause.

Further considering the complexity of the gesture of awakening from the Sistine Chapel in that first moment of Caravaggio's widespread acclaim achieved in the Contarelli Chapel, we see an almost slow-motion effect in the movement of Christ's extended hand. It appears as though he has lifted it slowly and tentatively, in apparent contradiction to his aggressive summons to an unlikely follower. But the meaning of the symbolism in *The Calling of Matthew* is inescapable, with the epithet 'the new Adam' reinforced by another detail in the composition. The hand of Christ is centered below the cruciform shape constructed by the window casements above it; the message of Christ's mission is anchored by the association of his hand to a reminder of his future execution. The juxtaposition is emphasized by its isolation within the empty space, with a beam of raking light above, plus an additional burst that hits the hand directly, lifting it from the shadows. The motif is closely echoed in the brightly lit hand of Saint Peter, placed just below that of Christ and repeated with variation in the extended index finger of Matthew. The future martyr's facial expression proclaims a startled 'Who, me?' even as his pointing finger is frozen in bewilderment, while yet hoping not to be the object of the summons.

Recent scholarship has questioned the identification of Matthew with this figure, but this doubt is unwarranted. The man's age, his elegant and costly outfit (including a gold medallion pinned to his black beret), along with the lighting that emphasizes his face and hand, unambiguously show him to be the one singled out by Christ's unwelcome call. He is the central focus of the seated group and the pronounced illumination that catches his features and gesture connect him to the other principal protagonists in this story. The three crucial figures of Christ, Peter and Matthew, all display their hands with pointing index fingers; those of the other characters in the scene are either hidden or at rest, or fiddle with coins and eyeglasses. Further confirmation of Matthew's identity is attested by the repetition of this figure in variations on Caravaggio's composition found, for example, in paintings by Bernardo Strozzi (Fig. 24) and Hendrick ter Brugghen. The appropriations are sound evidence of the impact of Caravaggio's treatment of the biblical narrative, as attractive to these northern artists (respectively Genoese and Dutch), as they were shocking to Roman eyes.

An openness to northern cultures in fact distinguished Caravaggio's first circle of patrons, which predisposed them to appreciation of the artist's style. We recall that Cardinal Del Monte, Venetian by birth, was introduced to Caravaggio's work by the dealer Costantino Spata, whose shop was located near the French national church, San Luigi dei Francesi. The most conspicuous residents of the neighborhood militated in a 'liberal political faction' backing Pope Clement VIII (reigned 1592–1605), connected to French interests as opposed to Spanish concerns, the two major powers with contrasting claims in Italy.[14] Their united political allegiances were echoed by a shared participation in the religious community fostered by Filippo Neri's Oratorians.[15] This environment, connected in turn to Federico Borromeo's reforming spirit, marks profoundly the religious imagery of Caravaggio, both through his patrons' connections and his own cultural formation in Milan; commonalities that nurtured Caravaggio's attunement to the sensibilities of his early enthusiasts.

One more extremely important family with particularly close personal ties to Neri and the Oratorians, the Mattei, were conspicuous initial champions of Caravaggio. Within a year after the completion of the Contarelli Chapel, Caravaggio had moved into the palazzo of Asdrubale Mattei on the via delle Botteghe Oscure. Located just beneath the Campidoglio, Caravaggio's new situation was only slightly distant from the San Luigi neighborhood, but a step up in status. During this same year, 1601, Asdrubale's brother, Ciriaco Mattei, commissioned Caravaggio to paint *The Supper at Emmaus* (Plate 23), now in London's National Gallery. The confidence gained through the realization of the Contarelli canvasses is apparent in this painting. It is more manageable in size than the huge narratives composed for the chapel, yet much more ambitious than the earlier easel paintings. Its subject, again taken from the New Testament, presents an array of interpretive challenges. In meeting the new demands set before him, Caravaggio renewed the strategy that had assisted him in earlier tasks. He turned again to Michelangelo's frescoes in the Sistine Chapel; on this occasion he targeted the figure of Christ on the altar wall, around whom the final judgment of mankind swirls.

Michelangelo labored over *The Last Judgment* (Plate 22) from 1536–41, during the papacy of Paul III (1468–1549). This Pope was almost an exact contemporary of the elderly artist, ascending to the throne of Saint Peter when he was 66 years old, to all appearances fragile in health. Although his reign was expected to be brief, the accomplished statesman and highly intelligent strategist fooled the Curia by flourishing throughout his 15-year tenure as Pope. The former Cardinal Alessandro Farnese, a scion of the influential Roman family, Pope Paul was a steadfast benefactor of the city of Rome, helping to restore it after the ferocious Sack of 1527. He was consumed by the desire to have Michelangelo create art and architecture to enrich Pauline Rome and amplify the magnificence of his rule. It was a propitious association, even beyond acts of patronage. Paul's agenda for meaningful reexamination of Catholic practices and ecclesiastic structures, his sympathy for several of the doctrinal points raised by the Protestants and his desire for reconciliation with them, were the strains of Catholicism most sympathetic to Michelangelo.

The artist's style spoke to Farnese's cultural formation and esteem for ancient imperial Rome, which he saw as his ancestral heritage. The cultural values of Paul III stemmed from his humanistic training; he had been the student of the esteemed scholar Pomponio Leto (1428–98). Farnese was deeply nourished by the literary and philosophical currents that stirred Michelangelo during his time in the Medici household. It was precisely in the Florentine culture of neoplatonism that these two men from such different

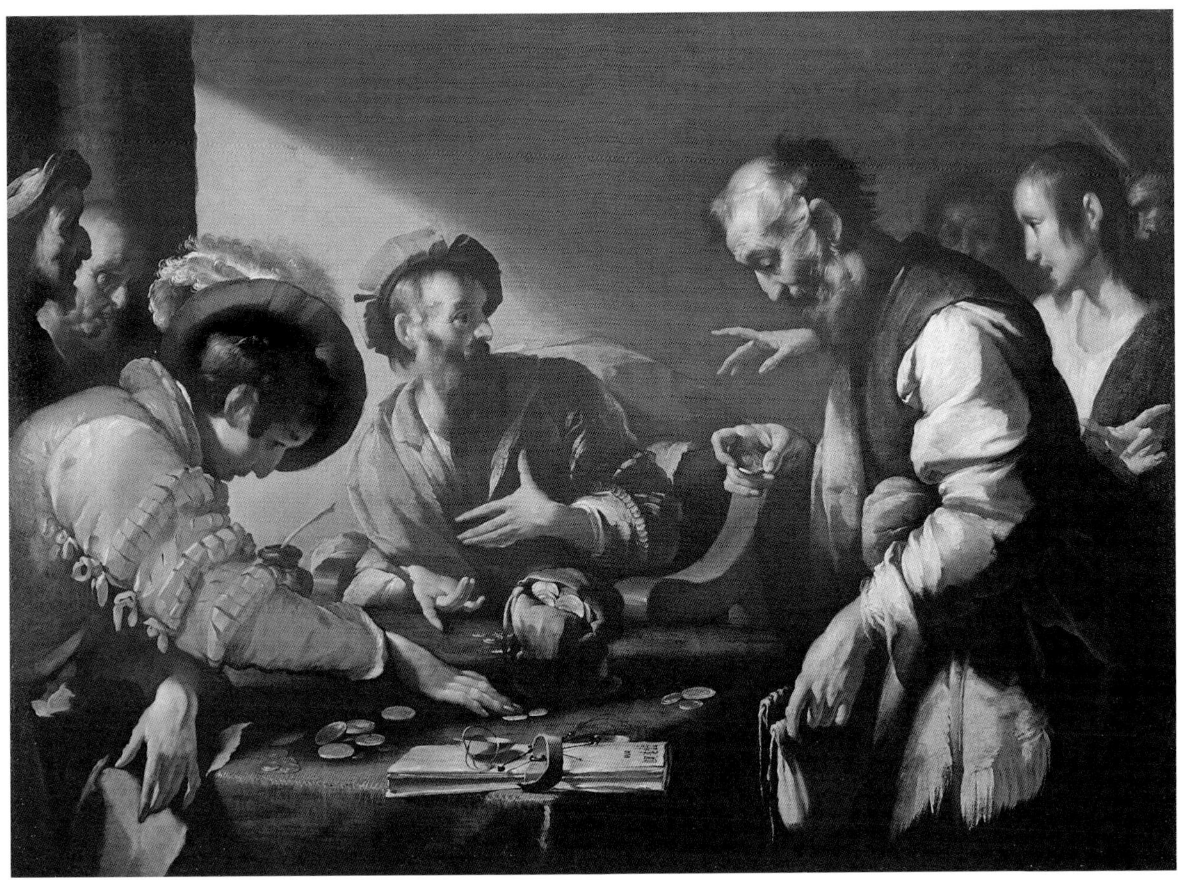

24 Bernardo Strozzi, *The Calling of Saint Matthew*, *c.*1620, oil on canvas, 139.1 × 187 cm (54¾ × 73 ⅝ in), Worcester Art Museum, Worcester, MA, Museum purchase, 1941.1

backgrounds actually shared a point of personal history. In 1486, Alessandro Farnese had arrived in Florence to spend the next three years immersed in the stimulating intellectual environment created by Lorenzo de' Medici, enjoying the privileges of his friendship and exchanges with his entourage. Michelangelo stepped into the same situation, albeit from a far lower social level, a mere two years after Alessandro's return to Rome. The memories of their idyllic time with Il Magnifico must have been a cherished common bond.

Michelangelo's work on the immense altar wall in the Sistine Chapel was first envisioned by Pope Paul III's predecessor, but the new pope assumed the task with relish at the start of his reign. Correspondence reveals that he followed the project with a keen eye, requesting that the artist accompany him on a visit to see the progress. Upon completion, Paul paid the artist the most unequivocal compliment possible: he immediately commissioned more frescoes for his adjacent chapel, as we will see. Paul's hands-on patronage is important to bear in mind when discussing the *Last Judgment*, because the fresco eventually became controversial. Although Michelangelo produced an unforeseen result, innovative and challenging both in its pictorial vocabulary and

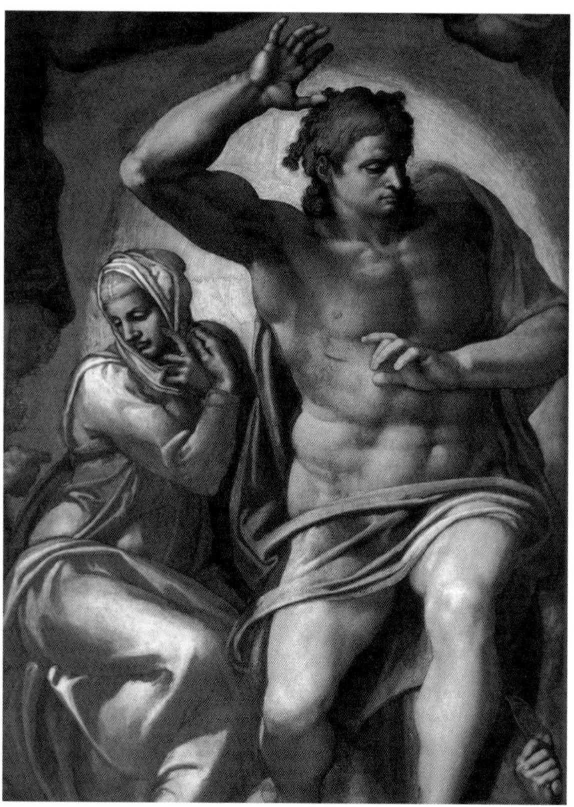

25 Michelangelo, Christ and Mary, detail, *The Last Judgment*, 1536–41, fresco, 1370 × 1220 cm (539 3/8 × 480 5/16 in), Sistine Chapel, Vatican, Rome

the presentation of its subject, when the fresco was unveiled it was deemed to be more than acceptable by the occupant of Saint Peter's throne, who had called it into being.

Yet the iconography is daring in many significant details. The portrayal of Christ, the supreme protagonist of the image, is unexpected (Fig. 25); it does not follow the Renaissance conventions of bearded face and slight build, modestly garbed in flowing robes. Michelangelo's choice has been connected to the use of Apollonian imagery to represent the Savior, metaphorically placing him as the Sun around which the range of humanity orbits as it awaits judgment. The general resemblance of Christ's stance to the stride of the *Apollo Belvedere*, the sun god, suggests the comparison; however, the thick, overtly muscled body transforms the model with a more vehement and aggressive characterization. Given Michelangelo's supreme care in his choice of figural types and the precision with which he fashioned them, specific reasons lay behind this non-standard representation of Christ as Judge. A textual source for Michelangelo's unusual iconography has recently been discovered in the *Iudicium Dei* [God's Judgment] written in 1505 by Giovanni Sulpizio (1440–after 1508?), a scholar of Latin literature and an intimate of Paul III from his youth.[16] The poem envisions Christ the Judge as blindingly splendid, brighter than the sun, with a terrifying gesture, standing in the midst of an angelic choir, with Mary beside him. Sulpizio's poem provides a convincing point of departure for Michelangelo's imagery and further personalizes the fresco by its references to an author dear to the patron.

The primary sources, while not mentioning Sulpizio's poem, parallel its interpretation of Christ as awesome Judge. Condivi simply says the Son of God appears in majesty; Vasari more specifically refers to 'a countenance proud and terrible', echoing the characterization found in the poem. It is instructive that neither Vasari nor Condivi provide elaborate defenses of the iconography of the *Last Judgment*, when we have seen that Michelangelo used the latter to respond to grievances and set the record straight, unambiguously replying to criticisms of his behavior and his art. Instead, Condivi prefaces his introduction to the fresco by noting it has been reproduced in so many prints that a description is superfluous. Vasari follows suit in his account. We are accustomed to thinking of *The Last Judgment* as a lightning rod that garnered the fury of later detractors, but the reverse is also true, especially during Michelangelo's lifetime. Parallel to vilification of the work by a segment of critics lies unabashed praise of *The Last Judgment* as surmounting the loftiest pinnacle attainable by art in the depiction of the human form. Condivi's text is epigrammatic in its tribute: 'Suffice it to say that, apart from the sublime composition of the narrative, we see represented here all that nature can do with the human body.'[17]

Caravaggio would not have concurred; he was determined to develop convincing alternatives in the delineation of the human form based on nature. Yet his approval of at least some aspects of his predecessor's pictorial solutions in *The Last Judgment* is evident in his *Supper at Emmaus* (Plate 23). Caravaggio selected Michelangelo's clean-shaven Christ, which had received unfavorable comments from critics, as the model for the Savior in the painting for Ciriaco Mattei. The predilection for a beardless Christ occurs in Early Christian iconography, a period whose simplicity and proximity to the roots of its beliefs became a beacon for Catholic reformers, particularly in Borromean and Oratorian circles. Mattei actively favored these groups and may have requested or encouraged the audacious representation. The early 17th century was a contentious time in Roman culture; newly founded religious orders militated for their views of how to promulgate Catholicism, with sacred art a weapon in their arsenal. Caravaggio had 'besotted' his adherents (in Baglione's opinion) just as he had attracted vocal opponents and the skirmishes involved not so much the doctrinal messages (decided by his patrons) but how he conveyed them. The unidealized naturalism of Caravaggio's style was coopted by the partisans of his religious art as the visual expression of their reformed approach to Catholicism, in which literal representation of sacred texts, straightforward presentations and an emphasis on the common denominator in humanity were valued above all other factors. The declining suitability of Michelangelo's Renaissance style to the requirements of a certain sector of resurgent Catholicism made Caravaggio's unanticipated, dramatic handling of religious narratives materialize as heaven sent.

Mattei, who as we recall owned the Capitoline *Saint John the Baptist,* received another astonishing example of Caravaggio's capabilities in his rendition of *The Supper at Emmaus,* where Christ reveals his identity to the disciples who have failed to recognize his post-Resurrection presence. Recognition came, as recorded in Luke's gospel (Luke 24: 30–35), as Christ broke and sanctified the bread during a shared supper. Caravaggio combines the revelatory gestures of Christ with the vivid responses of the two disciples. The force of their astonishment is conveyed straight to the viewer by theatrical gestures that appear to threaten physical contact. The disciple wearing a pilgrim's badge, the shell of Saint James, fully extends his arms in a manifestation of openness to the disclosure of Christ's identity. The gesticulation allusively mimes, perhaps unconsciously, the stretched limbs of crucifixion, with outspread fingers that thrust toward the viewer. The startled companion is no less demonstrative and begins to leap from his seat. Upon consideration it is an ineffective action which serves to illustrate his confusion; it also captures a brusque movement that, in the fiction of the painting, will push the chair out into the space where the viewer stands. These strategies of immediacy within the composition are reinforced by other telling details couched in humble everyday references, including a tear in the disciple's jacket, about to be worsened by his jutting elbow and the basket of fruit that precariously straddles the table's edge.

The lighting is as pronounced as the emotions portrayed on the canvas. Strong shadows are cast while the dazzling white of the tablecloth illuminates the central area of the composition; it shares the glow suffusing the figure of Christ. Surprisingly, the sturdily graceful hands of Christ, which establish the fundamental meaning of the scene, are made mysterious by seeming to glimmer from within pale shadows. They are eloquent in their Eucharistic disquisition, one hand reaching out in benediction, the other hovering over the bread. The arrangement is a purposeful modification of Caravaggio's prototype. Michelangelo fashioned his Christ as an irate Judge, whose right hand rises to cast out the wicked while his left beckons to the righteous in a calming gesture. Although this interpretation has been disputed in the specialized literature, Condivi is unequivocal about the characterization:

> Above the angels with their trumpets is the Son of God in His majesty, with His arm and mighty right hand raised in the manner of a man who wrathfully damns the guilty and banishes them from His presence to eternal fire; and, with His left hand held out toward His right side, it seems as if He is gently gathering the righteous to Him.[18]

Caravaggio's Christ retains the fluidity of his model's left hand with fingers poised over the bread, but he transforms the right into an incipient benediction. The Savior's visage is infused with a serenity that very few of Caravaggio's personages have; its riveting equanimity is proper to the glorified state of Christ, although his features remain unidealized.

Depicting this event convincingly through markedly humble types, the bewildered innkeeper and poorly dressed, unprepossessing disciples giving the impression of having been transcribed from life, Caravaggio pushed sacred iconography into a new realm. The device of seating figures around the table, used so successfully in earlier works, was now demanded by the narrative; its comfortable derivation from daily experience is bolstered by the familiar food on the table, a blend of a tavern meal mixed with the Eucharistic symbols of bread, wine and grapes. Similarly, the timeless robes that distinguish Christ are placed in proximity to the rough clothes of the contemporary poor and the slightly finer, but still workaday garb of the host. The immediacy of the presentation with half-length figures, unconventional for paintings of religious history, is further brought to bear on the viewer by the limited compositional space, with the bodies tightly packed and near to us despite the table, unrelieved by any superfluous elements. It must have been an intoxicating, thrilling result for the painter and his audience.

This hypothesis can be gauged by the fact that five years later, under circumstances that could not have been further removed from the first flush of his major successes, Caravaggio expunged the conspicuously daring elements from a second version of the *Supper at Emmaus*, now in the Pinacoteca di Brera, Milan. There is far less emotional outpouring in the later work; rather, a meditative atmosphere permeates a somber darkness, where gravitas replaces excitement, spatial fireworks and still life bravura are eschewed and the references to Michelangelo's beardless Christ with his prodigious gestures have disappeared. Caravaggio had left the privileged Roman environment of intense disquisitions on spiritual truths and the impassioned theological interests of connoisseur benefactors, who were also high-ranking clergy. His art was to be forged under very different circumstances after fleeing the papal city in 1606. But in the brief span of his Roman career, commended and coddled by passionate patrons who commissioned and facilitated paintings that were challenging, yet perfectly suited to his talents, Caravaggio had conquered a vast territory in the terrain of religious art.

The speed of Caravaggio's progress in Rome was extraordinary, both as a painter and as a celebrity. His sensational accomplishment in San Luigi dei Francesi was followed at once by a request from Tiberio Cerasi (1544–1601), a cleric of notable standing in Vatican affairs, the Treasurer General of the Apostolic Camera (Papal Treasury). In September 1600, a mere three months after the paintings in the Contarelli Chapel were opened to the public, Cerasi offered Caravaggio a contract to paint his family chapel in the church of Santa Maria del Popolo. The venerable site was connected to many distinguished families and their artists. Raphael had worked there for the prominent Sienese banker, Agostino Chigi; Pinturicchio decorated a chapel for the Della Rovere family, which as we have seen, was closely associated with the church; and Raphael's epoch-making portrait of Pope Julius II was displayed there above the papal coffin while the remains of the pontiff lay in state. Caravaggio was now to join this select group with paintings planned for the lateral walls of the Cerasi Chapel, adjacent to the main altar of the church.

Monsignor Cerasi envisioned a showcase for the artist's recently acclaimed skills by following the established tactic of a *paragone*, an approach we have seen indulged by other patrons. Not only were Caravaggio's canvasses positioned to flank an altarpiece commissioned from his existing rival, Annibale Carracci, but the legacy of Michelangelo Buonarroti also hovered over the very subjects of Caravaggio's contributions. In 1541, Pope Paul III had requested Michelangelo paint the unusual combination of the *Conversion of Saint Paul* and the *Martyrdom of Saint Peter* on opposite walls in a newly constructed chapel, referred to as the Pauline Chapel in honor of its patron. This chapel lies just beyond the Sistine Chapel in the Vatican complex. The identical pairing was commissioned for the Cerasi Chapel, following the same placement along facing walls; both sets of paintings are large in scale within a relatively restricted viewing area.[19] Caravaggio took up the challenge and triumphed once more. Although, just as in the Contarelli Chapel, it took him more than one attempt to conceive an approach that proved to be truly revolutionary, a worthy successor to Michelangelo's own unconventional interpretations.

Caravaggio continued to eschew the fresco medium and painted his first version of the scenes on cypress panels, approximately 237 × 189 cm (93 5/16 × 74 7/16 in). These at least are the dimensions of the single extant panel of the original pair, preserved in the private Odescalchi Collection, showing the *Conversion of Saint Paul* (Plate 24). We do not know exactly when these panels were completed, although a final payment was made to the artist in November 1601, six months after Tiberio Cerasi's sudden death. It is certain, however, that in 1605, when the installation is documented, Caravaggio had produced a second, entirely different set of paintings stretched on canvas supports. With a return to his accustomed medium came a complete rethinking of the compositions; Caravaggio wrought radical changes that vivified the drama of decisive episodes in the lives of the two saints.

As the first version demonstrates, Caravaggio began with a more discursive approach to the story, packing the pictorial space with a tight knot of intertwined people, plants, armaments of soldiers and a horse in frenzied motion. Even the figure of Christ is interwoven in the mix, having descended from the heavens, arms outstretched with hands reaching down towards the soldier, who has been thrown to the ground. In this crowded grouping Caravaggio conveys the details of the narrative from the Acts of the Apostles, describing how Saul, a militant persecutor of Christians, is struck by blindness as he travels to Damascus (Acts 9:1–20). A thundering voice questions him, 'Why do you persecute me?' Through this miraculous intervention, Saul becomes Paul, embracing the creed of his former enemies; the blindness retreats upon the illumination of his new faith. By either his own choice, or the request of the patron, Caravaggio's figure of Paul echoes that of Michelangelo's work (Fig. 27), particularly in the unusual sprawling posture with torso slightly twisting and half rising. But whatever the requirements, Caravaggio did not follow his model in the idiosyncratic choice of portraying Paul as being converted late in life. The abundant, grizzled beard, painted so conspicuously, is an unexpected feature of Michelangelo's protagonist in the Pauline Chapel, whose advanced age is further attested by the solicitous care with which he is cradled by a younger companion rushing to his aid. The characterization is haunting and so attuned to the burdens of advanced age that weighed on both patron and artist, some have seen the figure as a kind of symbolic self-portrait of its maker. Caravaggio respectfully supplied his saint with a similarly long and bushy beard, but painted it in the ruddy colors of a man just reaching maturity.

Beyond the isolated borrowing of the central figure, however, the Odescalchi panel contains several of Caravaggio's developing ideas, with the action concentrated in the foreground and conveyance of the miraculous through earthly means. These are found, for example, in Paul completely covering his eyes to indicate his blinding and the bright light concentrated on his torso, arising from within to signify the interior illumination that will establish his faith. The arrival

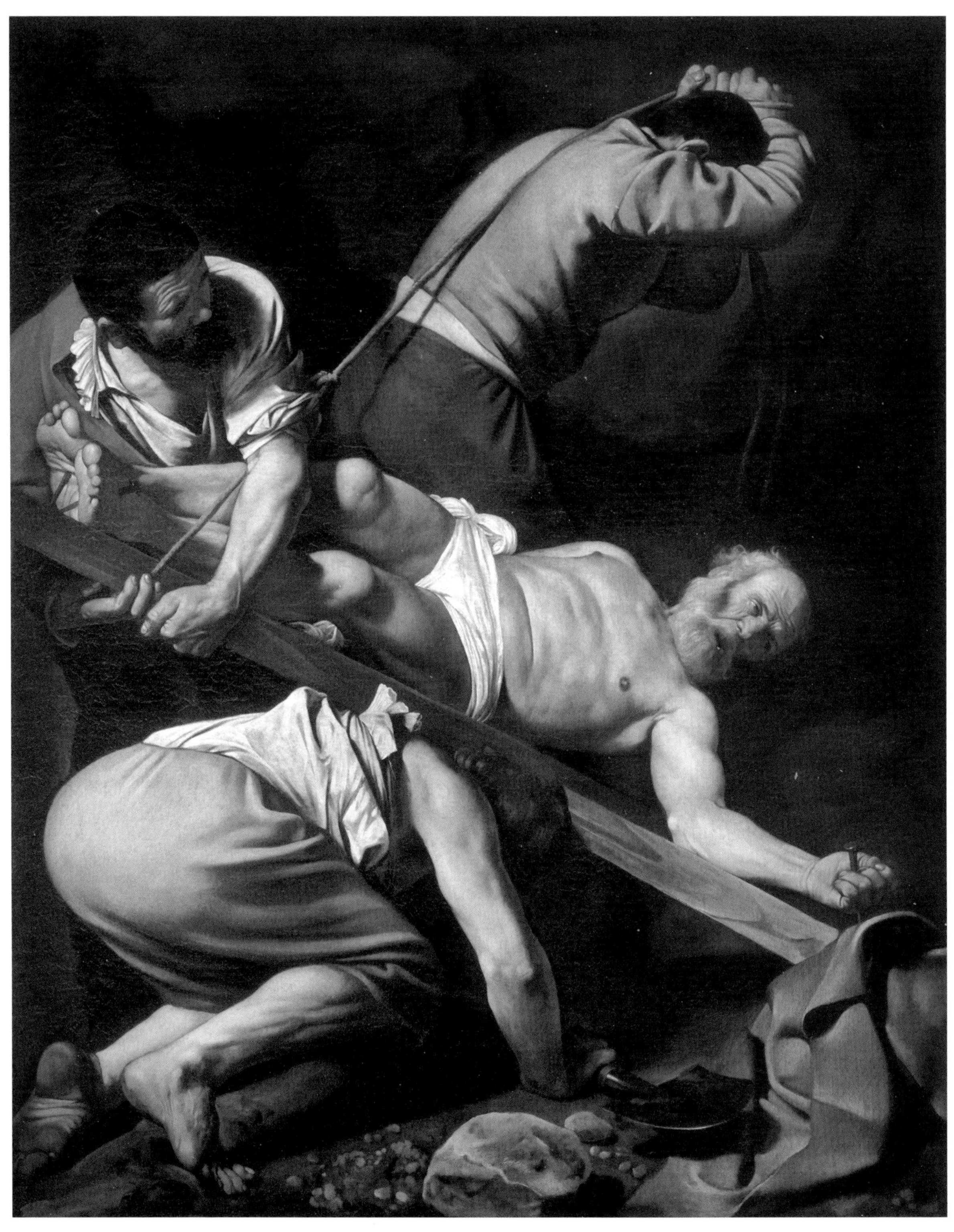

26 Caravaggio, *Crucifixion of St Peter*, 1604–5, oil on canvas, 230 × 175 cm (90 9⁄16 × 68 7⁄8 in), Santa Maria del Popolo, Rome

of the sacred figures also is conveyed in surprisingly concrete terms. Gone is the dazzling shaft of light that envelops Michelangelo's mighty figure of Christ, reverberating along his arm on a direct path to the ground on which Saul has collapsed. In contrast, Caravaggio's Christ, wrapped in a dark, heavy mantle, has descended from his celestial home literally on the dense wings of his angel. The two foreshortened figures form an indivisible pairing, bound together by an angelic arm clasping Christ's torso, with a grip gaining leverage from the bough of a tree that appears to impede their forward motion. Saul is straddled by a companion-in-arms who raises lance and shield against the heavenly onslaught, while falling back on another soldier cowering against his own shield, with gauntlet hovering over his head for further protection. This very physical description of divine impact, while furthering Caravaggio's explorations of translating sacred stories into human terms, was not enough to satisfy the artist.

We do not know if the panel would have been found acceptable by the original patron, who may or may not have seen the completed version prior to his death. Nor, without the help of relevant documentation, can we say if four years passed from the time of payment without the heirs demanding the completed paintings or exacting new ones from the artist. We are left with the material evidence showing us only that Caravaggio drastically re-thought his commission and pushed his handling of the narrative components to an unforeseen level of mastery by the time the paintings were finally installed on 1 May 1605. The final versions are as shocking in their design as they are effective.

Caravaggio's second treatment of the conversion of Saint Paul is unprecedented; it communicates the story on a visceral level, encapsulating the text into a totally internalized experience of the protagonist (Plate 25). The militant Saul, about to be transformed into Paul, lies on the ground flooded by light that reflects off his torso onto his face and uplifted arms. The muscled torso rests inertly within the torrent of folds formed by the cloak beneath him. The details of his brightly colored military costume and accessories fill the entire foreground, whose cramped space presents a drastically foreshortened body, with the figure's head projected just at the edge of the pictorial space. This was calculated for maximum impact in the actual space of the chapel, which is constricted and the fixed placement of the canvas sets the painted head nearly on a collision course with that of the viewer. We become witnesses across the centuries to the enlightenment of the former antagonist, the total focus of a representation that provides neither textual details nor elaborate iconographies. The devout must bring the story with them; the image is an invitation to meditate on the mystery of salvation symbolized by the figure of Paul. The audacious choice to fill two-thirds of the canvas with the shining flank of the horse and the coarse corporeality of its handler forfeits all other potentially distracting details and brings the event down to earth with a visual thud no less resounding than Paul's supine contact with the ground. Caravaggio has managed to convey an intangible spiritual transformation through a massing of palpable forms.

The radical minimalization of the unessential is even more pronounced in the scene Caravaggio dedicated to *The Crucifixion of Saint Peter* (Fig. 26). The martyrdom of Catholicism's first pope is reduced to a close-up view of Peter's resisting body impaled on a cross and the exertions required of three laborers to elevate the gibbet with its human burden. While nothing remains to inform us about Caravaggio's initial design for the panel treating this subject, the painting that stands in Santa Maria del Popolo demonstrates the enduring influence Michelangelo had on Caravaggio. The Pauline fresco treating *The Crucifixion of Saint Peter* (Plate 26) is a stunning conception of a scene not frequently illustrated in Renaissance art. Despite the vast amount of wall space to be covered (approximately 20 × 21 ft), the composition thrusts the cross aggressively toward the viewer, set on a diagonal presenting a full extension of the impressively muscular body of the elderly saint. As the cross rises and begins to orient Peter head downwards, he awkwardly jerks his head

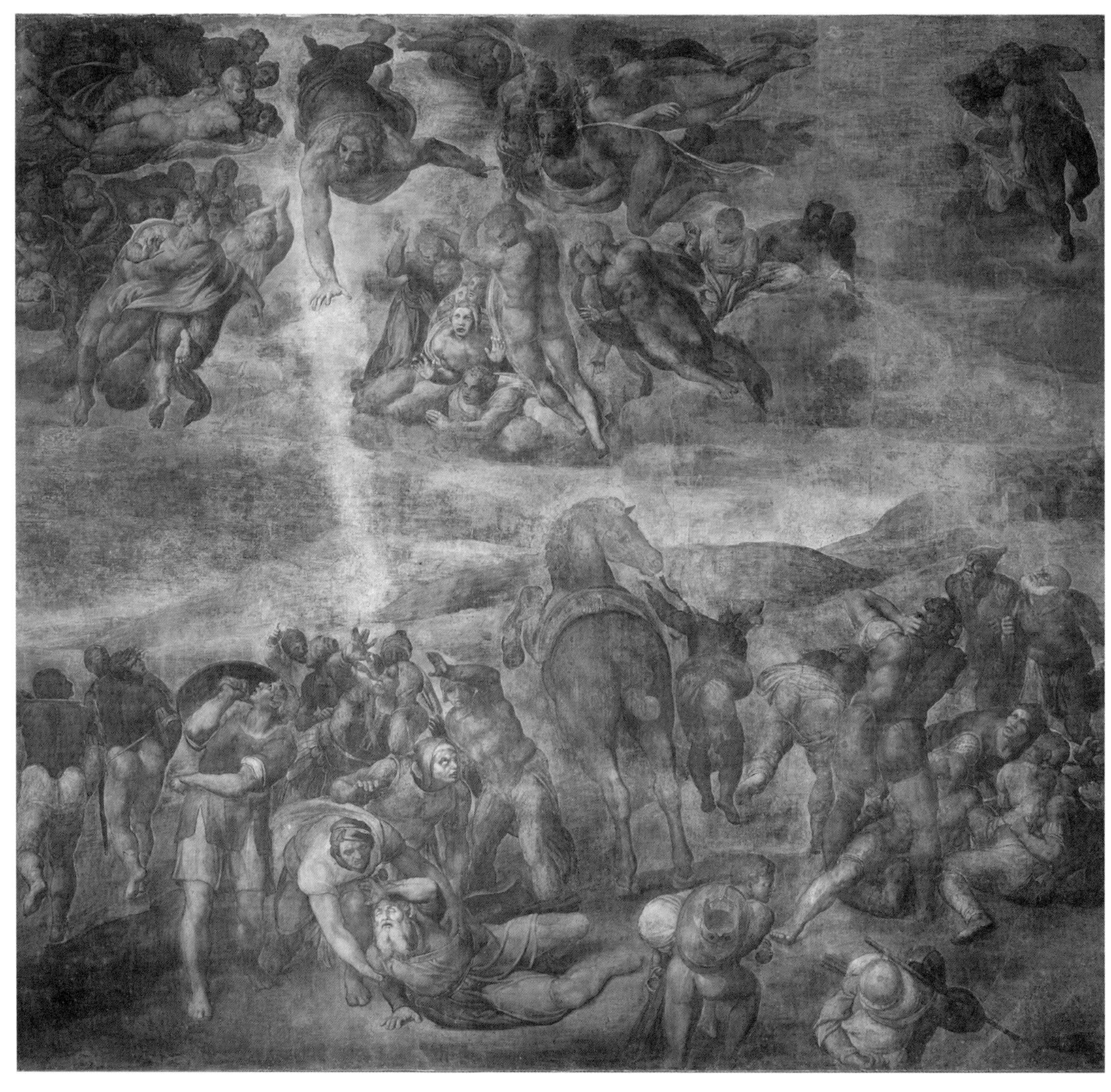

27 Michelangelo, *The Conversion of Saint Paul*, 1542–45, fresco, 625 × 661 cm (246 1/16 × 260¼ in), Pauline Chapel, Vatican, Rome

out pugnaciously, darting a rancorous glare toward the viewer. He is not reacting against the upending of the cross, since texts explain that he demanded this additional humiliation to differentiate his execution from imitating too closely the crucifixion of Christ. Whether the source of his anger is the physical torment, the irrevocable ending of his ministry, or his human despair at his impending death, it is an unexpected characterization and hits like a punch. Peter's rage projects directly at the viewer who would meet it inescapably in the confined space of the chapel.

While we have no certainty that Caravaggio experienced Michelangelo's volatile Saint Peter at first hand on the wall of the Pauline Chapel, which has always had a restricted audience, Cerasi's elite Vatican position would have enabled the artist to gain admission. The results argue that he did. Memory of the original effect could then have been easily buttressed by consulting print versions of the frescoes issued shortly after completion.[20] The striking impetus to Caravaggio's imagination is evident in his inspired re-imagining of Michelangelo's forceful interpretation of Saint Peter, which pushed him to reinvent the motif, intensifying the dramatic force with his distinctive stylistic vocabulary.

Caravaggio's interaction with Michelangelo's composition went beyond the surprising portrayal of the saint.[21] In addition to adopting Peter's angry countenance, the younger artist responded to the motif of toil that Michelangelo employs as an ancillary compositional device. In the Pauline fresco, the labor of lifting the cross bearing the figure gives cohesion to the focal grouping within the scene. Numerous helpers struggle to drag the cross into a hole in the center of the foreground, whose preparation is only just being completed by a bending figure still hollowing out the interior. Tools lie on the ground as symbols of the task. In the Cerasi Chapel, in contrast, Caravaggio retains only the tip of the digger's spade and turns his crouching form around so that we are confronted by his rump and bare, filthy feet. He literally 'puts his back into his work', aiding two other laborers who are, with considerable struggle, hefting the weight upwards. Taking Michelangelo's minor motif as his starting point, Caravaggio concentrates on the physical effort required to raise the cross and magnifies it into the controlling concept of his representation to create a wholly unexpected, unorthodox interpretation.

Caravaggio situates the action uncomfortably close to the observer, causing an even more intense confrontation with the torment of the glowering martyr than does Michelangelo's prototype; it shows us with an increased emphasis the fatigue involved in carrying out the sentence of death. Caravaggio presents the momentous execution as an iteration of lowly details: the strain of the rope across the shoulders of the topmost figure, whose shirt rides up in the process; the exaggeratedly furrowed brow of a figure who seems to shout an order to hoist, despite his mouth being obscured in shadow; his uncomfortably positioned hands with veins bulging; the crumpled shirt of the crouching man and the rippling skin on his leg as he strives to push upwards.

Michelangelo's magisterial composition amasses and controls half a dozen groups of figures that fill the enormous dimensions of the Pauline Chapel wall, skillfully varying their types and actions to provide an internal cohesion for each cluster of witnesses to the barbarous event. Caravaggio took an entirely different route in order to monumentalize the scene for the much more modest span of the Cerasi family chapel. He successfully transformed Michelangelo's audacious conception from a universal, heroic saga into a brutal tale of local murder. With this transmutation, Caravaggio forged an image that spoke forcefully to reforming factions within the Church. His art was valued by those newly concerned with fostering representations of sacred texts and spiritual subjects that were calculated to shatter the emotions rather than beguile the intellect. Caravaggio achieved this with an uncluttered staging performed by people who look real enough to have walked into the church from the Roman streets outside.

5

Renaissance Reckoning in Portraits and Self-Portraits of the Two Michelangelos

The testimony of portraiture affords a path of inquiry into the shaping and transmission of public personas. While just as 'constructed' as any other artistic vehicle, portraiture and self-portraiture are eloquent articulations of opinion. The surviving portraits of Michelangelo and Caravaggio provide us with the keen observations of their contemporaries, immediate in their impact but enigmatically layered in meaning. The two artists' self-portraits describe, often in a covert manner, how they viewed themselves and their situations. In the extant corpus of their works, neither of the two Michelangelos has left an independent transcription of his features; each included his face within the setting of larger narratives, imparting a meaning to his presence that outweighs a mere record of his appearance.

Did either of the two Michelangelos ever supply a personal directive to the viewer, indicating his estimation of his own work, imparting an interpretive key? The surprising answer is that they both did so once, in the same way, with similar intention. In a single instance each artist emblematically signed his work, Michelangelo at the start of his career and Caravaggio at the end. The fundamental reason – shared across time, but in different places and under circumstances poles apart – was a particular pride in the work signed. Common to both cases is the desire to proclaim authorship in a public manner, to tie the maker indivisibly to its invention and fabrication and to document the identity of the artist in connection to a major, monumental achievement.

Michelangelo signed his name on the strap on Mary's garment in the Saint Peter *Pietà* (Plate 4 and Plate 27). Vasari, as we recall, embroidered an anecdote, resonant with amusing insinuations, around the fact. Yet the unenhanced report in his first version of the artist's biography reveals the uncomplicated impetus: Because of the 'love and the labor' he put into it, Michelangelo was satisfied with the work and well pleased *with himself* for having made it.[1] I emphasize the element of self-congratulation, because it is often disregarded in English translations. The patterns of Michelangelo's creative life tell us how rare this was. He was often in despair about his work and even more often dissatisfied with himself; but upon completing the stupendous feat of carving the *Pietà*, Michelangelo indulged an auto-celebration. His stunning interpretation of a traditional motif and demonstration of the highest level of virtuosity in carving and finishing the stone to a silken surface, makes the young artist's pride in his accomplishment understandable. It did astound his contemporaries. Vasari sings its praises equally in both editions:

> To this work let no sculptor, however rare a craftsman, ever think to be able to approach in design or in grace, or ever to be able with all the pains in the world to attain to such delicacy and smoothness or to perforate the marble with such art as Michelagnolo did therein, for in it may be seen all the power and worth of art.[2]

Vasari might be accused of hyperbole, until we look back at comparable sculpture in Rome just before 1500; Michelangelo's accomplishment was breathtaking and the impact has not been diminished by time. What is generally not considered, despite its crucial relation to the signature, is that by creating an unquestionably paramount sculpture, Michelangelo was fulfilling the precise terms of his contract. It was negotiated by his Roman friend and supporter Jacopo Galli, who brokered several commissions for the artist. The contract drawn up by Galli pledges that Michelangelo 'will make the said work within one year, and it will be the most beautiful work in marble that may be found today in Rome, and that no master-sculptor working today could make it'.[3] He was so confident of his young protégé's limitless ability that Galli guaranteed results: he would personally reimburse the client's outlay if there were any question of whether the stipulations had been met. The patron of the sculpture was illustrious and discerning: the French Cardinal Jean de Bilhères, who was eager to leave a singular legacy for Rome in the Chapel of the French Kings connected to Saint Peter's Basilica. He wanted the installation to coincide with the jubilee year of 1500, to be seen by the crowds of the French faithful who would make the pilgrimage to the papal city. It is, incidentally, an intriguing parallel to Caravaggio's first public Roman commission in San Luigi dei Francesi, exactly 100 years later, timed to receive the influx of French Catholics during the jubilee year of 1600.

The signature confirms the successful conclusion according to the terms of the contract and no one disagreed. Michelangelo, however, never one to be tempted by unrestricted vainglory, qualified his accomplishment. The phrase he inscribed formally in Latin is 'MICHAEL.A¯GELVS.BONAROTVS.FLORENT. FACIEBA', meaning 'Michelangelo Buonarroti the Florentine was making'. The unexpected 'imperfect' form of the verb negates the sense of completion of the simple past tense ('made'), indicating instead 'making over a period of time'. The choice was not only deliberate, but reprised a classical paradigm. Pliny's *Natural History* is once again the source, recording that the most renowned Greek painters and sculptors signed their works as a declaration that no work of art, no matter how marvelous, was ever truly finished. The practice of truncation that Pliny cites is unfortunately usually followed when quoting him.[4] The complete text makes it clear that Pliny posits the premise in the Preface to his volumes as a preemptive strike against any shortcomings eventually perceived in his accounts:

> I should like to be accepted on the lines of those founders of painting and sculpture who, as you will find in these volumes, used to inscribe their finished works, even the masterpieces which we can never be tired of admiring, with a provisional title such as Worked on by Apelles or Polyclitus, as though art was always a thing in process and not completed, so that when faced by the vagaries of criticism the artist might have left him a line of retreat to indulgence, by implying that he intended, if not interrupted, to correct any defect noted.[5]

An excerpt is usually quoted to underscore the fallibility of human creation. However, the passage goes on to make a further point, crucial to the reception of the work: it provides the artist with a rebuttal to future critics. Michelangelo was undoubtedly clever enough to apply Pliny's complete, two-pronged exposition to his *Pietà*, philosophically admitting to human limitation, while strategically putting all pundits on alert that he would have attended to their objections, had he only been given the time.

Michelangelo not only emulated his forerunners, but as always when citing his ancient exemplars, devised a way to outdo them. He deliberately carved the word *faciebat* without the final 't', feigning an unanticipated lack of space on the strap of Mary's garment. In reality, the 'accident' was premediated. The incomplete spelling not only refers to, but actually demonstrates, the concept of incompletion taken from Pliny, most likely acquired by way of Poliziano's tutelage.[6] Even a sculpture with a flawless, gleaming surface and figures of impeccable anatomy stops short of its ultimate realization. The signature has it both ways; the artist takes due credit and announces his creation at the same time that he demurs about the ultimate completion of human fabrication. This also furnishes him with an implied line of defense against critics.

Caravaggio was not troubled by similar musings. He proudly, if somewhat disquietingly, signed the great work painted in Malta in 1608, the *Beheading of Saint John the Baptist*.[7] It was placed in the Oratory of San Giovanni Decollato (commemorating the martyrdom by decapitation of Saint John the Baptist) to announce Caravaggio's investiture as a Knight of the Order. The artist's pride was due as much to his new status as to his completion of the most monumental painting of his career. It was most likely created as his offering to the Order upon entry. The subject is thus directly tied to the occasion of the painting's completion and its location, but it also forms an eerie connection to other representations of decapitation in the painter's oeuvre, including the biblical scenes of Judith slaying Holofernes and David with the severed head of Goliath. Popular throughout the 16th and 17th centuries, the theme received a new impetus with the desire for graphic renditions of biblical heroism and Christian martyrdom favored by the Counter-Reformation church. The violence and murder contained in the stories, however, would have had profound resonance for Caravaggio and he seems to have used these subjects, especially toward the end of his life, for personal meditation as well as to fulfill his audience's expectations. The signature on the *Beheading* is indeed an intimate reflection of the artist (detail, Plate 30).

The words are more abbreviated than in Michelangelo's *Pietà* signature, but placed just as surprisingly and even more conspicuously. We find Caravaggio's ominous inscription 'f. Michel An' at the bottom of the canvas in the center foreground, the letters flowing from a pool of blood spurting from the martyr's gashed neck. The sanguinary color is a counterpoint to the bright red of John's mantle overlying an animal skin, the same attributes found in Caravaggio's earlier representations of the Baptist. Now, however, the artist's personal relation to the Saint takes on special meaning as a Knight in the Order dedicated to his devotion. It is worth pondering if the truncated signature is also a reminiscence of an artistic forerunner, Buonarroti's missing 't' of *faciebat*. The ambiguity of the small 'f' initiating Caravaggio's inscription has been interpreted by some as standing for *fecit*; the sole letter could easily suggest this, or indeed *faciebat*, as well as *frate*, Caravaggio's appellation as a knight. It should be kept in mind that *frate* [brother] is more commonly shortened to *fra*, indicating an intentional variation on the part of the artist. Why not write out 'Fra', especially as the title is so meaningful in the context of both the image and the signature? Or, why not place the 'f' after the name, in the conventional format for *fecit*? Arguably because the artist wanted to suggest both meanings by using only the shared letter.

Caravaggio's choice to precede his name with the ambiguous 'f' is not the only puzzle. Why stop with a partial signature when there is plenty of space in the foreground to write out his name in full? The explanation may well be that Michelangelo Merisi continued to recall his predecessor, especially in a moment of triumph and conceived an *imitatio* of

Michelangelo's performance of the disappearing letter in the single signature of his own career. Further, in this exceptional case, Caravaggio announced himself simply as 'Michel Angelo'. Just as Buonarroti left his '*faciebat*' incomplete, Caravaggio's letters stop at the 'n' of Angelo, trailing off in a smear of blood, outdoing his model both in brevity and ferocity. We know that the highly visible inscription confused a French traveler enough to mistake one Michelangelo for the other. Nicolas Bénard recorded in his diary of 1616 having seen 'a most excellent work by the hand of the late Michel-Angelo as attested by his signature'; he believed it to be the Florentine. It seems the young Parisian's hosts allowed the ambiguity to pass, a mere eight years after the scandal of Caravaggio's flight.[8]

Whether or not the multiple valance was intended, the 'f' preceding Caravaggio's name can assuredly be read as *frate*, a specific rank in the echelon of the Order of Saint John. The immense importance of the title may not be immediately appreciated by modern viewers; for Caravaggio it was hard won and of enormous significance. It was, by a long mark, the closest he could hope to arrive at a social status approaching nobility. The Order was rigorously exclusive; the Grand Master had to obtain special permission to enroll Caravaggio, not only because of his criminal record as we have noted, but also because his investiture involved the use of a non-noble category, 'the habit of Magistral Obedience', which de Wignacourt himself had suspended four years previously.[9] Even harder for us to evaluate, and ultimately impossible to understand, is the spiritual significance that being a member of the Order had for the artist. In his life of contrasts, Caravaggio's deepest religious convictions remain unknowable, attested only by the conviction with which he painted religious subjects. For all these reasons, Caravaggio's signed proclamation is celebrative rather than swaggering. Its appearance in blood is macabre, yet beyond the ostensible gore, it is a symbolic sharing in John's martyrdom, in the 'baptism of blood' by which one's sins can be cleansed.[10]

It is the ultimate tragedy of Caravaggio's life that he was unable to sustain the weight of observing the Order's strictly enforced rules.[11] Almost immediately after having received his habit, Caravaggio transgressed through involvement in a brawl to the damage of a high-ranking, aristocratic Knight. For this he was imprisoned and might have been penalized by temporary suspension or fine, as happened to several others involved. However, Caravaggio turned this setback into an irrevocable crime by escaping from prison and leaving Malta without authorization. This unsanctioned departure from the Knights of Malta, as with all military organizations, was considered unpardonable. Caravaggio was immediately defrocked and the sorrowful ceremony took place in the Oratory beneath the imposing image of the martyrdom of Saint John displaying Brother Michel Angelo's once triumphant signature, now disgraced, yet not erased.

We have seen that in literary sources Michelangelo Buonarroti was apostrophized as 'divine' from an early date and his art hailed as miraculous. While Caravaggio's violent conduct never allowed for this play on an angelic name, he was quickly and consistently praised as an eminent painter, starting in Rome from at least 1600 when his contract for the Cerasi Chapel referred to Caravaggio as *egregius in Urbe pictor*. Another very early comment, written in 1603 by the Netherlandish artist Karel van Mander, opens without equivocation: 'There is also a certain Michael Angelo of Caravaggio who is doing remarkable things in Rome.'[12] Further along in the text the author continues to marvel: 'Already this Michael Angelo has achieved with his works great repute, honor and a name.' A perceptive artist, van Mander analyzes Caravaggio's commitment to copying nature, musing on the benefits and challenges presented by this method. A strict opposition is made between the merits of his art and the problematic comportment of the artist, proclaiming sententiously (if prophetically) that 'Mars and Minerva have never been the best of friends.' Three years before Caravaggio killed a man, van Mander warned that fighting and creating were incompatible.

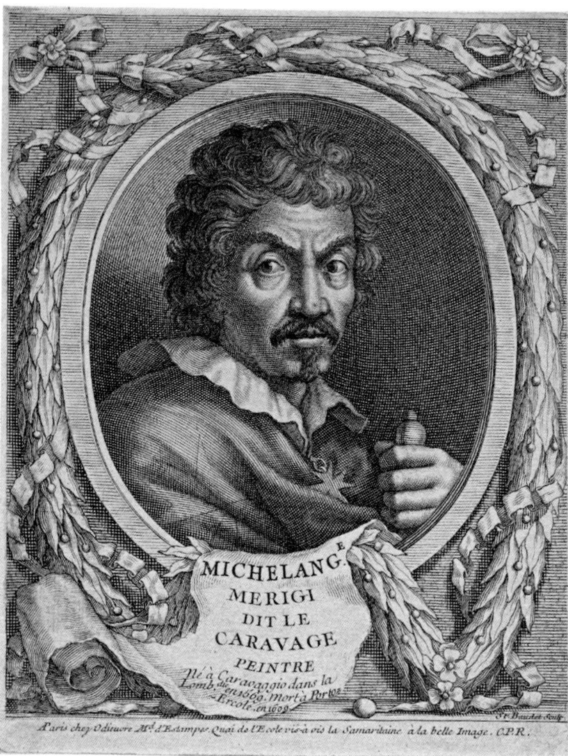

28 Etienne Baudet, *Portrait of Michelangelo Merisi da Caravaggio*, etching with line engraving, 16.7 × 12.7 cm (6 9/16 × 5 in), The State Hermitage Museum, St Petersburg

At the time of writing, Caravaggio had not yet become a murderer; perhaps this permitted van Mander to end his account by giving Caravaggio's art the highest praise: 'as regards his way of painting, it is such that it is very pleasing in an exceedingly handsome manner, an example for our young artists to follow'. After 1606 it proved impossible for biographers to separate Caravaggio's art from his life and his criminal behavior colored even the most serious accounts.

A major voice during the second half of the 17th century, Giovanni Pietro Bellori indulged invective against both Caravaggio's art and his person, although his biography also includes passages of reasoned assessments and appreciation for the strengths of Caravaggio's style. Far beyond Bellori's passionate upholding of classicism, a clearly personal distaste for Caravaggio's behavior pushed the writer into lapses of judgment that overshadow his more cogent arguments. Bellori denigrates Caravaggio's art through an attack on his person, making the artist's forceful dark palette a distorted mirror image of his physical traits:

> Caravaggio's ways [of painting] went along with his physiognomy and appearance; he had a dark [*fosco*] complexion and dark [*foschi*] eyes, and his eyebrows and hair were black; this coloring was naturally reflected in his paintings. His first manner, sweet and pure in color, was his best, and he achieved a supreme level of merit in it, and showed himself to be, with great praise, a most excellent Lombard colorist. But afterward, driven by his own temperament, he retreated to the dark manner which, similarly, is disturbed and contentious.[13]

This passage is disturbing on every level, describing Caravaggio's dark coloring in such a way that it evokes evil. Rather than the more straightforward *scuro*, Bellori uses the word *fosco* for the artist's skin and eyes, which conjures a surly and menacing quality, putting both the artist and his work in a bad light. He then sets the shady person and his shadowy palette in opposition to a 'sweet and pure' precedent. The insidious use of the word 'naturally' further corrupts the statement, disguising the author's prejudice as a phenomenon occurring in nature rather than a calculated insult. Since images give visual form to ideas, it is not surprising that a portrait conforming to Bellori's presentation of the artist's character presides at the opening of the biography in the 1672 edition of *Le vite de' pittori, scultori e architetti moderni* (Fig. 28). The subject's face is modeled in such way as to make an unpleasant contrast between the brightness of the forehead and darkness of the cheeks and chin; the eyebrows arch in exaggerated angles; the mouth is set in a graceless pout. In sum, the impression of a villain is rendered, reinforced by lines scored on the forehead and under the eyes, bolstered by the turbulent movement of hair and garments. The characterization is completed by the discreet but telling detail of the artist's fist wrapped around a sword hilt – no longer the property of a gentleman, but the weapon of an assassin. Similarly, the medallion of the Maltese cross hanging from under his collar, almost obscured by shadows and folds, is transformed from being a sign of Caravaggio's ascendance to knighthood into the stigma of having been defrocked from the noble Order of Saint John.

Fortunately, the physiognomic terms of Bellori's disparagement have not been followed by later critics. But if the engraving delineates a face to match Bellori's distaste, it was most likely refashioned from a more sympathetic image of Caravaggio drawn by Ottavio Leoni (1578–1635). Leoni's portrait (Chapter 1, Plate 2) is particularly valuable since it stands alone as the one extant record of Caravaggio's appearance that could have been the result of personal acquaintance. Rendered in graphite, red chalk and white gesso on blue paper, the skillful likeness conveys its subject's concentration, alertness and wariness. It is the basis for all the portraits of Caravaggio that followed, beginning with a less compelling version by Leoni himself. The second of Leoni's portraits was perhaps made in commemoration after the artist's death, since his features are thinner and more haggard and a Maltese cross has been added to his mantle.[14] The authority of the colored portrait, in addition to its visual impact, comes from its placement in a series of the most notable personages in early 17th-century Rome carried out by Leoni, who was in a position to know. He was attached for a time to the household of Cardinal Del Monte and might have known Caravaggio from that connection. But the lack of other first-hand documentation of Caravaggio's appearance and demeanor defies expectation and explanation, especially given Caravaggio's fame and notoriety, the clout of his style and the reputed importance of portraiture in his own output. Despite his contentious behavior and eventual outlaw status, it would seem likely for those artists who admired his work and imitated it to have memorialized him in some way. However, if portraits from life were made, none apart from Leoni's (and the variations in paint and prints based on it) have come down to us.

Caravaggio filled the gap by giving us a number of images of himself. They appear in his paintings in various ways and the practice has caused numerous faces to be singled out as self-portraits, some more convincing than others.[15] A few are indisputably the artist's image, introduced seamlessly into several compositions; in these cases, their relation to the painted narrative is always significant. In other less conclusive instances, the artist might well have used his own features as a basis for a figure in lieu of a model, but with slight alterations that signal us not to read the image as autobiographical.

This is arguably the case with the *Saint Francis in Meditation*. There are two known versions, of which the one in the Palazzo Barberini is the original (Fig. 29). The painting is a haunting presentation of Francis rapt in prayer as he contemplates a skull. His face is presented at an angle to the pictorial surface, so that both the face and entire right side of the saint are suffused with a bright light against the prevailing darkness. The dark, close-cropped hair and beard recall those of the artist, as does the nose with its strong line etched down toward the mouth. The eyes are veiled in their contemplation, but their shape and brows do not conform to those of Caravaggio's other portraits, nor does the more pronounced elongation of the face. The painting dates to around 1606; recent research suggests it may have been completed when Caravaggio first fled Rome in May of that year and was hiding nearby under the protection of the Colonna.[16] Given what we know of Caravaggio's practices, it is a reasonable assumption that he would use himself as a model, along with painting from memory, under these circumstances. A study that has further clarified the artist's working method posits his painting strictly *dal vivo* [from life]

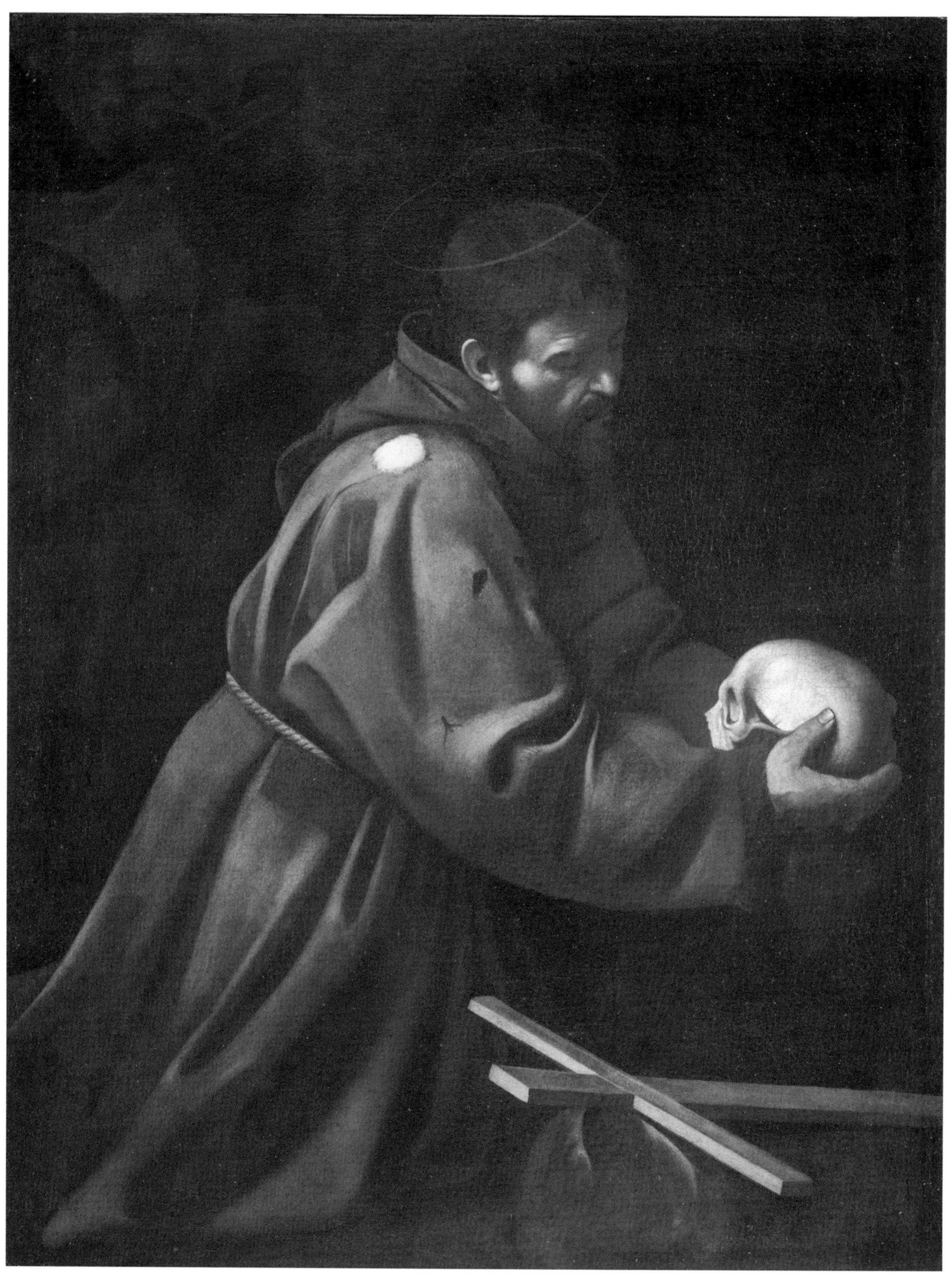

29 Caravaggio, *Saint Francis in Meditation*, *c*.1606–7, oil on canvas, 123 × 92.5 cm (48 7/16 × 36 7/16 in), Galleria Nazionale d'Arte Antica, Palazzo Barberini, Rome

as a first step in his compositions and then painting a second, more finished layer, where modifications were made.[17] This might well account for some of the more dubious 'self-portraits', which began with study from a mirror and ended with changes when the artist did not want to paint himself as a participant in the narrative.

Caravaggio presented himself most dramatically and identifiably in his first major public commission, *The Martyrdom of Saint Matthew* (Fig. 30, detail of Plate 21; Chapter 4). We see the artist running in the background, moving toward the engulfing darkness, fleeing the ensuing chaos as Matthew is attacked. His face is brightly lit, but even brighter is the light that falls on his naked left hip, haunch and leg, not covered by the brown cape he has thrown around his torso. This seldom remarked detail tells us that the artist has painted himself into the story as one of the proselytes awaiting baptism. Showing himself as terrified, he hastily departs with all the others who are too frightened to give aid to the victim. Yet he looks backwards with a conflicted expression of deep concern and regret.

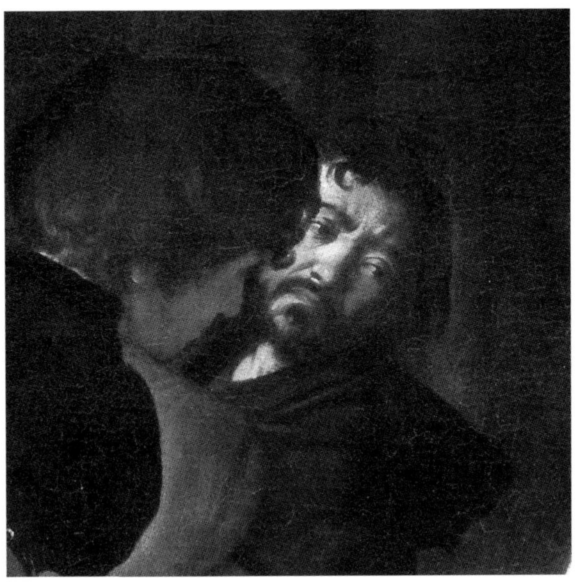

30 Caravaggio, self-portrait, detail, *The Martyrdom of Saint Matthew*, 1599–1600, oil on canvas, 323 × 343 cm (127 3/16 × 135 1/16 in), Contarelli Chapel, San Luigi dei Francesi, Rome

The trepidation of the character in the drama played by Caravaggio calls for a pronounced frown, heavy-lidded, half-closed eyes and a grimace pushing his brow into furrows. These are features that also connote melancholy according to physiognomic conventions, endowing Caravaggio's features with the attributes of the melancholic creator, burdened by lofty thoughts that are unrealizable. As we will see, this was a characterization given to Michelangelo and I believe it influenced Caravaggio in this particular portrait, proudly incorporated into a major work. He shared a similar coloring and wore his dark hair and beard short, a constant feature in likenesses of Michelangelo. If the allusion was intentional, it remains a subtle suggestion, whereas painting himself into the composition as a participant in the sacred history was deliberate and functions at a more complex level of ideation.

Renaissance artists developed the practice of including their portraits within narrative scenes and it proves to have captured the audience, involving them in a shared game of detection. The personalized additions most often are akin to a signature, with recognizable faces simply attesting to the identity of the work's maker. In religious stories, however, a self-portrait might become a prayer, placing the artist in a group of believers, or as a witness to salvation history. The self-image can become more complex if we are meant to see the artist disguised as an actual participant in the sacred story, which then alludes to private aspirations through emulation of the character being impersonated. Michelangelo was reticent about revealing himself explicitly in his art and incorporated disguised self-portraits, as we will see, in only a few instances. Caravaggio, in contrast, showed a marked interest in this convention and as we have come to expect from him, in a few instances gave the custom an innovative twist. He does not use his own features simply to inhabit the role of a saint or historical personage, but

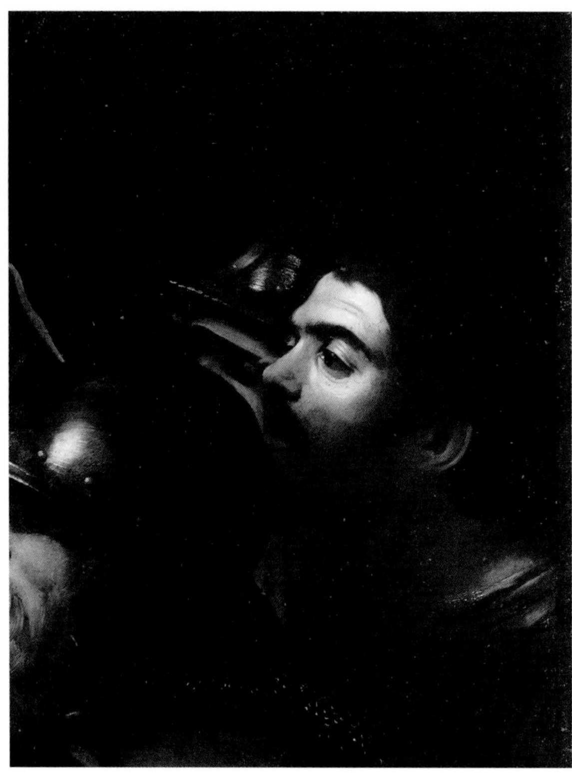

31 Caravaggio, self-portrait, detail, *The Taking of Christ*, 1602, oil on canvas, 133.5 × 169.5 cm (52 9/16 × 66¾ in), National Gallery of Ireland, Dublin

thinks himself into the scenario of his own painting. He envisions the sacred story, invents its actions and imagines himself taking part in a specific way. It is, perhaps, an extension of his creed to paint from life, an approach that encouraged him to use his own life as part of the reckoning. It is not a common component in 17th-century art.

This highly personalized approach is also found in *The Taking of Christ* (detail, Fig. 31) from 1602, not long after the completion of *The Martyrdom of Saint Matthew*. Caravaggio places his likeness at the extreme right of the composition, reacting to the skirmish with an intense concentration and open mouth, as though utterly disconcerted by what he sees happening. In the crowded group of seven men only the countenance of Christ is as luminous as the self-portrait. Light floods Caravaggio's face from a lantern held aloft, partially hidden by one of the soldier's helmets. The conception is literally dazzling. The artist's brush elucidates the scene, so that his depiction may enlighten the viewer; within the story of the painting, the artist portrays himself as the bringer of light, making certain that the dark deed of Judas is revealed to all. By playing a part in an enactment of the passion of Christ, Caravaggio attests to his role as an artist, one who commits his skill to the service of his religion, painting from life to give life to sacred history.

Several years later, Caravaggio added a close variation of this self-portrait to one of his final paintings, *The Martyrdom of Saint Ursula* (Banca Intesa Sanpaolo Collection, Palazzo Zevallos Stigliano, Naples). Carried out as a commission from the Genoese aristocrat Marcantonio Doria while Caravaggio was in Naples after his flight from Malta, the scene is a crowded composition of half-length figures, recalling the *Taking of Christ*. But on this occasion Caravaggio does not conceive of himself as a protagonist; rather, he imagines himself struggling to observe the action, despite being in proximity to it, gaping in an even more pronounced way at the cruelty he strains to witness. Only his head is visible, emerging from darkness behind the saint as she bends to inspect her fatal wound. Caravaggio's features are fully illuminated once more, but he is not the source of light as in the earlier painting. In this case, the insertion of Caravaggio's semblance acts to reinforce his authorship of the martyrdom's commemoration in the manner of a signature. The canvas bears testimony to Ursula's faith and her fate, just as his appearance within the scene indicates his imaginative witnessing of the sacred event. In this frantic moment toward the end of Caravaggio's life, the faces of all the figures tend to be generalized types that have appeared frequently in his previous paintings, suggesting inspiration from memory rather than models. His repetition of an earlier self-portrait may well have been based on pictorial recollection as much as a mirrored reflection, especially if the image had been painted after Caravaggio's face was lacerated in an ambush while leaving a Neapolitan tavern, which according to one contemporary, rendered him unrecognizable.

It is distressing to think of this anguished climax to a career begun with such promise in Rome just a decade-and-a-half earlier. We should recall the playful and prickly self-image as Bacchus that the artist created at the start of his Roman years (Chapter 2; Plate 8). Despite the camouflage of costume and pallor, it presents a convincing representation of Caravaggio's features, along with an entertaining rumination on the qualities of the deity of wine. We have seen how Bacchus, most impressively embodied in Michelangelo's sculpture (Chapter 2; Plate 6), was a focal point for Renaissance neoplatonism as a symbol of the spirit-enhancing 'divine frenzy', which unleashed creativity. By presenting himself in the guise of Bacchus almost immediately upon arriving in Rome, Caravaggio claimed the god as a tutelary deity for himself and his art, but with a new meaning. His transgressive treatment of the *Bacchino malato* de-emphasizes the concept of transcendent inebriation and replaces it with the all-too-human effects of over-indulgence in drink. Allusions to decidedly carnal Bacchic reveling replace spiritual revelation; if a frenzy ensues, the results are more likely to be ignominious than ingenious.

Or so the most obvious reading of the *Bacchino malato* might propose. From the outset, Caravaggio played with the artistic patrimony he inherited from his Milanese training under Simone Peterzano. In that sophisticated workshop, Caravaggio would have been aware of the Renaissance traditions of Bacchic imagery and its derivation from the classical canon.[18] It is not much of a stretch to imagine his willful allusion to the commonly known proverb cited by Pliny '*in vino veritas*' [in wine there is truth] and his decision that his Bacchus, god of creativity, would stand for the truth found in painting from nature.[19] Caravaggio's teasing perception of himself in relation to the god of wine

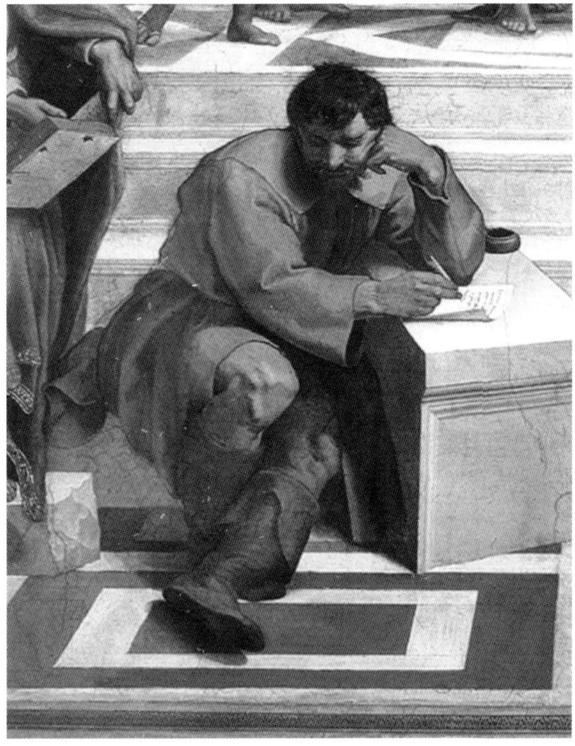

32 Raphael, Michelangelo as Heraclitus, detail, *School of Athens*, 1509, fresco, width at base 770 cm (303 ⅓ in), Stanza della Segnatura, Vatican, Rome

can be found again in the Uffizi *Bacchus* (Chapter 2; Plate 5). Although the deity in this painting does not have Caravaggio's features, the artist set a self-portrait within a reflection on the surface of the sparkling glass decanter. Not easily legible in reproduction, the tiny portrait was discovered and documented after a modern restoration of the painting, revealing that the canvas destined for the Medici collection was cunningly signed by the artist, immersed in the wine offered by Bacchus. One wonders if the Grand Duke was made aware of Caravaggio's almost invisible, lurking presence within Del Monte's gift, a concealed declaration of the new Michelangelo's arrival in Florence.

The Tuscan Michelangelo never imagined himself mirrored in the more dissolute aspects of Bacchic mythology and in general was much more reticent about marking his works with his features, whether hidden or evident. Painful awareness of his ungraceful appearance together with his avowed love of physical beauty may have conditioned his rejection of self-portraiture in his works, a silence broken on only a few occasions. In contrast, he revealed himself most intimately in his large corpus of poetry, clearly feeling more compelled to portray himself through rigorously constructed words instead of images, attaining a high level of artistry in the process. However, by way of compensation, Michelangelo's contemporaries left us many versions of the master's appearance, delineating very personal views of their preeminent fellow artist. As opposed to the literary sources we have followed, not all characterized him as divine.

One of the earliest portraits of Michelangelo is among the most revealing, both of the painter and the subject. It is a 'disguised' portrait, a convention that uses the recognizable face of a contemporary to portray a personage from history. In his epochal frescoes for the apartments of Pope Julius II in the Vatican, Raphael (1483—1520), at the age of about 25, endowed a depiction of the ancient philosopher Heraclitus with the features of Michelangelo (Fig. 32). At the same moment, Michelangelo was also working for the pope on a major project, painting the nearby Sistine ceiling; he was the older and more established of the two artists, but the enormously talented Raphael was blazing his own trail to success in Rome. An intense rivalry was inescapable and each artist engaged the competitiveness in his own manner. Michelangelo tried to guard his extraordinary work from prying eyes and spoke ill of the newcomer. Raphael, with an elegant mixture of admiration and one-upmanship, found ways to scrutinize Michelangelo's work in progress and appropriated what was most useful to his own strong artistic vision.

The results can be seen in the portrait placed within Raphael's *School of Athens*. The robust figure of Heraclitus is formed in homage to Michelangelo's muscular style, while the marble block upon which he leans alludes to the artist's prowess as a sculptor. Similarly, the sheet of paper with verses acknowledges Michelangelo's gifts as a poet. Yet all the compliments are double-edged, albeit in a very subtle way. The impressive corporeality of the philosopher/artist demonstrates Raphael's ability to paint perfect human anatomy on par with his exemplar. The marble block signals Michelangelo's achievements as a sculptor, but the short garment and rough boots – in striking contrast to the refined antique togas in which the other philosophers are dressed – indicate the physical labor involved in working the stone and are distinctly contemporary workaday gear. Michelangelo's well-known features, with dark hair and short beard, may seem benignly portrayed; yet the characterization of deep, meditative thought, along with the untouched stone and pen stopped in mid-air, can just as easily be read as a kind of creative paralysis. The downcast, shadowed eyes look away from his work. The gesture of head resting on hand has a long iconographic history, regularly indicating sleep, but often symbolizing a kind of somnolence of the spirit, or melancholy stemming from a creative block. A teasing, conceptual 'rock-solid block' may be presented to us here, symbolized by the marble fragment that supports the lethargic Michelangelo/Heraclitus.

Raphael, so intellectually sharp in his inventions, manages simultaneously to praise and poke fun at his subject from within the same skillfully realized image. In some ways the scale seems to tip in favor of acclaim, since the figure is relatively isolated in the foreground and large in scale for being so close to the viewer. But even this ostensible tribute can be understood as its very opposite. We have long known from technical analysis that the figure was an afterthought; the original plaster of the fresco was scraped away and the area showing Heraclitus/Michelangelo was added in a second period of work. It is quite possible that Pope Julius specifically asked Raphael to include the features of Michelangelo in the fresco, which already contained disguised portraits of many other important artists and

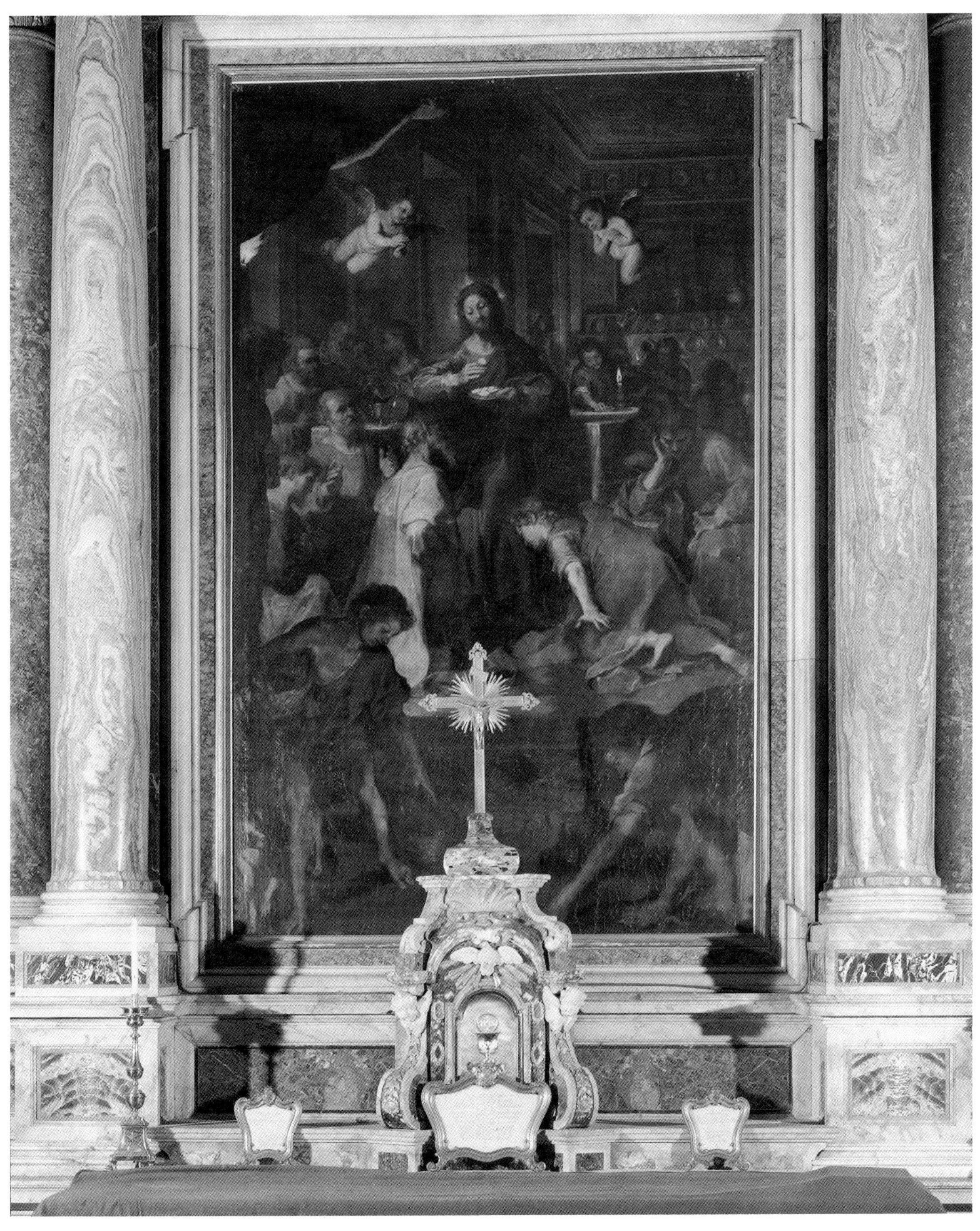

33 Federico Barocci, *Communion of the Apostles*, 1603–8, oil on canvas, 290 × 177 cm (114 3/16 × 69 11/16 in), Santa Maria sopra Minerva, Rome

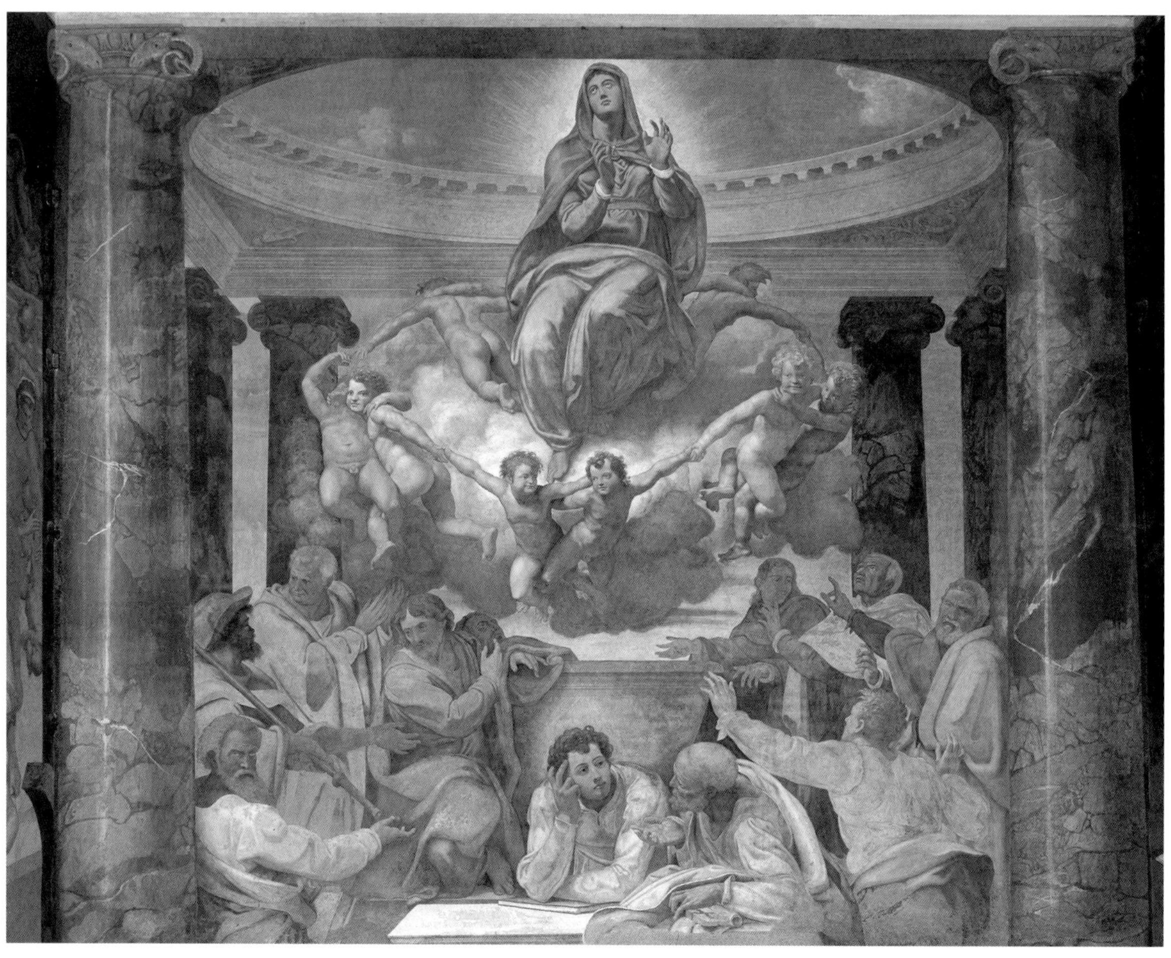

34 Daniele da Volterra, *Assumption of the Virgin*, 1548–50, fresco, Trinità dei Monti, Rome

writers of Julius's Vatican court.[20] As a perfect courtier and inestimable painter, Raphael figured out how to satisfy the Pope's desire to commend fittingly a rival artist but with the inclusion of 'editorial comments' that qualify the praise.

If Raphael's characterization suggests his subject's tormented spirit, a later artist cited the image in a full-fledged denunciation of Michelangelo's artistic heritage. Federico Barocci (*c.*1535–1612), like Raphael, was born in Urbino, where he lived and worked, only twice traveling briefly to Rome. However, Barocci's art had a significant presence in the city, with two important altarpieces painted for the Chiesa Nuova, whose major benefactors were Filippo Neri and those associated with his Oratorians. Neri held Barocci's paintings in high esteem and especially admired his *Visitation*, commissioned for a major chapel in the Chiesa Nuova.

Having been accredited in the Chiesa Nuova, Barocci received other commissions in the Oratorian sphere. Neri had been the confessor of Ippolito Aldobrandini (1536–1605), who later ruled as Pope Clement VIII. Influenced by Neri's example, Clement commissioned

Barocci to paint a major altarpiece for his family chapel in the Roman church of Santa Maria sopra Minerva and in 1608 the *Communion of the Apostles* was installed (Fig. 33). The subject isolates the moment during the Last Supper when Christ shares the blessed bread with his apostles, to the exclusion of Judas. Other examples of this extrapolation from the more ubiquitous Last Supper iconography do exist, but it is not a common theme.

Barocci marked the subject indelibly by the way he devised one of the most visible figures in the crowded scene. Placed alone at the extreme right of the painting (on Christ's left), the Savior's betrayer has been given the unmistakable likeness of Michelangelo as it appears in Raphael's *School of Athens*. The position of the figure is copied precisely, down to the nearly hidden stone block that sustains the arm on which the head of Judas rests. Only the orientation is reversed; the right hand of Judas now cradles his head, while the left conspicuously holds the shameful attribute of the traitor, the bag of silver received in payment for his perfidy.

The appropriated figure openly pays tribute to Raphael, a revered predecessor and countryman from Barocci's home town of Urbino; but the venom expressed against Michelangelo is unprecedented. It has been interpreted as a condemnation of Michelangelo's personal religious views, adhering to the *Spirituali* sect of Catholics half a century earlier; a hint of his less orthodox views may be involved.[21] It is not likely, however, that a papal commission would have involved making a polemical point about the religious views of an artist, no matter how famous, in the iconography of an altarpiece. The pope was exacting about the doctrinal content and indeed requested changes. But when it came to fashioning the figures, it was the artist's decision. While Pope Clement took an unfavorable view of Michelangelo's fresco of the *Last Judgment* and more favorably upon censorship, it took a practitioner to conceive the visual comment by means of the double-edged *imitatio*. Barocci's appropriation of Raphael's portrait of Michelangelo is more convincingly seen as a *parti pris* of one artist against another's style and its undue influence, with perhaps an added overlay alluding to the unorthodoxy of Michelangelo's religious beliefs, as seen from a later perspective.

We do not know if Clement would have enjoyed or approved the cruel pun, for he died a few years before the completion of the painting. Earlier, he had followed progress on the work from drawings provided by Barocci and imposed changes in the iconography touching on theological points.[22] The extant drawings do not include the figure of Michelangelo/Heraclitus/Judas and thus provide no basis for speculation on that point. What is clear, however, is that following a long-established tradition of art commenting on art, Barocci engaged the convention of quoting a valued master and adding an embellishment to the borrowing. In this instance, he gave the practice an unusual twist, manipulating the citation to insult a much-praised artist whose style he personally rejected. Perhaps the appropriation also declares the alliance of Barocci the Urbinite in the historical rivalry between Michelangelo and Raphael. If Michelangelo was a critic of Raphael, then Barocci returned the volley. He was a partisan of harmonious Raphaelesque forms as opposed to the sculpted anatomies of the Michelangelesque manner. Perhaps Barocci's malevolent, little-disguised portrait of Michelangelo as Judas declaims first of all that the Tuscan's highly lauded and imitated style was, in fact, traitorous to art.

Barocci's well-aimed, vicious broadside in the disguised portrait of Judas/Michelangelo is an anomaly. More typical was the bestowal of laudatory characterizations upon the artist, as in a portrayal of Michelangelo in the role of a faithful apostle who not only witnesses Mary's ascent into heaven after death, but points out the marvel to the viewer. This disguised portrait appears in the *Assumption of the Virgin* for the Della Rovere Chapel in Santa Trinità dei Monti in Rome (Fig. 34). Daniele da Volterra (*c.*1509–1566) painted the fresco in 1550, including the portrait in homage to the older artist whose close friend and

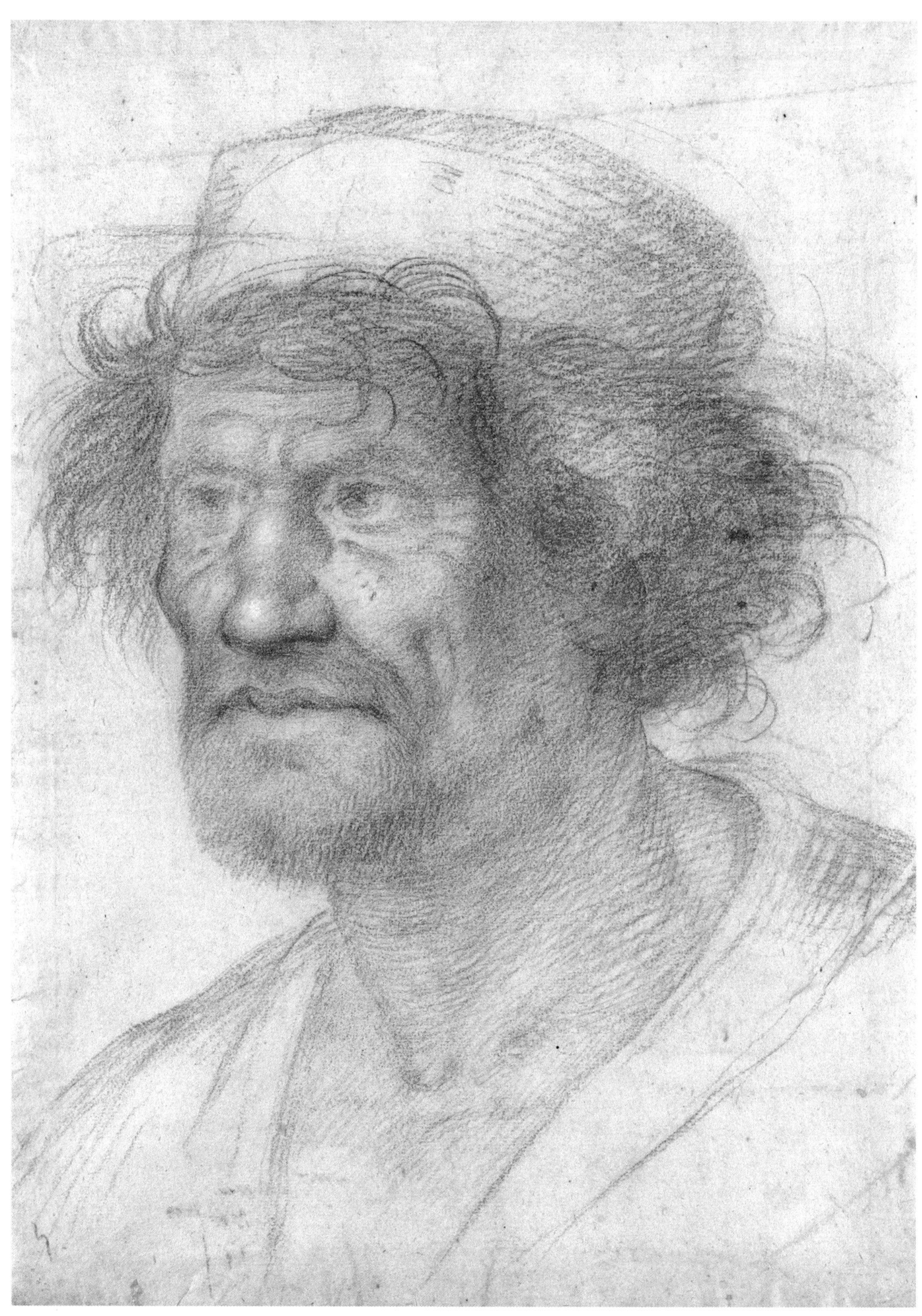

35 Fra Bartolommeo, *Portrait of Michelangelo Buonarroti*, *c.*1515–17, red and black chalk drawing, 26.4 × 37.3 cm (10 ⅜ × 14 11/16 in), Museum Boijmans Van Beuningen, Rotterdam

follower he had become during the previous decade. The detailed drawing of the head, pricked for transfer to the painting, is the basis for the portrayal in the fresco (Plate 1). It shows us a most sympathetic, elderly man – one might say a grandfatherly type – whose creased brow and averted eyes indicate the reticence of a thinker, whose deep meditations are connected to a noble spirit. It could not be further from the impersonation of the apostate Judas whose introversion results from treachery.

Numerous artists who esteemed Michelangelo's art, both during his lifetime and after, have left us independent portraits of Michelangelo as a distinguished professional artist. Although most are idealized, one stands out as a more objective likeness of the working artist. Fra Bartolommeo (1473–1517), a leading talent in Florence, where he was born and spent his life, produced an expressive drawing of Michelangelo, caught as if in a moment of reflection (Fig. 36).[23] From 1500, Fra Bartolommeo was a monk in the Dominican Order in the convent of San Marco. He was a draftsman of exceptional quality, whose style successfully navigates the shared pictorial objectives of his friend, Raphael, with the impact of Michelangelo's monumental figural style. Bartolommeo experienced Michelangelo's Roman art first hand during a visit in 1513 and renewed his acquaintance in 1516, when the sculptor returned to Florence to design the facade of San Lorenzo for his Medici patrons. The portrait is thought to be from this period, just before the death of Fra Bartolommeo in 1517.

The red and black chalk employed for this drawing, a medium in which the artist achieved great mastery, enlivens the carefully observed appearance of the subject. An intensity approximating the frenzy of the artist's creative spirit is obtained through a focus on the contours of the face with its expressive lines, furrows and hollows that animate craggy, congenial features. Even the indentation of Michelangelo's notoriously broken nose is demarcated, but subtly, without slipping into caricature. The wild jumble of dark hair, kept from eruption by the minimally sketched worker's cap, is a foil for the penetrating stare, fixed on a vision seen only by the portrait's subject. Magically, Michelangelo's self-avowed ugliness is described with nobility, enabling it to register the strength of his steadfast imagination. Fra Bartolommeo's decision to allude to the sculptor's unleashed creative forces through a disheveled appearance comes closest to the only eye-witness account we have of Michelangelo at work. During his travels in Italy, Blaise de Vigenère, an erudite Frenchman (and author of a treatise on secret codes), paid a visit to Michelangelo. Most unusually, the distinguished guest was permitted to watch the artist at work and not surprisingly, was astounded enough by his experience to record it. His report begins like a formal witness statement: 'I have seen Michelangelo, although more than sixty years old and no longer among the most robust, knock off more chips of a very hard marble in a quarter of an hour than three young stone carvers could have done in three or four.'[24]

He goes on to marvel at the skill and control of the artist as he furiously attacks the stone with 'impetuosity and fury'. The words of de Vigenère reinforce the effect of Michelangelo on his contemporaries, his '*terribilità*' [awesomeness, formidability], which applied both to his works and to his comportment.

Other artists who were close friends of Michelangelo chose to depict him in a more genteel manner, even when referring to his professional identity. A painting that has recently come to scholarly attention with a convincing attribute to Sebastiano del Piombo (1485/6–1547), shows Michelangelo as a vivacious middle-aged gentleman.[25] It is dated to around 1520, when Michelangelo would have been 45 years old and Sebastiano a decade younger, during a particularly close period in their friendship that had been developing over the last half-dozen years and a fecund time for their collaborative practice. Michelangelo's iconic short, dark, curly hair and beard identify him, as does his furrowed brow, although in this instance the lines are less emphatic. His nose is not disfigured, although a

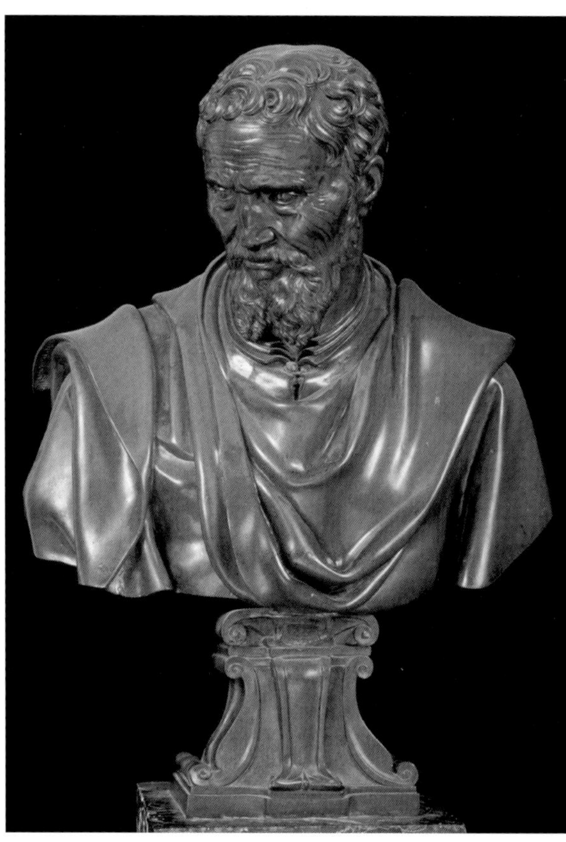

36 Daniele da Volterra, *Bust of Michelangelo*, 1564–66, bronze, Bargello Museum, Florence

passage of highlighting below its bridge gently alludes to the blemish. Departing from the norm, Sebastiano has the eyes of his subject engage the viewer directly and composes the twisting figure of the artist in a lively fashion. The movement further addresses the spectator, since the artist turns to share two pages of sketches contained in his large notebook, proudly directing our attention to his work with a very 'michelangelesque' hand.

Sebastiano has left us an unusual depiction of his partner in art. Known by his contemporaries for the *terribilità* both of his personality and his work, Michelangelo is here exemplified as an elegantly dressed but approachable expert, happy to share his work and exchange views. In reality, Michelangelo tended toward secrecy, fearful of colleagues' poaching and intent on hiding the labor-intensive process of creation.[26] Vasari tells tales of the older artist extinguishing candles to cloak his sketches, even burning drawings in order to obscure signs of the struggle involved in the realization of his ideas. Perhaps Sebastiano's unexpected characterization of Michelangelo constitutes a record of professional bragging about his own privileged position. In several instances Sebastiano received drawings directly from the master to execute in paintings and was a valued collaborator until the mid-1530s. As distinct from Michelangelo's public persona and behavior, the qualities Sebastiano experienced stem from his friend's more intimate side: a warm and prosperous professional, ready to impart his knowledge with good grace. Or at least this is the story implied by Sebastiano's amiable depiction.

Vasari mentions four portraits of Michelangelo in different media and posits them as the prototypes on which numerous copies were based.[27] Not by chance, all four were made by Tuscan artists; the biased criterion silently reinforces Michelangelo's roots. With regard to paintings, Vasari cites one produced around 1520 by Giuliano Bugiardini (1475–1554), a fellow apprentice during Michelangelo's years in Ghirlandaio's workshop. Now in the Casa Buonarroti, the bust-length portrait poses Michelangelo turning toward the viewer wearing an intricately wrapped white turban.[28] The head-gear is a mark of the sculptor at work, swathed against his exertions and the flying marble dust. In this instance, the elaborately delineated turban is a symbolic attribute, for the artist is presented as a gentleman, well-dressed, with a calm demeanor, not in any way engaged in hammering or chiseling. The depiction strives to be ceremonial and commemorative, rather than anecdotal. Unfortunately for the artist's intentions (but to our delight), Vasari supplies the anecdote. In the *Life* of Bugiardini, he recounts with relish a hilarious scenario of Michelangelo sitting for his portrait. The story begins as the master is invited, after two hours' posing, to inspect Giuliano's progress:

> 'Michelagnolo, if you wish to see yourself, get up and look, for I have now fixed the expression of the face.' Michelagnolo, having risen and looked at the portrait, said to Giuliano, laughing: 'What the devil have you been doing? You have painted me with one of my eyes up in my temple. Give a little thought to what you are doing.' Hearing this, Giuliano, after standing pensive for a while and looking many times from the portrait to the living model, answered in serious earnest: 'To me it does not seem so, but sit down again, and I shall see a little better from life whether it be true.' Buonarroti, who knew whence the defect arose and how small was the judgment of Bugiardini, straightaway resumed his seat, grinning. And Giuliano looked many times now at Michelagnolo and now at the picture, and then finally, rising to his feet declared: 'To me it seems that the thing is just as I have drawn it, and that the life is in no way different.' 'Well, then', answered Buonarroti, 'it is a natural deformity. Go on, and spare neither brush nor art.'[29]

The story allows Vasari his own depiction of Michelangelo in the guise of indulgent friend, responding with probity and humor to the limitations of a childhood companion.

The other painted portrait on Vasari's list is by Jacopino del Conte (*c.*1515–1598); it is most likely the version that survives in an unfinished state in the Metropolitan Museum of Art.[30] Only the sculptor's head and left hand are completed, although the pose of the half-length figure is indicated. The conception appears to be indebted to Sebastiano del Piombo's portrait, but with a more regal attitude conceded to the artist, imagined as a patrician. The portrait is usually dated to *c.*1547, when work may have come to a halt due to a rupture in the relations of the two artists. The rift would certainly have soured Jacopino's desire to continue the idealized, flattering approach with which he originally conceived the tribute to an eminent artist, an erstwhile but now embittered friend.

The final word, however, was reserved for a faithful acolyte, Daniele da Volterra, who executed a bronze bust based on Michelangelo's death mask. Given the possibility of obtaining multiple originals from the bronze casting method, it is not surprising that this likeness, both authoritative and intimate, has numerous closely related examples and many copies and variations. Michelangelo's nephew Lionardo, having commissioned two castings, was involved in seeing to the completion of the bronzes in Daniele's workshop after the artist's death in 1566. The example in the Bargello Museum (Fig. 36), is one of the strongest versions of the bust, a moving rendition that belies the advanced years of the aged titan, felled two weeks short of celebrating his 89th birthday. All of the hallmarks noted in the earlier portraits are present, taken from the mask or artfully manipulated so that the iconography of Michelangelo's appearance was set with authority and tenderness. Daniele's poignant bust is the reason we always imagine Michelangelo as elderly and pensive, with a network of creases on his large forehead attesting to the force of his imagination and staring eyes that see only internally. The close-cropped curls defining hair and beard recall the compactness of classical carving and like an ancient bust marred by time, the flaw of his broken nose is featured as a testament to authenticity rather than as a defect. No artist could ask for a more touching tribute.

Yet Michelangelo has told us what he valued in a portrait and it was not necessarily a strict physical likeness, nor even an exalted one. He was delighted to receive a medal cast with his features, designed by Leone Leoni (1509–90); it is the fourth example in Vasari's group of paradigms (Fig. 37). A sculptor born in Arezzo who gained major success working in Milan, Leoni identified with his Tuscan origins throughout his life and the Florentine classicizing tradition in his art.[31]

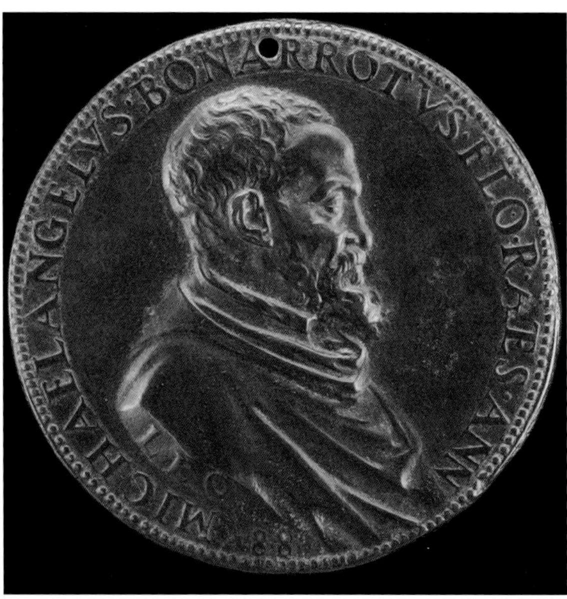

37 Leone Leoni, *Portrait Medallion of Michelangelo*, 1562, bronze, diameter 5.9 cm (2 5/16 in), National Gallery of Art, Washington, D.C., Samuel H. Kress Collection

After Michelangelo's recommendation had helped him to obtain an important commission, Leoni thanked his distinguished sponsor with this very personal gift. The portrait medallion, a format popularized in the Quattrocento, copied the ancient Roman practice of placing a likeness of the emperor in strict profile on coinage minted during his reign. Renaissance versions honored rulers and citizens of status by repeating the imperial formula on medals, casting faces in profile on the obverse and an *impresa*, a personal emblem that combined an image with a motto, on the reverse.

Leoni's medal, designed in 1561, follows a gratifying convention, presenting a stylized but recognizable portrayal of the eminent artist in profile. When the medal is reversed, a figure that alludes both to Michelangelo's appearance and to his figural style in art is set within a narrative scene. He is partially clothed in flowing drapery and grips a staff as he is led by a dog along rocky terrain. Vasari describes this personage as blind, which is a credible reading, but no elaboration is given. The purposeful stride, cap and accessories suggest a pilgrim's journey, while around the rim of the medal a verse from a Davidic psalm appears: *Docebo iniquos vias tuas, et impii ad te convertentur* [Then will I teach transgressors your ways, and sinners will return to you].[32] Following the conventions of *imprese*, the import of the combined image and phrase (referred to as the 'body and soul' of the device), had a private meaning for Michelangelo, who apparently collaborated on its invention. Vasari informs us that Leoni fashioned the reverse 'to please' Michelangelo, who was in turn most appreciative.

The source of the verse would have been widely recognized in Michelangelo's time as part of Psalm 50, known as the *Miserere*, from its opening plea for mercy. It is the most celebrated of the seven penitential psalms in the canon, stirring in its language of abject contrition and expectant renewal. Starting with the reign of Pope Leo x, Psalm 50 was set to music numerous times specifically for performances in the Sistine Chapel during Holy Week. A 1518 version by Costanzo Festa (*c.*1490–1545) is the earliest known, although the most famous was composed by Gregorio Allegri (*c.*1582–1652) for Pope Urban viii in the 1630s. A setting by the Franco-French composer, Orlande de Lassus (1530/32–1594), was immensely famous in the years around the time that Michelangelo was painting in the Pauline Chapel.[33] Although the precise date of Lassus's composition is not known, it most likely belongs to his time in Italy, from 1545 to 1554. While in Rome, Lassus was a guest in the household of Antonio Altoviti, the Archbishop of Florence and thus in Michelangelo's social orbit. It seems he also had an empathy with the artist's religious sphere, attested by a motet dedicated to Cardinal Reginald Pole, published in 1556. The popularity of the *Miserere* in Rome at mid-century may have become linked in Michelangelo's memory to the impact it made at the end of the 1400s through an extended mediation written by Savonarola as he awaited execution. Smuggled out from the monk's cell, it was published in 13 editions in Latin and Italian, before 1500.[34] Michelangelo had been indelibly marked by the preaching of the fiery Dominican monk and it remained a facet of his more mature religious formation.

We can therefore imagine Psalm 50 to have been a fundamental text for Michelangelo's religious thought. Its theme explores the acknowledgment of guilt, the promise of clemency and praise in response to the gift of restoration. The psalm in its entirety has been authoritatively glossed as 'an extended *confession* of sin and an *anticipation* of a new life grounded in divine forgiveness'.[35] The verse singled out by Michelangelo gives voice to the psalmist after having received the gift of being cleansed from sin; in gratitude, he will praise God and teach others how to be restored to spiritual health. In choosing the passage that promises specific actions in response to his cleansing, the artist stresses his future deeds rather than his past sins. A reading of the image must work in harmony with the clear statement of the motto. For this reason, I interpret the combined words and narrative scene to indicate the leadership of the pilgrim, led by his faith (*Fides*, or *fido* as symbolized by the dog), progressing along the correct path to salvation. Personalizing the practices of teaching and praising to Michelangelo's life, the suggestion that he will accomplish this through his art becomes inescapable. This is particularly convincing since, at the time the medal was cast the multi-faceted, 82-year-old artist was projecting the dome for Saint Peter's Basilica, unsalaried by his own stipulation, conceiving the work as direct service to God.

The image on the reverse of the portrait does not give us any reason to describe the man as blind; we base this reading on Vasari's report. Certainly, the author may have had inside information on the *impresa*; however, if this were the case, Vasari likely would have given a much more complete exegesis, emphasizing his insider's knowledge of the puzzle. But perhaps he, like all who subsequently try to fathom the device, was blocked by the avowed nature of the *impresa* as memorably defined by Paolo Giovio: 'neither so obscure it would take a sibyl to interpret it nor so clear it could be comprehended by the vulgar'. The last word is best understood as 'unlettered' and indeed, another rule of *imprese* was that the motto had to be in a language different from that spoken by the owner. The reason for the secrecy stems from the symbolic purpose of the device as 'an outward display of the bearer's inner truth'.[36] In this curious quasi-heraldic custom, the owner broadcasts a proclamation whose significance is never fully disclosed, but always reveals enough to indicate something noble. This is admirably suited to what we know of Michelangelo's personality and aspirations: the medal existed in multiple copies, distributed to announce the fame of the subject, while the exposure of his 'soul' was veiled by symbolism.

Psalm 50 contains several further clues to explain its appeal for Michelangelo's personal meditation. The psalm is traditionally contextualized as a cry from the soul of King David after the prophet Nathan confronted him on his adultery with Bathsheba. Thus the specific sin demanding atonement is carnal in nature; sexual transgression underlies the pleas for forgiveness expressed in the psalm, although it is not specifically named in the prayer. This would encourage Michelangelo privately to reflect on his own sins of the flesh, while publicly pronouncing only the verse that pledges propagation of the righteous path after acknowledgment of sin and its merciful forgiveness. The connection to David's progress from confessed sinner to redeemed king would have been a powerful inspiration for the artist, who had seen him as a model from the time he carved the colossal statue of the biblical hero.

The self-identification is well-known from revelatory lines written on a sheet of studies.[37] The words 'David with his sling, and I with my drill' are followed by his signature, attesting with palpable pride and optimism the 29-year-old sculptor's belief in his inevitable triumph in the challenging commission. Michelangelo's art would prevail through his dexterity in wielding

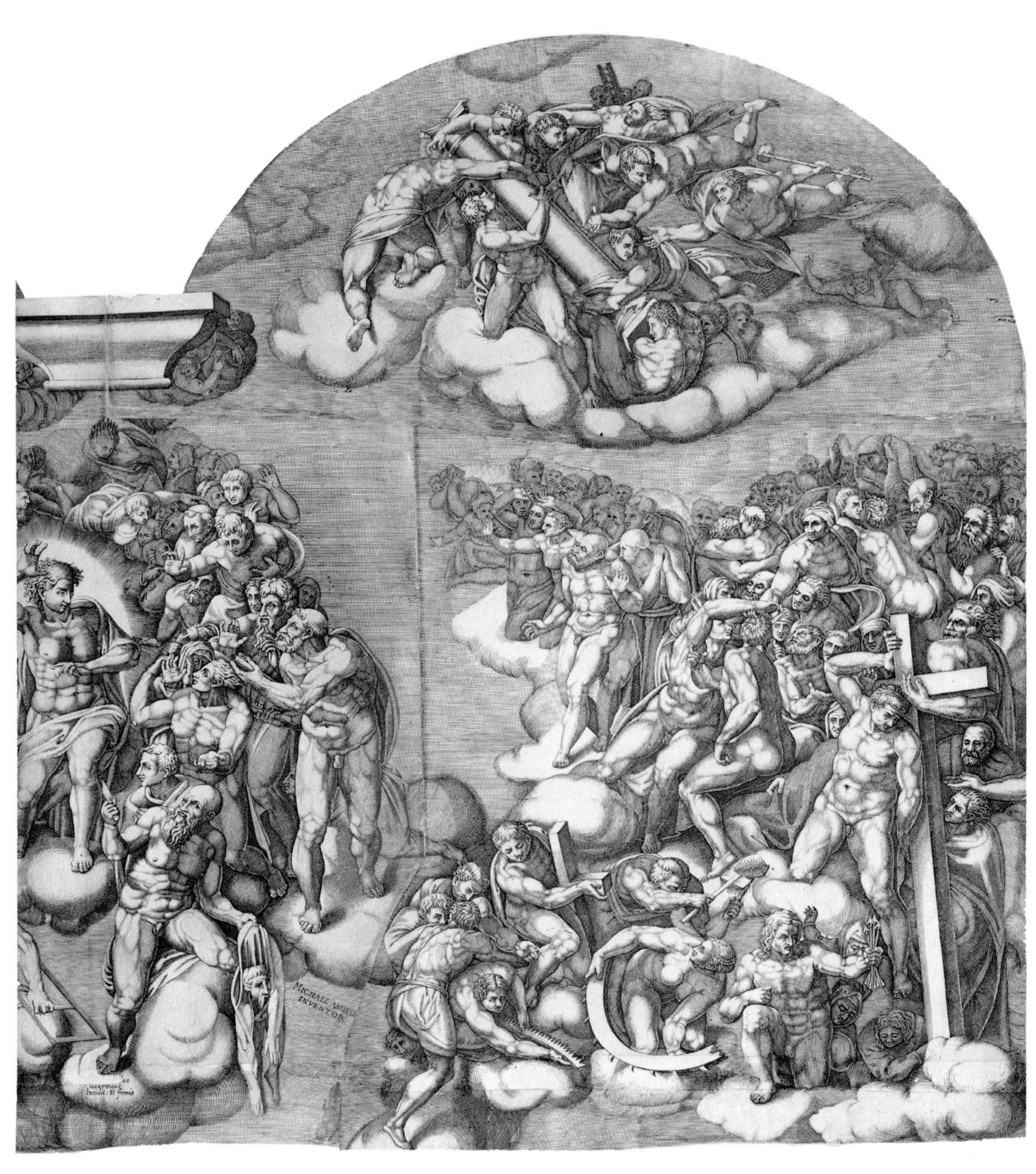

38 Nicolas Beatrizet, *Michelangelo's Last Judgment*, detail,1562, engraving, Metropolitan Museum of Art, New York

his tools, just as David's slingshot overcame the giant Goliath. At a gloomier time in his later life, the artist extended his affinity to the mature King David, burdened by sins and seeking forgiveness.

Meditation on the forgiveness of sins was a constant in Michelangelo's religious practices, especially under the influence of the *Spirituali*. He was tormented by his acute sense of sinning and fearful of his unworthiness, motifs found often in his sonnets. In several, Michelangelo yearns for a casting off of his flesh to liberate his soul, with gripping and graphic imagery. A poem from *c.*1530 ponders: 'Now that time is changing and sloughing off my hide [*scorza*], / death and my soul are still battling', while an earlier verse already contains the prayer 'and may my soul, stripped of its old habit / and of everything human, be restored to life'. A madrigal written *c.*1538–41 opens with the metaphor of skin being scraped away: 'From what sharp, biting file / does your tired skin keep growing thin and failing, / O ailing soul?', followed by allusions to the speaker's casting off his 'mortal veil' and changing his 'hide'.[38] This meditation on the body as a *velo* / *pelo* [veil/skin or hide] was written precisely at the time Michelangelo was painting the *Last Judgment*. On this occasion the artist took his poetic musing on the human condition and applied it directly to an image in his fresco by imbuing the flayed skin of Saint Bartholomew with aspects of his own face (Plate 28).

This disguised self-portrait is so concealed that it was not openly remarked upon by Michelangelo's contemporaries, which has caused recent questioning of its credibility. However, in dealing with historical art it is never a strong position to argue from a lack of information, given how much has been lost; in case of doubt, it is best to work from the context of what is known and contained in the art itself.[39] We do, in fact, have a striking attestation in support of the identification. It is found in an engraving of the *Last Judgment* by Nicolas Beatrizet (1515–66), who used ten sheets to reproduce the oversize image. In the section containing Saint Bartholomew (Fig. 38), Beatrizet acknowledges the creator of the original fresco, conspicuously engraving in bold letters MICHAEL ANGELVS INVENTOR beside the face on the flayed skin. The printmaker made the features on the pelt more explicit than they are in the painting, giving life to the eyes, more structure to the nose and detailing a proper coiffure. Beatrizet recognized his source in 1562, while Michelangelo was still living, which permits us to do the same today. The separation of the large letters recording the 'inventor' from the small script identifying Beatrizet as the engraver, placed to the left below a cloud, further indicates the significance of the inscription adjoining the flayed skin; it labels the allegorical portrait.

We know that Michelangelo used the metaphor of sloughing off skin in his poetry to symbolize the shedding of mortality to attain everlasting existence. We can see that there is a face in the flaccid, deteriorated skin, otherwise so formlessly painted, and that it does not repeat the features or coloring of the face of Saint Bartholomew whose 'mortal flesh', severed during his martyrdom, it is supposed to be. Rather, the short, curly hair that we clearly see is iconic in depictions of Michelangelo, as is the furrowed brow. And the nose, boldly formed by a few bold strokes, is always a point of emphasis in images of the artist. The configuration, necessarily suggestive rather than factual, stops just short of being a self-portrait; this is called for by the nature of its disguise within lifeless flesh. It is a very clever avoidance of close likeness by an artist who avoided frank self-portraiture. The image is like enough to make it self-referential, a metaphor in paint equivalent to those found in Michelangelo's poetry and like them, a prayer for salvation. Technical study of the *giornate*, the division of the fresco by each day's section of painting, shows the area with Bartholomew's flayed skin to be the last undertaken.[40] This significant fact encourages us to see the passage as a final declaration of the artist, filled with self-doubt, but with a measure of hope that sin could finally be shed; an emblematic signature after four years of labor on the fearsome fresco of the final reckoning.

Michelangelo's self-presentation as a disintegrating pelt to be discarded in exchange for a spiritual essence is antithetical to his illustrious and formidable public image. Caravaggio offers us a similarly unexpected and crushing self-condemnation in one of his most powerful self-portraits, using his features to paint the decapitated head of Goliath (Plate 29) in a painting usually dated to the last year of Caravaggio's life. In contrast to the silence surrounding Michelangelo's barely decipherable provocation, Caravaggio's blatant and violent use of his own features was recognized by his contemporaries. Although acknowledged, the fact was not further remarked upon nor interpreted, which should prevent us from drawing too many conclusions about the paucity of documentation around Michelangelo's much more subtle self-reference. It is entirely possible that along with other models, Caravaggio had Michelangelo's example in mind when he devised his portrait as a severed head held out toward the viewer, dangling from the hand of his antagonist.[41]

While the gruesome self-mutilation is most often discussed as an expression of Caravaggio's remorse for the murder he committed, and/or fear of its punishment, an interpretation exclusively linked to autobiography diminishes the meaning of the painting. As in his other works, Caravaggio's iconography stemmed from the conventions of his time even as he altered them and *David with the Head of Goliath* is no exception. While his predecessors (as we saw with Michelangelo) and contemporaries often saw David as an exemplar and at times identified with him, Caravaggio turned that practice on its head (literally) to equate himself instead with Goliath. The inversion was daring and very unsettling, but it was quickly absorbed into the vocabulary of art. In 1613, the Florentine court painter to the Medici, Cristofano Allori (1577–1621), adapted Caravaggio's *concetto* for another biblical subject of decapitation, *Judith with the Head of Holofernes*. In Allori's version, his lover portrays Judith, while the severed head with which she confronts the viewer is the artist's own effigy. The popularity of the bravura painting is attested by two autograph versions and several studio copies; it was Allori's most famous work.[42]

Caravaggio's *David and Goliath* was intended for Pope Paul V, the pontiff who was in the process of deciding to grant Caravaggio a pardon for his crime, which lends undeniable poignance to the artist's brutal pictorial confession of villainy. He does not identify himself with the hero, as Michelangelo did with *David*, but it is important to note that by playing the role of Goliath, Caravaggio both indicts himself as a felon and presents himself as victim. History has bequeathed few details surrounding the homicide on that ill-fated night, yet it is clear that Ranuccio Tomassoni was anything but blameless in the events that led up to his death. If we want to admit some measure of autobiography into the choice of subject, the painting's function as an added plea to Caravaggio's petition for clemency may well enter in. But to balance this in terms of its meaning purely as a work of art, the older Michelangelo's disguised self-portrait, hanging precariously between heaven and hell on the wall of the Sistine Chapel, which was after all the Pope's chapel, would have been a very apt paradigm, perhaps the most moving and decisive of all that Caravaggio appropriated and transformed.

If Vasari was silent about Michelangelo's symbolic self-depiction as a pared and sagging veil of human flesh, he discreetly confirmed the artist's self-portrait in the guise of Nicodemus, part of the sculpted group of figures in a work known as the Florentine *Pietà* (Fig. 39). The information was conveyed in a letter to Michelangelo's nephew Lionardo on 18 March 1564, exactly one month after the artist's death, concerning the funeral arrangements.[43] Vasari shared the observation only in this personal communication and did not include it in his expanded biography published four years later. This suggests a certain amount of privacy was reserved for the self-portrait, which had originally been intended by Michelangelo as part of his burial monument; the self-portrait is one of the reasons Vasari believed the artist's intention should be honored. The history of this *Pietà* is complex and exceptional in the artist's oeuvre, perhaps to be expected in a sculpture of such personal meaning. It is the single instance of Michelangelo carving a self-portrait that is straightforward in appearance, even if its inclusion in the sculpture is staged behind a curtain of symbolism.[44]

The grouping imagines the inert and awkwardly bent body of the dead Christ supported and mourned by his mother and intimate followers, Mary Magdalene and Nicodemus; the latter specifically identified by Condivi. It is a devotional piece that focuses attention on the ruins of Christ's humanity, which will lead to the salvation of the faithful. The concept is traditional, yet inventive in isolating the figures from the setting and symbolism of either the crucifixion or the burial chamber, although their arrangement implies the actions of a deposition scene. The selection of the participants is also singular; although they all appear in narrations of the events subsequent to Christ's death, there is no story that detaches Mary, Mary Magdalene and Nicodemus from the several other disciples involved in the retrieval, transport and burial of the Savior. The assemblage was Michelangelo's choice.[45] While the presence of Mary and Mary Magdalene needs no explanation, the artist's emphasis on Nicodemus, ostensibly a less important follower, placing him at the pinnacle of the huddled mourners, calls for special attention.[46]

Nicodemus appears several times in the gospel of John, described as a Pharisee who became a disciple of Christ after going secretly, under cover of darkness, to hear his teachings; he took part in Christ's burial (John 3:1–21; 7:50; 19:39). A tradition grew outside of the biblical texts, categorizing Nicodemus as a sculptor, connected to legendary works of art. He was a fitting personage to carry Michelangelo's features, professing devotion to Christ and piety to Mary by embracing them above his final resting place. It is a touchingly conceived symbol, which Michelangelo created, as both Vasari and Condivi tell us, 'for his own pleasure'.

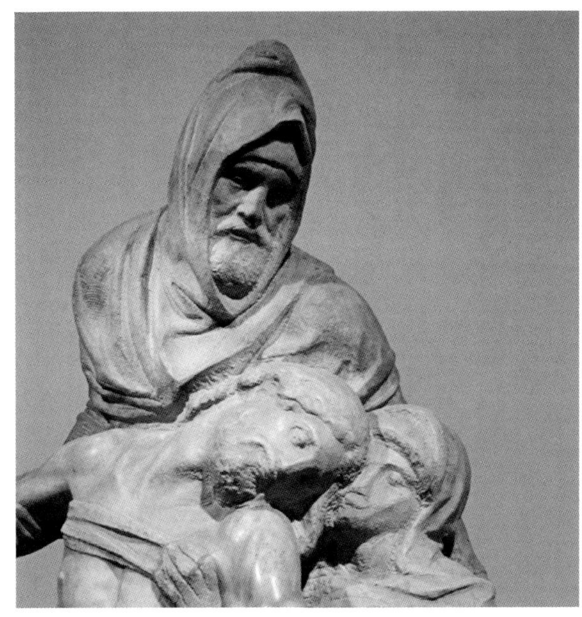

39 Michelangelo, Nicodemus, detail, *Pietà (Deposition)*, *c.*1550, marble, height 226 cm (89 in), Museo dell'Opera del Duomo, Florence

That is far from how the project eventually progressed. Michelangelo began carving the block in 1547, likely moved by the death of Vittoria Colonna to think even more deeply about his own inevitable passing. This led to the design of a funerary sculpture. Around 1555, however, Michelangelo turned against the piece, 'attacking' it with ferocity, so that Christ's left arm and leg were mutilated; one shattered, the other completely removed. The unfinished figures were abandoned and on request, Michelangelo gave the ruined piece to his friend Francesco Bandini. Vasari, who attests to the damage, mentions an imperfection in the marble and the sculptor's annoyance with the pressure of completion, motivations both vague and unconvincing for such desperate actions. Studies have hypothesized troubling iconographic issues as the reason, particularly the potential for misinterpretation of a mystical metaphor that alludes to Mary as the

Bride of Christ.[47] The evocation of a spiritual union through carnal imagery, in this case by placing the leg of Christ upon Mary's thigh, is linked to classical iconography. Such imagery, still fundamental to Michelangelo's symbolic system late into his art, might well have outraged some viewers. The leg is entirely missing from the Florentine *Pietà* as it survives today, even after steps toward completion were attempted by one of Michelangelo's assistants, which adds credibility to the interpretation.

Recently, a further interpretive point related to the changing temper of Catholicism after the mid-16th century in Italy has been explored.[48] Given the covert behavior of Nicodemus in his dawning acceptance of Christ, his name was used in the 16th century to refer to those who stayed within the ranks of Catholicism, but clandestinely accepted some of the Protestant arguments concerning points of doctrine. Michelangelo, in his close ties to the *Spirituali*, could easily have belonged to this category. Whether he began his self-portrait in forthright emulation of the biblical sculptor who accompanied Christ to the tomb, or if it was a cryptic reference to his creed at a time when he was particularly involved with the thinking of the *Spirituali*, by 1555 it would have become a dangerous confession to make. Calvin's pejorative use of the term 'Nicodemite' in a treatise of 1544, which quickly began to circulate in Latin and Italian translations, would have been enough to alarm any artist whose intention was to feature Nicodemus in a positive or neutral light. The grouping that Michelangelo had envisioned to include a pious rendering of himself, joined with Christ and Mary in death, was abandoned in anger and frustration.[49] Surprisingly, it was left to Caravaggio to complete the thought. He reconsidered Michelangelo's self-portrait as Nicodemus and created his own version of the artist's masked presence in a major altarpiece executed for a chapel within the Church of Santa Maria in Vallicella, known as the *Chiesa Nuova* [New Church], a core site of the Roman Catholic Reformation.

Caravaggio's *Deposition* (Plate 31) was commissioned by Girolamo Vittrice in memory of his uncle Pietro, a long-term employee in service to the Vatican, after his death in 1600. It is possible the artist signed a contract almost immediately; he worked on the painting from 1602–4. During this same period Caravaggio was occupied with the *Saint John the Baptist* and *Amor Vincit Omnia*; the art of Michelangelo was very much on his mind. Taking up the traditional subject of the removal of Christ from the cross, Caravaggio refocused it, closely following the path of Michelangelo, with emphasis on a compact group of figures grieving as they struggle to support the Redeemer's dead body. The differences, however, are striking. Where the sculpted *Pietà* displays grief as an interior state that paralyzes and wounds, the painted scene exposes it as a force propelled, flung and hurled outward by the mourners in a dynamic orchestration of movement. Caravaggio designed the painting to be a forceful competitor against the preexisting sculpture. In this instance, as in his other early works, the painter strove to develop his style of naturalism in an argument, rather than a dialogue, with his predecessor.[50]

There is, however, one point of agreement in the *paragone*: Caravaggio's representation of the inert body of Christ, defined with a more heroic, exposed anatomy than is usually found in the artist's corpus, owes its ennoblement to a reflection of its counterpart in Michelangelo's *Pietà*. In Caravaggio's painting, the impressive physicality of the Savior – almost nude and bathed in a strong light that reflects from the winding sheet – is thrust toward the viewer for contemplation. It is in marked contrast to the bending, plebian figure grasping the legs of Christ – precariously, open-mouthed, as if in fear of them slipping from his hold. Prominent on the central axis of the composition, the face of this figure is riveting. It is caught in the act of confronting the viewer, frozen in the moment it turns to look out to us. It is the only face that engages the public; it is easily readable, surrounded by the red of Saint John's mantle and the features are reminiscent of a well-known physiognomy. The short, dark, curling hair and beard, the lined forehead with deep indentations between deep-set eyes all consistently appear in portraits of Michelangelo.[51] Additionally, Caravaggio includes an ear of a distinctly large scale, which conforms to Vasari's comment about Michelangelo's appearance. There is one more glaring physical trait: Nicodemus/Michelangelo is given the pronounced hump of kyphosis, a condition usually known as 'hunchback'. Until recently this curious anomaly has not been noted in studies of the painting.[52] The curvature is more pronounced than would be occasioned by the stooping posture, with its protuberance evident between the tearful face of the Magdalene and the projected, highlighted elbow of Nicodemus. This detail is Caravaggio's invention, an unknown motif in the context, so we must assume the artist had a reason for characterizing Michelangelo as a *gobbo* [hunchback].

The supposition gains an unexpected affiliate in the sonnet Michelangelo wrote while painting the Sistine Chapel, where, in a mocking description of the ruination of his body from the torturous toil, he wrote:

> I' ho già fatto un gozzo in questo stento,
> come fa l'acqua a' gatti in Lombardia,
> o ver d'altro paese che si sia,
> c'a forza 'l ventre apicca sotto il mento.
> La barba al cielo, e lla memoria sento
> in sullo scrigno, e 'l petto fo d'arpia,
> e 'l pennel sopra 'l viso tuttavia
> mel fa, gocciando, un ricco pavimento.[53]

> I've grown a goiter from this labor, as do peasants from the water they drink in Lombardy, or whatever other similar place. As a result, my belly sticks to the underside of my chin. With beard toward the sky, I feel the base of my skull lying on my hump, and I make my breast that of a Harpy. My dripping brush, continuously held above my face, makes it a sumptuous pavement.

Michelangelo's imagistic Italian employs the archaic *memoria* for *nuca* [the base of the skull] and the bulge of his back is a *scrigno*, which comes from the Latin word for a cylindrical container to hold letters and manuscripts. The ancient *scrigno* was given a Renaissance form and function as a small box for jewelry, usually encrusted with gems. The term reinforces the mixture of classical allusions (in the image of the Harpy as well) with comedic antics. The splattering of paint paving the artist's chest is echoed in the sparkling jeweled *scrigno* of his hunched back. The Latinate *scrigno* has a Tuscan equivalent, *gibbo*, found in Dante, referring to a 'rounded protuberance'.[54] In colloquial Italian it corresponds to *gobba* and thus to the 'hump' that deforms Michelangelo in his sonnet and Nicodemus in Caravaggio's painting.

We have come across the term before, in the tale of Michelangelo's Vatican *Pietà*, when Lombards mistakenly attributed the sculpture to the Milanese Cristoforo Solario, known as Il Gobbo (see Chapter 1). Vasari's anecdote, we recall, poked fun at the 'provincial' Lombards, while providing a memorable (if spurious) explanation for Michelangelo's exceptional addition of his signature to the *Pietà*. The Lombard Caravaggio may have privately conceived his response, conflating Michelangelo with Il Gobbo and having the last laugh in response to the legend.[55] In this he followed a hallowed tradition of artists devising insider editorial comments that did not disrupt the public meaning of the work. Caravaggio had it both ways, employing traditional iconography of the subject for general comprehension, but disclosing private meanings readable only to the few. The appending of secular, often humorous (even wicked), comments to sacred imagery was a practice arrogated by Medieval artists and illuminators of religious art, an indulgence continued and transformed in the Renaissance.[56] Caravaggio wrought a further variation, integrated so skillfully into the demands of his naturalistic style that it did not cause a rupture. The figure of Nicodemus fits seamlessly into the artist's preferred cast of laborers and peasants, ill-clad, with bare legs and feet. That he could commandeer his established rustic type to humanize the 'divine' Michelangelo was an added bonus. Just like Raphael, Caravaggio honors Michelangelo in the painting while at the same time he diminishes him.

Apart from the possible meanings latent in the *gobba* of Nicodemus, the choice of this biblical figure mirrors Michelangelo's selection of his own alter ego. Caravaggio would have had every opportunity to gain access to the sculpture, since Cardinal Benedetto Giustiniani, Vincenzo's brother, was an intimate of the Bandini family, who still owned the Florence *Pietà* at that time and displayed it in their Roman garden.[57] Caravaggio acknowledged his predecessor's identification with the legendary sculptor by repeating it, only to skew the likeness with a subtle pejorative detail. The *gobbo* can in theory be related to a reference from one of Michelangelo's humorous poems and one of Vasari's anecdotes; two sources too relevant to be attributed purely to happenstance. But what of the other hint of disreputability attached to the name of Nicodemus as the Counter-Reformation took aim at dissidents? Without crediting Caravaggio with the interests of a theologian, we can certainly ascribe a polemic position to him, both in art and in the general tenor of reform that permeated the Oratorian community. The Oratorians are known to have been as exacting about iconography as they were about religious doctrine; if they were aware of the veiled depiction of Michelangelo, they might have applauded it. We should recall Federico Barocci and his portrayal of Michelangelo as Judas displayed in a commission for Pope Clement VIII; the comparison gives us another measure of the parameters Caravaggio would have been allowed in creating his work.

The study of the various ways in which other artists portrayed Michelangelo and Caravaggio and how they represented themselves, enriches us with an immediate connection to the status they held in their profession and their societies and in their own estimation. These visual documents provide the closest approaches we can make, even if the roads demand maps and signposts which we try to read from existing evidence and deduce from historical context. Often it is surprising that contemporaries of the two Michelangelos saw them so differently from the way we do; sometimes it is astonishing that our assessments are so similar. Although we can never be certain that what we glean from the art tallies with what was originally intended, our attempts to grapple with its evidence and its impact keep the art vital, a living force in its physical existence and in cultural memory.

Caravaggio's art demonstrates a lasting determination to assimilate and supersede the idealized perfection of Michelangelo's style and to replace it with a passionately professed method of copying nature in order to create art. The accident of his sharing the name 'Michelangelo' internalized that rivalry. It erupted at different times in different ways, but it appears to have simmered throughout Caravaggio's career, right to the end. The ubiquity of the Tuscan's achievement and affirmation in Rome (the chosen arena of both artists) and Caravaggio's need to measure himself against the 'divine artist', drove him to compose astonishingly inventive dialogues with his predecessor in his paintings. We have seen the varying tones taken in Caravaggio's pictorial discussions, from impudent to ingenious, from frank appropriation to fierce inversion, from paying homage to hurling insults – in sum, an entire range from contemptuous to reverential. Caravaggio's art, innovative, provocative and profound, would not have been the same if he had not needed to contend with Michelangelo's awesome, refined and deeply spiritual patrimony.

If both their lives had quantities of torment, they experienced their tribulations very differently. Michelangelo approached his art as a struggle and was vanquished over and over again by its demands, as attested by his unfinished works. Yet he was so driven that the battles he set for himself in producing art resulted in a monumental corpus of excellence in drawing, sculpture, painting, architecture and poetry. Caravaggio was focused on, and straightforward in his approach to the act of painting. Despite his disorderly life, he seems to have always delivered his commissions to their patrons without anxiety. Yet Caravaggio had a wretchedly self-destructive force within his personality which gained the upper hand even in the moments when his exceptional talent and stellar reputation were established enough to provide him with security and stability. These divergent traits ensured that Michelangelo Buonarroti ended up as a wealthy, landed gentleman, the patriarch and supporter of his family, even if the persona he wanted to propagate was that of a loner plagued by poverty. Caravaggio, in contrast, did not accumulate wealth, was in frequent trouble with the law, lived several years of his short life on the run as a felon and behaved disastrously when he finally had the opportunity to elevate his status with knighthood. If Michelangelo could be steeped in the fury of creation, Caravaggio was too often embroiled in all too human rage. In the end, then, we are quite correct in distinguishing between the 'two Michelangelos' by empowering the first to retain an appellation that alludes to an angel, sharing something of the divine, while permitting the younger Michelangelo to be named 'Caravaggio' in a more grounded mode, with proud reference to his earthly origins.

Notes

1 INTRODUCING THE TWO MICHELANGELOS

1 For a vibrant meditation on the significance of artists' names, see Barolsky, *Why Mona Lisa Smiles.* The author's 'trilogy' of studies is an excellent introduction to these issues, and also establishes many of the points I take up with regard to Michelangelo in relation to Vasari and Condivi throughout the present book. See also Barolsky's *Michelangelo's Nose* and *Giotto's Father.*

2 Characterized by Hirst as the 'first offprint' in 'First Biographers', p.67; Hirst also provides an important discussion of the relationship of Vasari's and Condivi's texts. Also see Pon, 'Michelangelo's *Lives*', pp 1015–37.

3 Vasari, *Lives of the Painters, Sculptors and Architects*, p.642.

4 Although in the end, Michelangelo also took issue with some of Condivi's formulations. With an assistant, Tiberio Calcagni, as amanuensis, he dictated corrections to the publication. See Elam, in Condivi, *Vita di Michelagnolo Buonarroti*, pp XXIII–XLVI.

5 Hirst, in Condivi, *Vita*, pp VI–IX; and 'First Biographers', pp 71–4.

6 Michelangelo's cartoon is in the British Museum, London; see Wilde, *Italian Drawings*, pp 114–16.

7 Mancini, in Friedlaender, *Caravaggio Studies*, p.258.

8 Carducho, in Enggass and Brown (eds), *Italy and Spain, 1600–1750*, p.174.

9 Caravaggio's baptismal record was found in the parish registry of Santo Stefano in Brolo, Milan. See Carminati, 'Caravaggio da Milano', p.29.

10 Vasari, *Lives*, p.643.

11 Baglione in Friedlaender, p.234.

12 Condivi, *The Life of Michelangelo by Ascanio Condivi*, p.108; this was restated emphatically in his conversation with Calcagni, who quoted him in the *postille*: 'Questo ho io fatto sempre, e se tu vòi prollungar la vita, non lo usare o pure quanto puoi 'l meno.' See Condivi, *Vita*, 23, p.XXII and pp XLIV–V.

13 See Marini and Corradini, 'Inventarium', pp 162–3; and Bassani and Bellini, 'La casa, le "robbe"', pp 70 and 73, where Caravaggio's friendship with the book dealer, Ottaviano Gabrielli, is noted as a possible source for the books.

14 Berra, *Il giovane Caravaggio in Lombardia*, p.246; the date is either 1604 or 1605.

15 See Muraoka, *The Path of Humility*, esp. Chapter 2.

16 ibid., p.5.

17 Berra, first in an article and then in a major book, offers thoroughly reasoned discussions of an enormous number of documents on all aspects of the artist's family and early life in the town of Caravaggio, as well as documents concerning his later life. My view of Caravaggio's background and the dates I give in the following pages are based on Berra's invaluable book, *Il giovane Caravaggio in Lombardia.*

18 Calvesi's pioneering work on the Colonna family in relation to Caravaggio in *Le realtà del Caravaggio* has now been amplified by Berra, *Il giovane Caravaggio*. For Costanza, see esp. Chapter 16; also see Baernstein, 'In my own hand'.

19 Berra, *Il Giovane Caravaggio*, p.293.

20 ibid., pp 305–8.

21 For an introduction to Colonna and her sonnets dedicated to Michelangelo, see Brundin, *Vittoria Colonna*.
22 Condivi, *Vita*, p.60, and *postilla* 21, p.XXII.
23 Spata was incorrectly called 'Valentino' in Baglione's text; see Vodret, *Caravaggio: The Complete Works*, p.18.
24 Condivi, *Life of Michelangelo*, p.102.
25 Quoted in Giannotti, *Dialogi di Donato Giannotti*, p.45 (my translation). In the context of the dialogue, discussion of the sonnet causes the participant 'Michelangelo' to demur about being praised.
26 ibid.
27 Baglione, in Friedlaender, p.236.
28 Mancini, in Friedlaender, p.257.
29 Baglione, in Friedlaender, pp 235–6.
30 For a full discussion of the passage in Vasari, see Pestilli, 'Lombard Critics', pp 21–30.
31 Giovio, *Michaelis Angeli vita*, p.15.
32 Vasari, *Lives*, vol. 1, pp 40–41.
33 For a discussion of the sonnet see Chapter 5 and note 52.
34 Pestilli, 'Lombard Critics', p.25.
35 Rowland and Charney, *The Collector of Lives*, p.307.
36 See Hirst, *The Young Michelangelo*, p.14.
37 Cadogan, 'Michelangelo in the Workshop', p.31.
38 For substantial information on Peterzano and his work, see Terzaghi, 'Peterzano, Simone'.

2 MYTHOLOGICAL CHARACTERS AS AGENTS OF PROVOCATION

1 Bellori, in Friedlaender, p.245.
2 Pliny, *Natural History*, Book 34, p.173.
3 ibid., Book 35, p.317.
4 Bellori, in Friedlaender, p.246.
5 Pico della Mirandola, quoted in Carman, 'Michelangelo's *Bacchus*', p.7.
6 Ramsden, *Letters*, vol. 1, p.3.
7 Risaliti and Vossilla, *Il Bacco*, p.41. My thinking about Cardinal Riario and his relation to the *Bacchus* is indebted to their thoroughly documented and convincing discussions.
8 ibid., p.25.
9 ibid., p.39.
10 Condivi, *Life of Michelangelo*, pp 21–3.
11 Freedman, 'Reflections on Bacchus', p.122.
12 Condivi, *Life of Michelangelo*, p.24.
13 ibid., pp 23–4.
14 Hirst, *Young Michelangelo*, p.32 for technical aspects of the carving; and Lieberman, 'Regarding *Bacchus*', pp 65–74 for superb photographs that capture the sculpture from all angles.
15 Francisco de Hollanda, *On Antique Painting*, pp 110–11.
16 Berra, 'Il *Bacco* degli Uffizi', p.59.
17 ibid., for a masterful discussion and overview of the scholarly arguments.
18 ibid., p.58.
19 ibid., p.59.
20 Barolsky, 'Michelangelo's Marble Faun', pp 113–16 for the tale of the faun as a 'novella of artistic origins', and on Vasari's contribution. Also see his *Michelangelo's Nose* for ideas regarding the story of the faun.
21 Condivi, *Life of Michelangelo*, pp 10–12.
22 ibid., p.12.
23 ibid., p.19.
24 Vasari, *Lives*, vol. 2, p.651.
25 Hirst, *Young Michelangelo*, p.23; also see pp 24–8 for an 'Excursis on The *Sleeping Cupid*'.
26 *Caravaggio: Final Years*, p.116.
27 ibid.
28 Stone, 'In Praise of Caravaggio's *Sleeping Cupid*', pp 165–77, presents the correspondence; he mentions the probable *paragone* with Michelangelo's work, and hypothesizes that Dell'Antella wanted Michelangelo the Younger to compose a poem on Caravaggio's painting. Berra, 'Il *Bacco* degli Uffizi', also refers to a *paragone* in his conclusion, p.82.
29 Condivi, *Life of Michelangelo*, p.19.
30 Christiansen, 'L'esempio davanti del naturale', esp. p.433; Gash, 'Maltese Inspiration', pp 253–66 for several examples of the artist studying other art in preparing his works.
31 Vodret, *Caravaggio: Complete Works*, p.182.
32 Warwick, 'Memory's Cut', pp 884–903, comments on the weapon, and suggests it came from the Maltese Order's armory.
33 Giovio, *Michaelis Angeli vita*, p.15; also see the introductory remarks about Giovio's not always positive '*elogio*', pp 4–8.
34 ibid., p.15.
35 Friedlaender, *Caravaggio Studies*, pp 89–94.

3 MICHELANGELO'S *IGNUDI* OF THE SISTINE CHAPEL, THEIR ANCESTORS, DESCENDANTS AND CARAVAGGIO'S SHOCKING RESPONSES

1 Condivi, *Vita*, 'Questi son certi ignudi, che sopra la già detta cornice . . . sostengano i medaglioni', p.33.
2 Talvacchia, 'The Word Made Flesh', pp 67–8 outlines the derivation, amplified in this discussion. De Tolnay, *Michelangelo*,

vol. 2, p.63 notes the relationship of the *ignudi* to traditional winged putti, and discusses a sketch (Fig. 231) demonstrating this was Michelangelo's first idea.

3 Condivi, *Life of Michelangelo*, p.48.

4 See Dempsey, *Inventing the Renaissance Putto*, for a masterful study of the subject. Bormand gives an overview of 15th-century *spiritelli* in Paolozzi Strozzi and Bormand (eds), *The Springtime of the Renaissance*, pp 111–17, with catalogue entries in Section IV.

5 La Malfa, 'The Chapel of San Girolamo', p.269.

6 Talvacchia on *spiritoni* and *spiritelli*, in 'Bronzino's *Corpus*', pp 52–8.

7 Dempsey, *Renaissance Putto*, pp 10–13.

8 Talvacchia, 'Bronzino's *Corpus*', pp 57–8.

9 See Israëls in Paolozzi Strozzi and Bormand (eds), *Springtime of the Renaissance*, pp 358–9.

10 Michelangelo's study of Lippi's frescoes is strongly suggested by several details. The wingless *putti* who lift ancient-style plaques above their heads find their equivalents in appearance and function in the Sistine figures who sustain the inscribed names of the Prophets. Lippi's Sibyls in the vault are echoed by those in the Sistine; his seated Delphic Sibyl, who consults a large book while turning to face the viewer, is a graceful forerunner of Michelangelo's more massive ancient Seer.

11 Steinberg, *Michelangelo's Painting*, pp 238–9.

12 Steen Hansen, *Michelangelo's Mirror* provides an illuminating discussion of artists in this context.

13 See Talvacchia, 'Bronzino's *Corpus*', pp 51–8; I draw on this work for the present discussion.

14 For the issue of ornament see Talvacchia, 'The Word Made Flesh', pp 64–9.

15 Condivi, *Life of Michelangelo*, p.48.

16 Dempsey, 'Et Nos Cedamus Amori', for the meaning of the decoration and its humor.

17 The Marchese also had keen interest in the sculpture of Michelangelo, discussing him in his *Discorso sopra la scultura*, and acquiring what is likely the first version of the Santa Maria sopra Minerva *Redeemer* for his collection, possibly in 1607. See Danesi Squarzina, 'The Bassano *Christ the Redeemer*'.

18 See Summers, *Michelangelo and the Language of Art*, for a discussion of *stupore*, pp 171–6.

19 Bassani and Bellori, 'La casa, le "robbe"', p.72.

20 Sandrart, in Friedlaender, p.265.

21 Friedlaender, *Caravaggio Studies*, pp 89ff.

22 As the following discussion will make clear, the subject of the painting is still open to question. Although perhaps most commonly referred to as *Saint John*, currently *Boy with a Ram* is also used to identify the Capitoline and the Doria Pamphilij paintings. For convenience I will refer to the painting as *Saint John*, while still reviewing arguments for other identifications; the case has not yet been closed, nor, given the nature of the painting, may it ever become definitive.

23 See Testa, 'La collezione di Ciriaco Mattei', in *Caravaggio e la collezione Mattei*, pp 29–38.

24 For Alberti's contribution see Barnes, *Michelangelo in Print*, esp. p.41. Also, for points about artists' ability to study and copy the ceiling frescoes, p.48.

25 Examples of the four engravings in the collection of the Metropolitan Museum can be viewed on its site, in the entries for Cherubino Alberti.

26 For a succinct overview of the documents and identifications see Guarino's entry in the catalogue *Caravaggio e la collezione Mattei*, pp 120–23.

27 Calvesi, *Le realtà del Caravaggio*, p.196. Originally published by Cozzi, 'Intorno al cardinale Ottavio Paravicino', with an extensive discussion; then emended with further information by Pupillo, who found a draft of Gauldo's reply, 'Di nuovo intorno al Paravicino'.

28 Von Rosen, 'Ambiguità intenzionale', strongly argues for ambiguity as Caravaggio's artistic strategy; she reviews the series of Saint John paintings and studies a group of close variations, also stressing the 'corrections', pp 63–77. See also Pavesi, 'Un nuovo "San Giovanni Battista nel deserto"', for Giuseppe Vermiglio's close variations with amendments for the Mattei and Borghese *Saint John*.

29 See Ostrow and Rudolph, 'Isaac Laughing', for a strong presentation of the argument.

30 Barroero, 'L'Isacco di Caravaggio', p.38; the author argues for identification of the figure as Isaac, and reminds us that in Genesis 22:6, the boy carries the wood on his shoulders to the altar, a clear prefiguration of Christ carrying the cross to his crucifixion.

31 Condivi, *Life of Michelangelo*, p.47.

32 Kimura, 'Analisi iconografica', pp 293–6.

33 Baglione, in Friedlaender, p.232; I have paraphrased the comments.

4 RELIGIOUS MESSAGES CONVEYED THROUGH BODY LANGUAGE, FROM IMPECCABLE HEROES TO IMPERFECT HUMANS

1 For a clear discussion of the Council and its effect on art see O'Malley, 'Trent, Sacred Images, and Catholics' Senses of the Sensuous', pp 28–48.

2 See Barnes, *Michelangelo's 'Last Judgment'* for a sustained discussion of reception centered on the Sistine fresco.

3 Saslow, *The Poetry of Michelangelo*, 107, p.239.
4 Talvacchia, 'The Word Made Flesh', pp 49–73.
5 Calvesi, 'Rapporto con i Mattei', in *Caravaggio e la collezione Mattei*, pp 17–28.
6 See Chapter 3; I have paraphrased the comment.
7 Borromeo, *Sacred Painting*, p.21.
8 Friedlaender, *Caravaggio Studies*, p.104.
9 Vasari, *Lives*, vol. 2, p.669.
10 Baglione, in Friedlaender, pp 234–5. I have emended 'smiling' to 'stifling laughter' in an attempt to render *sogghignando* more evocatively, which implies sneering or smirking.
11 Friedlaender, *Caravaggio Studies*, p.108.
12 Condivi, *Vita*, p.31 (my translation).
13 Saint Peter Canisius, writing in 1555, lists five precepts in his *Summa Doctrinae Christianae*; Saint Antoninus of Florence catalogued ten in his *Summa Theologica* of 1439. Catholic encyclopedia, entry 'Commandments of the Church', www.catholic.org/encyclopedia.
14 Friedlaender, *Caravaggio Studies*, p.101.
15 Calvesi, *Le realtà, passim*, and in 'Rapporto con i Mattei', pp 17ff.
16 Bussagli, 'Michelangelo e Sulpizio Verolano', pp 88–93. My information comes from this scholar's work in the discussion that follows.
17 Condivi, *Life of Michelangelo*, p.87.
18 Condivi, *Life of Michelangelo*, p.84; see Steinberg, *Michelangelo's Painting*, pp 135–7, for other interpretive possibilities.
19 Friedlaender, *Caravaggio Studies*, pp 3–33; his thorough discussion starts with the *paragone* of the two Michelangelos' commissions; for a more recent in-depth study of the Pauline frescoes see Steinberg, *Michelangelo's Painting*, pp 235–304.
20 Wallace, 'Narrative and Religious Expression', p.119; this article should also be consulted on the visual impact of the compositions *in situ*.
21 For further thoughts on Michelangelo's composition and its impact on Caravaggio, see Barolsky, 'Pontormo, Michelangelo, Caravaggio', esp. p.17.

5 RENAISSANCE RECKONING IN PORTRAITS AND SELF-PORTRAITS OF THE TWO MICHELANGELOS

1 Vasari, *Le vite de' più eccellenti architetti, pittori, et scultori italiani*, p.886.
2 Vasari, *Lives*, p.652.
3 Risaliti and Vossilla, *La Pietà Vaticana*, p.49. See for full information on the commission and its history.
4 An exception is Goffen, *Renaissance Rivals*, p.114.
5 Pliny, *Natural History*, Preface to Book I, 26–7.
6 See Pon, 'First Signature'; Wang, 'Michelangelo's Signature'; and Preimesberger, *Paragons*, p.91.
7 See Stone, 'Signature Killer' for a wide-ranging discussion of the signature. Also see Stone, 'The Context of Caravaggio's *Beheading*'.
8 For a full account of the confusion on this and other occasions, see Balsamo, 'Les Caravage de Malte', pp 151–3.
9 Sciberras, 'Due persone à lui ben viste', p.38. For the importance of heraldry see Stone, 'Signature Killer', pp 576–7.
10 Stone, 'Signature Killer', p.580.
11 My understanding of Caravaggio's crime and its consequences comes from Sciberras, 'Frate Michael Angelus in Tumultu'.
12 Van Mander, in Friedlaender, p.260. All quotations in the following discussion come from this passage.
13 Bellori, in Friedlaender, p.245 (my translation).
14 For the second portrait see Longhi, 'Volti della Roma caravaggesca', pp 35–9; for the colored drawing see Papi, 'Ottavio Leoni', pp 68–71.
15 For an overview see Dell'Orto, 'Self-Portraits', pp 225–32; for further thoughts, see Varriano, 'Caravaggio and Religion', in *Saints and Sinners*, ed. Franco Mormando, p.202.
16 Vodret in *Caravaggio. The Final Years*, p.151, and Vodret, *Complete Works*, pp 166–7.
17 McTighe, 'Caravaggio's Physiognomy' in *Representing from Life*, p.45.
18 For the relation to Giovan Paolo Lomazzo's *Self-Portrait*, and his Milanese Academy with its motto: 'Bacco ispiratori' see Cappelletti and Lemoine, *I bassofondi*, p.25, and Hermann Fiori, 'Il *Bacchino malato*', pp 91ff.
19 For these ideas as taken up by the *Bentvueghels*, see Cappelletti and Lemoine, *I bassofondi*, esp. Lemoine, 'Sotto gli auspici di Bacco', pp 23–41 and Morel, entry for the *Bacchino malato*, pp 128–31.
20 Talvacchia, *Raphael*, p.90.
21 See Verstegen, 'The Apostacy of Michelangelo', and 'Oratorian Orbit' for historical context and the appropriation.
22 Tomasi Velli, 'la *comunione di Giuda*', discusses the preparatory drawings and their iconography.
23 Fischer, 'Portrait Study', entry in *Fra Bartolommeo*, pp 294–6; I do not find the identification of a second portrait drawing convincing on the visual evidence.
24 Quoted in Wallace, *Michelangelo: The Artist*, p.145.
25 Barbieri, 'Chompare e amicho'.
26 Bambach, *Divine Draughtsman*, pp 258–9 for further discussion and examples of Michelangelo's secrecy.
27 ibid., pp 232–65.
28 Another version is attributed to Baccio Bandinelli (Louvre).
29 Vasari, *Lives*, pp 312–13.

30 I follow ideas found in Costamagna's entry in *Raphael, Cellini*, pp 337–8; cf. Bambach, *Divine Draughtsman*, p.256 for the attribution.

31 Cupperi, 'Leoni, Leone'. This author settles the question of Leoni's birthplace, disproving an earlier mistake that doubted his Aretine origin.

32 Psalm 50 in the Latin Vulgate, 51 when based on the Hebrew numbering. The cited translation is from the *New Revised Standard Version Bible*, Oxford University Press, Oxford, 1989, 51:13.

33 See James Haar's entry, 'Lassus [Orlando di Lasso], Orlande [Roland] de', *Grove Music Dictionary*, www.oxfordmusiconline.com/grovemusic.

33 Emily Fenichel, 'Penance and Proselytizing', p.132. This is the most thorough study of the *impresa*, with a wide-ranging discussion. Although having arrived independently at similar associations and conclusions, my analysis benefits from Fenichel's arguments. I differ in my reading of the relationship of the motto and image.

34 My understanding of the psalm follows the commentary (51:13) in Walter Brueggemann and William H. Bellinger, *New Cambridge Bible Commentary: Psalms*, Cambridge University Press, New York, 2014. I would like to thank Dr. Kathleen Talvacchia for suggesting this source, and for her remarks about the interpretation.

35 Zimmerman, *Paolo Giovio*, p.248.

36 Barolsky, *Michelangelo's Nose*, pp 46–8, and Fenichel, 'Penance and Proselytizing', pp 128ff, discuss the imagery of David.

37 The lines cited are from poems 33, 51 and 161 in Saslow, *The Poetry of Michelangelo*; his dating is used.

38 See Steinberg, *Michelangelo's Painting*, pp 220–28.

39 Barnes, 'Skin, Bones, and Dust', p.86; *passim* for a thorough overview of the arguments surrounding the flayed skin. Cf. Barnes, 'Metaphorical Painting'.

40 See the in-depth article by Stone, 'Self and Myth', on the relation of this image to Michelangelo.

42 The two autograph versions are in the British Royal Collection, and the Pitti Gallery. Filippo Baldinucci identifies the portraits in the biography of Allori found in his *Notizie de' professori del disegno*.

43 Vasari, *Der literarische Nachlass*, vol. 2, pp 59–60.

44 There is a tradition in the critical literature adducing Michelangelo's self-portrait in the face of Saint Paul in the *Conversion* fresco of the Pauline Chapel. I do not accept it on visual evidence, nor in terms of decorum. It would be unseemly for an artist, no matter how affirmed, to place his visage on the principal saintly protagonist in such a sacred setting. There is, however, the possibility that Michelangelo used stylized masks as self-referential in several works; see Paoletti, 'Michelangelo's Masks'.

45 Michelangelo most likely repeated his self-portrait as Nicodemus in the first phase of carving the later Rondanini *Pietà*; see Paoletti, 'The Rondanini *Pietà*', esp. pp 60–61.

46 See Kristoff, 'Michelangelo as Nicodemus' for views of Nicodemus in the 16th century, which informs my discussion.

47 Steinberg, 'Michelangelo's Florentine *Pietà*'. For differing interpretation, technical information, and overview of the controversies, see Wasserman, *Michelangelo's Florence Pietà*.

48 Kristoff, 'Michelangelo as Nicodemus', p.181.

49 See Wallace, 'Michelangelo, Tiberio Calcagni, and the Florentine *Pietà*', for the technical challenges of carving four figures in one block as part of the reason for abandonment.

50 Noted eloquently by Schütze, *Caravaggio: The Complete Works*, p.121.

51 See Preimesberger, *Paragons*, pp 83–107. He also argues for reading Caravaggio's *Deposition* as engaged in a *paragone* with Michelangelo.

52 Preimesberger points this out and directly poses questions about the characterization, *Paragons*, p.84.

53 Though well-known, this sonnet defies efforts to translate its images. Residori, *Rime*, pp 9–10, has come to the rescue; my prose translation is based on his notes. For example, the *gatti* of Lombardy refer to *contadini* in the slang of the time. Residori posits *gobba* as a metaphorical meaning of *scrigno* (see also note 54).

54 *Paradiso*, 21:109, referring to the 'hump' of Mount Catria in the Apennines. *Enciclopedia dantesca*, 1970, s.v. gibbo: 'un gonfio, il qual "gibbo" a Fiorenza "scrigno" si chiama'. (www.treccani.it/enciclopedia).

55 I assume Caravaggio had some familiarity with Vasari, from his time in Peterzano's studio, conversations in Rome, and perhaps directly from reading. See Gregory, 'Caravaggio and Vasari's *Lives*'.

56 See Michael Camille, *Image on the Edge: The Margins of Medieval Art* and Talvacchia, 'The Word Made Flesh', esp. pp 65–66.

57 Danesi Squarzina, 'Cristo *Uomo dei Dolori*', p.245.

Bibliography

PRIMARY SOURCES

Borromeo, Federico, *Sacred Painting/Museum*, Kenneth S. Rothwell (ed. and trans.), Harvard University Press, Cambridge, MA, 2010

Carducho, Vicente, from *Diálogos de la pintura*, in Robert Enggass and Jonathan Brown (eds), *Italy and Spain, 1600–1750: Sources and Documents*, Prentice-Hall, New Jersey, 1970

Condivi, Ascanio, *Vita di Michelagnolo Buonarroti*, Giovanni Nencioni (ed.), with essays by Michael Hirst and Caroline Elam, S.P.E.S., Florence, 1998

Condivi, Ascanio, *The Life of Michelangelo by Ascanio Condivi*, Alice Sedgwick Wohl (trans.), Louisiana State University Press, Baton Rouge, 1976

Friedlaender, Walter, 'Biographies and Documents', in *Caravaggio Studies*, Princeton University Press, Princeton, 1955, pp 227–314

Giannotti, Donato, *Dialogi di Donato Giannotti de' giorni che Dante consume nel cercare l'Inferno e 'l Purgatorio*, Deoclecio Redig de Campos (ed.), G.C. Sansoni, Florence, 1939

Giovio, Paolo, *Michaelis Angeli vita*, Charles Davis (ed. and trans.), FONTES 12, September 2008, pp 1–30, http://archiv.ub.uni-heidelberg.de/artdok/volltexte/2008/579

Hollanda, Francisco de, *On Antique Painting*, Alice Sedgwick Wohl (trans.), Pennsylvania State University Press, University Park, 2013

Michelangelo, *Rime*, Matteo Residori (ed.), Arnoldo Mondadori, Milan, 1998

Pliny, *Natural History*, H. Rackham (trans.), Books 33–35, Harvard University Press, Cambridge, MA, 1999

Ramsden, E.H. (trans.), *The Letters of Michelangelo*, 2 vols, Stanford University Press, Stanford, 1963

Saslow, James M. (trans.), *The Poetry of Michelangelo*, Yale University Press, New Haven, 1991

Vasari, Giorgio, *Der literarische Nachlass*, Karl Frey (ed.), 3 vols, G. Olms, Hildesheim and New York, 1982 (reprint of 1930 edition)

Vasari, Giorgio, *Le vite de' più eccellenti architetti, pittori, et scultori italiani*, Luciano Bellosi and Aldo Rossi (eds), Einaudi, Turin, 1986 (1550 edition)

Vasari, Giorgio, *Lives of the Painters, Sculptors and Architects*, Gaston du C. de Vere (trans.), with Introduction and Notes by David Ekserdjian, 2 vols, Alfred A. Knopf, New York, 1996

MODERN BIOGRAPHIES

Langdon, Helen, *Caravaggio: A Life*, Farrar, Straus & Giroux, New York, 1999

Wallace, William E., *Michelangelo: The Artist, the Man, and his Times*, Cambridge University Press, New York, 2011

WORKS CITED

Baernstein, P. Renée, '"In my own Hand": Costanza Colonna and the Art of the Letter in Sixteenth-Century Italy', *Renaissance Quarterly*, vol.66, no.1, 2013, pp 130–68

Balsamo, Jean, 'Les Caravage de Malte: le témoignage des voyageurs français (1616–1678)', in *Come dipingeva il Caravaggio*', Mina Gregori (ed.), Electa, Milan, 1996, pp 151–3

Bambach, Carmen, with essays by Claire M. Barry, Francesco Caglioti, Caroline Elam and Marcella Mariongiu, *Michelangelo: Divine Draughtsman and Designer*, The Metropolitan Museum of Art, New York, 2017

Barbieri, Costanza, '"Chompare e amicho karissimo": A Portrait of Michelangelo by his Friend Sebastiano', *Artibus et Historiae*, vol.28, no.56, 2007, pp 107–20

Barnes, Bernadine, *Michelangelo in Print: Reproductions as a Response in the Sixteenth Century*, Ashgate, Burlington, 2010

Barnes, Bernadine, 'Skin, Bones, and Dust: Self-Portraits in Michelangelo's *Last Judgment*', *Sixteenth Century Journal*, vol.35, no.4, 2004, pp 969–86

Barnes, Bernadine, *Michelangelo's 'Last Judgment': The Renaissance Response*, University of California Press, Berkeley, 1998

Barnes, Bernadine, 'Metaphorical Painting: Michelangelo, Dante, and the Last Judgment', *The Art Bulletin*, vol.77, no.1, 1995, pp 64–8

Barolsky, Paul, 'Pontormo, Michelangelo, Caravaggio', *Source*, vol.19, no.4, 2000, pp 12–17

Barolsky, Paul, 'Michelangelo's Marble Faun Revisited', *Artibus et Historiae*, vol.20, no.40, 1999, pp 113–16

Barolsky, Paul, *Giotto's Father and the Family of Vasari's Lives*, Pennsylvania State University Press, University Park, 1992

Barolsky, Paul, *Why Mona Lisa Smiles and Other Tales by Vasari*, Pennsylvania State University Press, University Park, 1991

Barolsky, Paul, *Michelangelo's Nose: A Myth and its Maker*, Pennsylvania State University Press, University Park, 1990

Barroero, Liliana, 'L'Isacco di Caravaggio nella Pinacoteca Capitolina', in *Bollettino dei Musei Comunali di Roma*, n.s. 11, 1997, pp 37–41

Bassani, Riccardo, and Fiora Bellini, 'La casa, le "robbe", lo studio del Caravaggio a Roma. Due documenti inediti dal 1603 e del 1605', *Prosepttiva*, vol.71, 1993, pp 68–76

Berra, Giacomo, 'Il *Bacco* degli Uffizi del Caravaggio e il riferimento al modello antico dell'Antinoo', in *Una vita per la storia dell'arte. Scritti in memoria di Maurizio Marini*, Pietro Di Loreto (ed.), Etgraphiae, Rome, 2015, pp 57–82

Berra, Giacomo, *Il giovane Caravaggio in Lombardia. Ricerche documentarie sui Merisi, gli Aratori, e i Marchesi di Caravaggio*, Fondazione Roberto Longhi, Florence, 2005

Berra, Giacomo, 'Il giovane Michelangelo Merisi da Caravaggio: la sua famiglia e la scelta dell' *ars pingendi*', *Paragone*, vol.41–2, 2002, pp 40–128

Brundin, Abigail, *Vittoria Colonna: Sonnets for Michelangelo*, University of Chicago Press, Chicago, 2005

Bussagli, Marco, 'Michelangelo e Sulpizio Verolano. La fonte letteraria del *Giudizio Universale*', in *Il rinascimento a Roma nel segno di Michelangelo e Raffaello*, Maria Grazia Bernardini and Marco Bussagli (eds), Electa, Milan, 2011, pp 88–93

Cadogan, Jean K., 'Michelangelo in the Workshop of Ghirlandaio', *Burlington Magazine*, vol.135, no.1078, 1993, pp 30–31

Calvesi, Maurizo, *Le realtà del Caravaggio*, Einaudi, Turin, 1990

Camille, Michael, *Image on the Edge: The Margins of Medieval Art*, Reaktion, London, 2019

Cappelletti, Francesca and Annick Lemoine, *I bassifondi del Barocco. La Roma del vizio e della miseria*, Officina Libraria, Milan, 2014

Caravaggio e la collezione Mattei, exh.cat., Electa, Milan, 1995

Caravaggio: The Final Years, exh.cat., Electa Napoli, Naples, 2005

Carman, Charles H., 'Michelangelo's *Bacchus* and Divine Frenzy', *Source*, vol.2, no.4, 1983, pp 6–13

Carminati, Marco, 'Caravaggio da Milano', in *Il Sole 24 Ore*, 25 February 2007, p.29

Christiansen, Keith, 'Thoughts on the Lombardy Training of Caravaggio', in *Come dipingeva il Caravaggio*', Mina Gregori (ed.), Electa, Milan, 1996, pp 7–28

Christiansen, Keith, 'Caravaggio and "L'esempio davanti del naturale"', *The Art Bulletin*, vol.68, no.3, 1986, pp 421–45

Costamagna, Philippe, 'Portraits of Florentine Exiles', in *Raphael, Cellini, and a Renaissance Banker: The Patronage of Bindo Altoviti*, Alan Chong, Donatella Pegazzano, Dimitrios Zikos (eds), Isabella Stewart Gardner Museum, Boston, 2003, pp 329–50

Cozzi, Gaetano, 'Intorno al cardinale Ottavio Paravicino, a monsignor Paolo Gualdo e a Michelangelo da Caravaggio', *Rivista Storica Italiana*, vol.73, no.1, 1961, pp 36–68

Cupperi, Walter, 'Leoni, Leone', entry in *Dizionario Biografico degli Italiani*, vol.64, 2005, www.treccani.it/biografico

Danesi Squarzina, Silvia, 'Cristo *Uomo dei Dolori* da Savonarola a Michelangelo', in *L'immagine di Cristo dall'acheropita alla mano d'artista: dal tardo medievo all'età barocca*, Christoph Luitpold Frommel and Gerhard Wolf (eds), Biblioteca Apostolica Vaticana, Città del Vaticano, Rome, 2006, pp 241–67

Danesi Squarzina, Silvia, 'The Bassano *Christ the Redeemer* in the Giustiniani Collection', *The Burlington Magazine*, vol.142, no.1173, 2000, pp 746–51

Dell'Orto, Giovanna, 'Caravaggio: Self-Portraits as Exploration of Living Reality', *Gazette des Beaux-Arts*, vol.138, 2001, pp 225–32

Dempsey, Charles, *Inventing the Renaissance Putto*, University of North Carolina Press, Chapel Hill, 2001

Dempsey, Charles, '"Et Nos Cedamus Amori": Observations on the Farnese Gallery', *Art Bulletin*, vol.50, no.4, 1968, pp 363–74

De Tolnay, Charles, *Michelangelo*, 5 vols, Princeton University Press, Princeton, 1969–71

De Tolnay, Charles, 'Le menu de Michel Ange', *Art Quarterly*, vol.3, 1940, pp 240–42

Elam, Caroline, 'Il giardino delle sculture di Lorenzo de' Medici', in *Il giardino di San Marco: Maestri e compagni del giovane Michelangelo*, Paola Barocchi (ed.), Silvana Editoriale, Milan, 1992, pp 157–71

Fenichel, Emily, 'Penance and Proselytizing in Michelangelo's Portrait Medal', *Artibus et Historiae*, vol.37, no.73, pp 125–38

Fischer, Chris, *Fra Bartolommeo: Master Draughtsman of the High Renaissance*, Museum Boijmans Van Beuningen, Rotterdam, 1990

Freedman, Luba, 'Reflections on *Bacchus*', *Artibus et Historia*, vol.24, no.47, 2003, 121–35

Friedlaender, Walter, *Caravaggio Studies*, Princeton University Press, Princeton, 1955

Gash, John, 'Caravaggio's Maltese Inspiration', *Melita Historica*, vol.2, no.3, 1998, pp 253–66

Goffen, Rona, *Renaissance Rivals: Michelangelo, Leonardo, Raphael, Titian*, Yale University Press, New Haven, 2002

Gregory, Sharon, 'Caravaggio and Vasari's *Lives*', *Artibus et Historiae*, vol.32, no.64, 2011, pp 167–91

Hall, Marcia and Tracy E. Cooper (eds), *The Sensuous in the Counter-Reformation Church*, Cambridge University Press, New York, 2013

Hermann Fiore, Kristina, 'Il *Bacchino malato* autoritratto del Caravaggio ed altre figure bacchiche degli artisti', in *Caravaggio. Nuove riflessioni*, Dante Bernini (ed.) Quaderni di Palazzo Venezia, vol.6, Fratelli Palombi, Rome, 1989, pp 95–134

Hirst, Michael, 'Michelangelo and his First Biographers', *Proceedings of the British Academy*, vol.94, 1996, pp 63–84

Hirst, Michael, *The Young Michelangelo: The Artist in Rome, 1496–1501*, National Gallery Publications, London, 1994

Kimura, Taro, 'Analisi iconografica del *San Giovanni Battista nel deserto* del Caravaggio della Galleria Borghese di Roma' *Artibus et Historiae*, vol.36, no.72, 2015, pp 283–304

Kristoff, Jane, 'Michelangelo as Nicodemus: The Florence *Pietà*', *Sixteenth Century Journal*, vol.20, no.2, 1989, pp 163–82

La Malfa, Claudia, 'The Chapel of San Girolamo in Santa Maria del Popolo in Rome. New Evidence for the Discovery of the Domus Aurea', *Journal of the Warburg and Courtauld Institutes*, vol.63, 2000, pp 259–70

Lieberman, Ralph, 'Regarding Michelangelo's *Bacchus*', *Artibus et Historiae*, vol.22, no.43, 2001, pp 65–74

Longhi, Roberto, 'Volti della Roma caravaggesca', *Paragone*, vol.21, 1951, pp 35–9

Marini, Maurizio, and Sandro Corradini, 'Inventarium omnium et singulorum bonorum mobilium' di Michelangelo da Caravaggio "pittore"', *Artibus et Historiae*, vol.14, no.28, 1993, pp 161–76

McTighe, Sheila, *Representing from Life in Seventeenth-century Italy*, Amsterdam University Press, Amsterdam, 2020

Mormando, Franco (ed.), *Saints and Sinners: Caravaggio and the Baroque Image*, McMullen Museum of Art, Chestnut Hill, MA, 1999

Muraoka, Anne H., *The Path of Humility: Caravaggio and Carlo Borromeo*, Peter Lang, New York, 2015

O'Malley, John W., 'Trent, Sacred Images, and Catholics' Senses of the Sensuous', in *The Sensuous in the Counter-Reformation Church*, Marcia B. Hall and Tracy E. Cooper (eds), Cambridge University Press, New York, 2013, pp 28–48

Ostrow, Steven and Conrad Rudolph, 'Isaac Laughing: Caravaggio, Non-traditional Imagery, and Traditional Identification', *Art History*, vol.24, 2001, pp 646–81

Paoletti, John T., 'The Rondanini *Pietà*: Ambiguity Maintained through the Palimpsest', *Artibus et Historiae*, vol.21, no.42, 2000, pp 53–80

Paoletti, John T., 'Michelangelo's Masks', *The Art Bulletin*, vol.74, no.3, 1992, pp 423–40

Paolozzi Strozzi, Beatrice, and Marc Bormand, *The Springtime of the Renaissance: Sculpture and the Arts in Florence 1400–60*, Mandragora, Florence, 2013

Papi, Gianni, entry 'Ottavio Leoni', in *Michelangelo Merisi da Caravaggio: Come nascono i capolavori*, Electa, Milan, 1991, pp 69–7

Pavesi, Mauro, 'Un nuovo "San Giovanni Battista nel deserto" della fase caravaggesca di Giuseppe Vermiglio', *Arte Lombarda*, n.s., no.160, 2010, pp 14–19

Pestilli, Livio, 'Michelangelo's *Pietà*: Lombard Critics and Plinian Sources, *Source*, vol.19, no.2, 2000, pp 21–30

Pon, Lisa, 'Michelangelo's *Lives*: Sixteenth-Century Books by Vasari, Condivi, and Others', *Sixteenth Century Journal*, vol.27, no.4, 1996, pp 1015–37

Pon, Lisa, 'Michelangelo's First Signature', *Source*, vol.15, no.4, 1996, pp 16–21

Preimesberger, Rudolf, *Paragons and Paragone: Van Eyck, Raphael, Michelangelo, Caravaggio, and Bernini*, Getty Research Institute, Los Angeles, 2011

Pupillo, Marco, 'Di nuovo intorno al cardinale Ottavio Paravicino, a monsignor Paolo Gualdo e a Michelangelo da Caravaggio: una lettera ritrovata', *Arte Veneta*, vol.54, no.1, pp 164–9

Risaliti, Sergio and Francesco Vossilla, *Michelangelo. La Pietà Vaticana*, Bompiani, Milan, 2015

Risaliti, Sergio and Francesco Vossilla, *Il Bacco di Michelangelo: Il dio della spensieratezza e della condanna*, Maschietto Editore, Florence, 2007

Rowland, Ingrid and Noah Charney, *The Collector of Lives: Giorgio Vasari and the Invention of Art*, W.W. Norton & Company, New York, 2017

Schütze, Sebastian, *Caravaggio: The Complete Works*, Taschen, Cologne, 2009

Sciberras, Keith, '"Due persone à lui ben viste": The Identity of Caravaggio's Companion as a Knight of Magistral Obedience', *Burlington Magazine*, vol.147, no.1222, 2005, pp 38–9

Sciberras, Keith, 'Frate Michael Angelus in Tumultu: The Cause of Imprisonment in Malta', *Burlington Magazine*, vol.144, no.1189, 2002, pp 229–32

Steen Hansen, Morten, *In Michelangelo's Mirror*, Pennsylvania State University Press, University Park, 2013

Steinberg, Leo, *Michelangelo's Painting: Selected Essays*, Sheila Schwartz (ed.), University of Chicago Press, Chicago, 2019

Steinberg, Leo, 'Michelangelo's Florentine *Pietà*: The Missing Leg', *The Art Bulletin*, vol.50, no.4, 1968, pp 343–53

Stone, David M., 'Signature Killer: Caravaggio and the Poetics of Blood', *The Art Bulletin*, vol.94, no.4, 2012, pp 572–93

Stone, David M., 'Self and Myth in Caravaggio's *David and Goliath*', in *Caravaggio: Realism, Rebellion, Reception*, Genevieve Warwick (ed.), University of Delaware Press, Newark, 2006, pp 36–46

Stone, David M., 'The Context of Caravaggio's *Beheading of Saint John* in Malta', *Burlington Magazine*, vol.139, no.1128, 1997, pp 161–70

Stone, David M., 'In Praise of Caravaggio's *Sleeping Cupid*: New Documents on Francesco dell'Antella in Malta and Florence', *Melita Historica*, vol.12, no.2, 1997, pp 165–77

Summers, David, *Michelangelo and the Language of Art*, Princeton University Press, Princeton, 1981

Talvacchia, Bette, 'The Word Made Flesh: Spiritual Subjects and Carnal Depictions in Renaissance Art', in *The Sensuous in the Counter-Reformation Church*, Marcia B. Hall and Tracy E. Cooper (eds), Cambridge University Press, New York, 2013, pp 49–73

Talvacchia, Bette, 'Bronzino's *Corpus* between Ancient Models and Modern Masters', in *Agnolo Bronzino: Medici Court Artist in Context*, Andrea M. Gáldy (ed.), Cambridge Scholars Publishing, Newcastle upon Tyne, 2013, pp 51–66

Talvacchia, Bette, *Raphael*, Phaidon Press, London, 2007

Terzaghi, Maria Cristina, 'Peterzano, Simone', entry in *Dizionario Biografico degli Italiani*, vol.82, 2015, www.treccani.it/biografico

Tomasi Velli, Silvia, 'Federico Barocci, Clemente VIII e la "comunione di Giuda"', *Prospettiva*, vol.87–88, 1997, pp 157–67

Varriano, John, *Caravaggio: The Art of Realism*, Pennsylvania State University Press, University Park, 2006

Verstegen, Ian, 'The Apostacy of Michelangelo in a Painting by Federico Barocci', *Source*, vol.22, no.3, 2003, pp 27–34

Verstegen, Ian, 'Federico Barocci, Federico Borromeo, and the Oratorian Orbit', *Renaissance Quarterly*, vol.56, no.1, 2003, pp 56–87

Vodret, Rossella, *Caravaggio: The Complete Works*, Silvana Editoriale, Milan, 2010

Von Rosen, Valeska, 'Ambiguità intenzionale. L'ignudo nella Pinacoteca Capitolina e altre raffigurazioni di San Giovanni Battista', in *Caravaggio e il suo ambiente: Ricerche e interpretazioni*, Sybille Ebert-Schifferer, Julian Kliemann, Valeska von Rosen and Lothar Sickel (eds), Silvana Editoriale, Milan, 2007, 59–85

Wallace, William E., 'Michelangelo, Tiberio Calcagni, and the Florentine *Pietà*', *Artibus et Historiae*, vol.21, no.42, 2000, pp 81–99

Wallace, William E., 'Narrative and Religious Expression in Michelangelo's Pauline Chapel', *Artibus et Historiae*, vol.10, no.19, 1989, pp 107–21

Wang, Aileen June, 'Michelangelo's Signature', *Sixteenth Century Journal*, vol.35, no.2, 2004, pp 447–73

Warwick, Genevieve, 'Memory's Cut: Caravaggio's *Sleeping Cupid of 1608*', *Art History*, vol.40, 2017, pp 884–903

Wasserman, Jack, *Michelangelo's Florence Pietà*, Princeton University Press, Princeton, 2003

Wilde, Johannes, *Italian Drawings in the Department of Prints and Drawings in the British Museum: Michelangelo and his Studio*, Trustees of the British Museum, London, 1953

Zimmerman, T.C. Price, *Paolo Giovio: The Historian and the Crisis of Sixteenth-Century Italy*, Princeton University Press, Princeton, 1995

Zöllner, Frank, *Michelangelo: The Complete Works*, Taschen, Cologne, 2014

Picture Credits

The publisher would like to thank the copyright holders for granting permission to reproduce the images illustrated. Every attempt has been made to trace accurate ownership of copyrighted images in this book. Any errors or omissions will be corrected in subsequent editions provided notification is sent to the publisher. The copyright holders for the photos are listed below.

bpk / Kupferstichkabinett, SMB / Jörg P. Anders: fig.5 and pl.13

Bridgeman Images: fig.10 *Lucca Cathedral, Italy* (© Giuliano Valsecchi); fig.12 *Casa Buonarroti, Florence, Italy*; fig.14 *Palazzo Vecchio (Palazzo della Signoria) Florence, Italy* (photo © Raffaello Bencini); fig.19 and 22, pls 14, 20, 28 and 32 Vatican Museums and Galleries, Vatican City fig.24 Worcester Art Museum, Massachusetts, USA fig.25 *Musei e Gallerie Pontificie, Musei Vaticani, Vatican City* © Mondadori Portfolio/Bridgeman Images; fig.26 *Santa Maria del Popolo, Rome, Italy, Museo Nazionale del Bargello, Florence, Tuscany, Italy* (photo © Raffaello Bencini); fig.32 (photo © Stefano Baldini); pl.4 *Basilica di San Pietro, Rome, Italy* (photo Luisa Ricciarini); fig.39 *Museo dell'Opera del Duomo, Florence, Tuscany, Italy* (photo: Luisa Ricciarini); pl.11 *Santa Maria Sopra Minerva, Rome, Italy*; pl.16 Nelson-Atkins Museum of Art, Kansas City, USA, pl.19 *San Luigi dei Francesi, Rome, Italy* (photo: Luisa Ricciarini); pl.22 *Musei e Gallerie Pontificie, Musei Vaticani, Vatican City* © Mondadori Portfolio/Bridgeman Images; pl.25 *Santa Maria del Popolo, Rome, Italy*

Creative Commons: fig.4, fig.8 (photo: Sailko); fig.9 (photo: Zello); fig.13 (photo: Vassil), pl.12

Elisha Whittelsey Collection, The Elisha Whittelsey Fund, 1959: figs 17, 18 and 38

Gallerie Nazionali di Arte Antica, MIBACT - Bibliotheca Hertziana, Istituto Max Planck for the History of Art/Enrico Fontolan: figs 20 and 29

The John and Mable Ringling Museum of Art, the State Art Museum of Florida, Florida State University: fig.3

KHM-Museumsverband: figs 16 and 21

Ministry of Culture: fig.7 and pls 3, 5, 7, 17

Ministry of Culture / Marucelliana Library of Florence: pl.2

Ministry of Cultural Heritage and Activities and Tourism - Regional Directorate for Museums of Tuscany – Florence: fig.6, pls 6 and 9

MiC – Galleria Borghese: pls 8, 18 and 29

Museum Boijmans Van Beuningen: fig.35

National Gallery of Ireland: fig.31

Scala, Florence © 2021: figs 1, 15, 27 and pls 26, 27 and 31; fig.11 Scala/FEC-Ministero Interno/Opera di S. Croce; fig.33 Photo Scala, Florence/Fondo Edifici di Culto - Min. dell'Interno; fig.34 Andrea Jemolo/Scala, Florence

National Galllery, London: pl.23

Picture Art Collection / Alamy Stock Photo: fig.2

Roma, Sovrintendenza Capitolina ai Beni Culturali: pl.15

St John's Co-Cathedral Foundation: pl.30

Sicilian Region, Department of Cultural Heritage and Sicilian Identity – interdisciplinary Museum of Messina: fig.23

State Hermitage Museum (photo by Vladimir Terebenin): fig.28
Teylers Museum Haarlem The Netherlands: pl.1

Index

Note: Italic page numbers indicate figures; page numbers followed by n refer to notes.